The Making of
American
Girl

Dedicated to Pleasant T. Rowland and Valerie Tripp, for opening windows into worlds with endless possibilities

Published by American Girl Publishing

26 27 28 29 30 31 32 LEO 10 9 8 7 6 5 4 3 2 1

Edited by Jodi Goldberg
Written by Janelle Asselin, Jodi Goldberg, Jennifer Hirsch, and Teri Robida
Creative Direction and Cover Design by Wendy Walsh
Designed by Leah Richards-Guha
Researched by Kathy Borkowski, Katherine Cartwright, Nina Roy, and Jolene Schulz
Photography by Janelle Asselin, Chris Hynes, Sydney Paulsen, Alexandra Trier, Jen Taylor, Adam Brown, Youa Awasthi, and Abigail Schaefer
Production by Jodi Knueppel and Kristi Lively

Special thanks to: Menzi Behrnd-Klodt, Dave Brophy, Blake Changnon, Carmen Connor, Mary Davison, Fran Greenman, Holder Printworks, Cole Koop, Charlie and Therese Maring, Heather Northrop, Isa Primavera, Samantha Sauer, Jill Sterrett, Katie Waller, and the Wisconsin Historical Society.

MO

PICTURE CREDITS

The following individuals and organizations have generously granted permission to reproduce their photographs, objects, and paintings:

Chapter 1: p. 2—*Newport News Daily Press*/Contributor/Tribune News Service via Getty Images (silversmith); David Kozlowski/Contributor/Moment Mobile via Getty Images (garden); Jeffrey Greenberg/Universal Images Group via Getty Images (girl); p. 3—Michael S. Williamson/*The Washington Post* via Getty Images (cooking demonstration); Jeffrey Greenberg/Universal Images Group via Getty Images (woman holding pot); p. 12—Used by permission of Renée Graef © 2025 (illustration); p. 15—Used by permission of Renée Graef © 2025 (illustrations); Louisa May Alcott (1832–1888), *Little Women*, 1878 edition, Houghton Library, Harvard University, AC85.Aℓ194L.1869 pt. 2aa (book cover); p. 16—William Matthew Prior (1806–1873), *Three Sisters of the Copeland Family*, 1854, oil on canvas, Bequest of Martha C. Karolik for the M. and M. Karolik Collection of American Paintings, 1815–1865, Museum of Fine Arts, Boston, 48.467 (portrait); p. 17—Wisconsin Historical Society, WHI-1947.1031, WHI-1951.2690, WHI-1967.200 (three dresses); p. 22—H. W. McVickar, artist, *Harper's Bazar: A Weekly Journal of Fashion Devoted to Every Interest of Woman and the Home*, 1895, New York [publisher not identified], https://www.loc.gov/item/2015645761/ (magazine); BooksR/Alamy Stock Photo (*Woman's Home Companion*); p. 23—*The Delineator*, vol. LXVII, no. 1 (January 1906), New York: Butterick Publishing Co., 1906, Public Domain Mark, Wellcome Collection, https://wellcomecollection.org/works/h8s5wnb2 (magazine); Steve Painter/Alamy Stock Photo (*Good Housekeeping*); BooksR/Alamy Stock Photo (*Ladies' Home Journal*); p. 26—Used by permission of Renée Graef © 2025 (illustration); p. 28—Used by permission of Renée Graef © 2025 (illustration); p. 32—Album/British Library/Alamy Stock Photo (painting); pp. 42–43—Sydney Rose Paulsen (photography).

Chapter 2: p. 61—Wisconsin Historical Society/Contributor/Archive Photos via Getty Images (servants); p. 68—Photo 12/Contributor/Universal Images Group via Getty Images (suffragette); p. 69—Bettmann/Contributor via Getty Images (ice cream parlor).

Chapter 3: p. 78—Helen Louise Allen Textile Collection (Q.P.US.0028), University of Wisconsin–Madison, Gift from the Estate of Professor Helen Louise Allen (quilt); p. 79—Universal History Archive/Contributor/Universal Images Group via Getty Images (portrait); Wisconsin Historical Society, WHI-1956.1947 (calico dress); Wisconsin Historical Society, WHI-1947.1030 (bonnet); p. 84—Knut Ekwall (1843–1912), *The Emigrants*, before 1912, oil on canvas, American-Scandinavian Foundation, Courtesy of Lena Biörck Kaplan (painting); p. 85—Jakob Kulle (1838–1898), *The America Letter*, 1881, oil on canvas, Swedish Emigrant Institute, Växjö, Sweden (painting); *New York—Welcome to the Land of Freedom—An Ocean Steamer Passing the Statue of Liberty: Scene on the Steerage Deck / from a Sketch by a Staff Artist*, 1887, print: wood engraving, Library of Congress, https://www.loc.gov/item/97502086/ (sketch); p. 86—*Ben Campbell, Steamship at Landing*, between 1852 and 1860, photograph, Library of Congress, https://www.loc.gov/item/2004664385/ (steamship); p. 87—Used by permission of Renée Graef © 2025 (illustration); pp. 92–93—Minnesota Historical Society (Dakota artifacts); p. 94—Sepia Times/Contributor/Universal Images Group via Getty Images (blizzard); p. 99—Made for Ella Maria Deacon (1811–94), *Friendship Quilt*, 1842, textile, Art Institute of Chicago, 1978.923, Gift of Betsey Leeds Tait Puth (quilt); p. 100—H. J. Perkins/Wisconsin Historical Society/Archive Photos via Getty Images (log cabin); p. 102—State Historical Society of North Dakota, B0338-00001, detailed (quilting bee); Wisconsin Historical Society/Archive Photos via Getty Images (barn raising); p. 106—Universal History Archive/Universal Images Group via Getty Images (beekeeping).

Chapter 4: p. 114—Courtesy of Valerie Tripp (photograph); p. 115—Alfred Eisenstaedt/The LIFE Picture Collection/Shutterstock (*Life* magazines); p. 121—Maginel Wright Barney (1877–1966), artist, and National War Garden Commission, funder/sponsor, *War Gardens over the Top. The Seeds of Victory Insure the Fruits of Peace*, c. 1919, photograph, [Washington, D.C.: National War Garden Commission], Library of Congress, https://www.loc.gov/item/95506484/ (seed packet); Library of Congress, Prints & Photographs Division, FSA/OWI Collection, LC-USE6-D-009197 (children in garden); p. 122—Nextrecord Archives/Archive Photos via Getty Images (postcards); Ann Cecil/Photo Resource Hawaii/Alamy Stock Photo (Hawaiian girl); p. 125—AFP/AFP via Getty Images (classroom); p. 129—Courtesy of Beverly Stevens (girls with blanket); p. 131—Louisa May Alcott (1832–1888), *Little Women*, 1878 edition, Houghton Library, Harvard University, AC85. Aℓ194L.1869 pt. 2aa (book cover); p. 133—*Members of the Women's Army Corps Identifying Incorrectly Addressed Mail for Soldiers, Post Locator Department, Camp Breckinridge*, 1943, photograph, Schomburg Center for Research in Black Culture, Photographs and Prints Division, New York Public Library Digital Collections, https://digitalcollections.nypl.org/items/510d47df-fa14-a3d9-e040-e00a18064a99 (sorting mail); Mondadori Portfolio/Contributor/Mondadori Portfolio Editorial via Getty Images (soldier with package); p. 134—Harold M. Lambert/Contributor/Archive Photos via Getty Images (family around radio); p. 137—FPG/Staff/Archive Photos via Getty Images (girls skating); Fox Photos/Stringer/Hulton Archive via Getty Images (children with ice cream); p. 139—Weegee(Arthur Fellig)/International Center of Photography/Contributor via Getty Images (pin the tail on the donkey); p. 140—Photo by Byron Filkins from the Cleveland Press Collections, Courtesy of the Michael Schwartz Library Special Collections, Cleveland State University (campers); p. 143—*Mulberry Harbor at Cherbourg, France*, June 1944, photograph, Library of Congress, https://www.loc.gov/item/2008680920/ (military vehicles); p. 144—Universal History Archive/Universal Images Group via Getty Images (homecoming poster); p. 145—Bettmann/Contributor/Bettmann via Getty Images (home perm advertisement); p. 146—Silver Screen Collection/MoviePix via Getty Images (show); p. 147—Bettmann/Contributor/Bettmann via Getty Images (soldier returning home).

Chapter 5: p. 151—Stephen Slaughter (1697–1765), *Portrait of Sir Edward Walpole's Children*, 1747, oil on canvas, given by Mrs. Eugene J. Carpenter and Olivia Carpenter Coan in memory of Mr. Eugene J. Carpenter, 1931, Minneapolis Institute of Art, 31.106 (painting); p. 152—Jean-Baptiste-Antoine de Verger (1762–1851), *Soldiers in Uniform*, 1781, Williamsburg, Virginia [publisher not identified, to 1784], photograph, Library of Congress, https://www.loc.gov/item/2021669876/ (soldiers); p. 153—IanDagnall Computing/Alamy Stock Photo (James Lafayette); Bettmann/Contributor via Getty Images (Phillis Wheatley, Abigail Adams); Collection of the Massachusetts Historical Society (letter); p. 158—Théodore Géricault (1791–1824), *Horsewoman*, 1820 or later, oil on canvas, Bequest of Mrs. Charles Wrightsman in honor of Mercedes Bass, 2019, Metropolitan Museum of Art, 2019.141.11 (painting); p. 165—The Colonial Williamsburg Foundation (milliner); p. 171—Johan Zoffany (1733–1810), *Mr and Mrs Dalton and Their Niece Mary de Heulle*, c. 1765–68, oil on canvas, Bequeathed by Alan Evans 1974, Tate, T01895 (painting); p. 175—George Romney (1734–1802), *Miss Juliana Willoughby*, 1781–1783, oil on canvas, Andrew W. Mellon Collection, National Gallery of Art, Washington, 1937.1.104 (painting); Historical Picture Archive/CORBIS/Corbis via Getty Images (battledore); p. 176—Benjamin Henry Latrobe (1764–1820), *An Overseer Doing His Duty near Fredericksburg, Virginia*, print, Maryland Center for History and Culture, 1960.108.1.3.21 (print); MPI/Stringer/Archives Photos via Getty Images (plantation wedding); © The Trustees of the British Museum (drum); Benjamin Franklin, *Join, or Die*, May 9, 1754, print: woodcut, Library of Congress, https://www.loc.gov/item/2002695523/ (poster); p. 180—Album/Alamy Stock Photo (woman in riding habit); p. 181—Brendan Sostak, The Colonial Williamsburg Foundation (photograph).

Chapter 6: p. 191—Illustration used by permission of Kimberly Shrack © 2025; photograph by Heather Lewis.

Chapter 7: p. 200—*Slippers (Bata Ileke)*, c. 1875–1925, Yoruba culture, Nigeria, Gift of Deborah Stokes and Jeffrey Hammer, Art Institute of Chicago/Art Resource, NY, 1991.385A-B; Connie Porter, *All-Bright Court*, 1991, New York: Houghton Mifflin Company (book cover); p. 201—Marvin Joseph/*The Washington Post* via Getty Images (Spencer Crew); p. 201—Zbigniew Bzdak/*Chicago Tribune*/Tribune News Service via Getty Images (Lonnie Bunch); p. 206—Miss Tyson, Slavery/Anti-Slavery Collection, Sophia Smith Collection, SSC-MS-00390, Smith College Special Collections, Northampton, Massachusetts (schoolgirl); p. 209—Eastman Johnson (1824–1906), *A Ride for Liberty—The Fugitive Slaves (recto)*, ca. 1862, oil on paperboard, Gift of Gwendolyn O. L. Conkling, Brooklyn Museum, 40.59a-b (painting); Theodor Kaufmann (1814–1896), *On to Liberty*, 1867, oil on canvas, Gift of Erving and Joyce Wolf, in memory of Diane R. Wolf, 1982, Metropolitan Museum of Art, 1982.443.3 (painting); p. 211—Heritage Images/Hulton Archive via Getty Images (classroom); p. 212—*Dress made by an unidentified enslaved woman*, 1845–1865, Virginia, United States, Collection of the Smithsonian National Museum of African American History and Culture, Gift of the Black Fashion Museum founded by Lois K. Alexander-Lane, 2007.3.4 (dress); p. 217—William L. Breton, *Bethel African Methodist Episcopal Church, Philadelphia*, Pennsylvania, United States of America, 1829, Philadelphia: Kennedy & Lucas's Lithography, print: lithograph, Library of Congress, https://www.loc.gov/item/2021670179/ (church); p. 219—*Dress*, American, 1860s, Gift of Miss Merle Munn, 1947, Metropolitan Museum of Art, Costume Institute, C.I.47.41.4 (plaid dress); p. 221—Sarah Ann Wilson (active mid-19th century), *Album Quilt*, 1854, New York or New Jersey, United States, Purchased with funds provided by Mrs. David W. Grainger, Art Institute of Chicago, 1999.509 (quilt); p. 223—Chip Somodevilla/Staff/Getty Images News via Getty Images (Smithsonian); p. 224—clu/Digital Vision Vectors via Getty Images (ice cream maker); p. 225—Courtesy of Connie Porter (photo of Aunt Ruth); p. 226—Khaneeros/stock.adobe.com (bunting); p. 228—Archive Photos/Stringer/Archive Photos via Getty Images (soldier); p. 230—*Fall suits for children*, The Miriam and Ira D. Wallach Division of Art, Prints and Photographs: Picture Collection, New York Public Library Digital Collections, https://digitalcollections.nypl.org/items/16bf3030-c543-012f-58dc-58d385a7bc34 (illustration); Buyenlarge/Archive Photos via Getty Images (family).

Chapter 8: p. 236—Education Images/Universal Images Group Editorial via Getty Images (washing wool); p. 237—Universal Images Group/Universal Images Group Editorial via Getty Images (bulto); p. 243—Édouard-Henri-Théophile Pingret (1788–1875), *China Poblana*, c. 1850, La Colección de Pintura del Banco Nacional de México (woman with jug); Courtesy of Jean Paul Tibbles (portrait); p. 247—Robert Alexander/Archive Photos via Getty Images (sheep); p. 251—Courtesy of Nuevo Mexicano Heritage Arts Museum, Santa Fe, New Mexico, Jack Parsons Photography, 1956.089 (writing desk); p. 254—*Wool-on-Cotton Colcha Embroidery*, 1840–1865, Former collection of Mary Cabot Wheelwright, E. Boyd Memorial Fund purchase for IFAF Collection, Museum of International Folk Art, FA.1975.28.1 (colcha cloth); p. 257—Edward S. Curtis, *Replastering a Paguate House, Paguate Village, Laguna Pueblo, New Mexico*, 1925, Courtesy of the Palace of the Governors Photo Archives (NMHM/DCA), Edward S. Curtis Collection, Negative No. 031961 (woman plastering house); p. 258—Sepia Times/Universal Images Group Editorial via Getty Images (Pueblo girls); p. 259—Heritage Images/Hulton Archive via Getty Images (Zuni houses); p. 263—*Violin*, 19th century, The Crosby Brown Collection of Musical Instruments, 1889, Metropolitan Museum of Art, 89.4.1312a,b (violin); p. 265—Gerald Cassidy (1869–1934), *View of the Santa Fe Plaza in the 1850s*, c. 1930, oil on canvas, New Mexico Museum of Art, Gift of the New Mexico Historical Society, 1977, 350.23P (painting); Used by permission of Bruce Hucko © 2025 (wagon photograph).

THE AMERICAN GIRLS COLLECTION
THE AMERICAN GIRLS COLLECTION
THE AMERICAN GIRLS COLLECTION
THE AMERICAN GIRLS COLLECTION
Pleasant company.
THE AMERICAN GIRLS COLLECTION
ling prec
period-in
f historically
haracter living in a specific w
PLEASANT COMPANY
AISLE SEAT
1 222
Tuesday
April 06, 1999
3:30 pm
$25.00
222
$25.00
Please arrive 15 minutes prior to be seated.
Ticket sales final. No refunds or exchanges.
Children under 6 are not permitted in the theater
Revue
American Girl Theater
111 East Chicago Avenue
Chicago, IL 60611
1-877-AG PLACE
ing precedents
Meet Kirsten
an american girl
t tells a story
other times in history.

Contents

1854

A Girl Company

Before there was American Girl, there was Pleasant Company. In the pages of this book, you'll read the story of how Pleasant Rowland created a collection of magical moments for girls—moments that strengthened the bonds between girls and their mothers, grandmothers, and aunts for generations. You'll see how Pleasant never wavered from the elegant simplicity of her original vision: to create a company for and about girls, a company that respected girls and took them seriously. Creating a business called Pleasant Company was not an end in itself, but rather the means by which Pleasant shared her belief that girls are intelligent and important people. "What we were really building was 'a girl company,' and anything that was good for girls was ours to give them," Pleasant recalls.

Through the pages of the Pleasant Company catalogue, Pleasant spoke *to* girls—not at them—directly and respectfully about the history of girlhood in America. She helped girls see they were part of a long line of strong, smart, confident, and courageous women who had an important role in the creation of this country and the future of this world. Pleasant presented stories to help a girl understand where she came from and spark conversations among the generations. She hoped a girl would go to her grandmother and say, "This character is the same age as you. What was your childhood like?"

Through the veil of the past, Pleasant gave glimpses of the timeless emotions and cherished traditions of girlhood. We all love our family and friends, we all struggle to find the courage to do what is right, and we sometimes push against cultural norms in the process. The emotional truths of joy, sorrow, compassion, disappointment, and hope are constant across time. The task of becoming who you truly are and learning how to use your unique talents is the same as it ever was.

Above all, Pleasant showed girls that they had their own important stories to tell, their own ideas to share. She wanted to help girls grow from hopes and dreams to aspirations and ambition, to know that their voices and their view of the world truly matter. She gave reassurance and inspiration and, without explicitly saying so, prompted a crucial question: "Now what are you going to do about it?"

Every girl mattered to Pleasant. She believed passionately that every girl has the power within her to make a difference and change the world. Whether a girl is quietly courageous like Kirsten, learning to be a leader like Molly, adventurous like Felicity, or building confidence like Josefina, Pleasant helped her realize the most empowering truth of all: She is the hero of her own story.

> “**I am so thankful there is a company that teaches girls** at a young age that they are **smart, strong, and beautiful just the way they are.** To this day, my American Girl dolls sit on a shelf in my room. Though my tastes have grown more mature, just as I have, I leave them out as a **reminder of my inner child** and my motivation for imagination. Thank you from the bottom of this **American girl's heart.**”
>
> KATIE, AGE 16, MINNESOTA

A Trip Back in Time

As a girl, Pleasant always wanted to visit Colonial Williamsburg, a living history museum in Virginia. Her parents had honeymooned there, and she remembers, "My sisters and I, when we were little, used to study the family album, and there was something about their wedding pictures and their honeymoon that just captured our hearts." So when her husband, Jerry Frautschi, invited her along on a business trip to Williamsburg in the early 1980s, she joined him.

Decades later, she recalls, "I had a truly seminal experience. Never did I expect to be blown away like I was. I loved everything about it! I loved the beautiful gardens. I loved the architecture. I loved sitting in the pew that George Washington had, standing where Patrick Henry had been in the governor's house . . . American history came alive."

As Pleasant strolled through the streets and buildings, with costumed interpreters demonstrating the arts of cooking over a fire, turning coins and other metals into useful new pieces, or making an elegant dress, she thought, *What a fantastic classroom of American history!* Families with children in tow filled the streets and buildings, and the kids were clearly fascinated with the clothing, tools, toys, and everyday items that had once been familiar aspects of life in America. Yet Pleasant noticed that most of the items sold in the gift shops and bookstores were for adults.

"I was seated under what is called a pleached arbor in colonial garden terms . . . and the idea came to me of a way to show that history is more than names and dates. It is the simple details of everyday life—the clothing our ancestors wore, the furniture they sat on, the dishes in their kitchens, the decorations in their parlors—that breathe life into history and inspire the imagination."

While completing her English major at Wells College, Pleasant had also taken many art history courses. She believes that this is what helped her create Pleasant Company: "I had learned history through pictures, and therefore the Colonial Williamsburg lessons and material culture really resonated with me in the same way." Being immersed in the homes, shops, gardens, and daily life of another era was the ideal way to learn about it.

As a former teacher and author of a popular early-elementary reading program, Pleasant knew how children learned and how to teach them—and, based on her own experience, there was a lot of American history that they didn't learn in school. Maybe she could teach it to them in a way that they would want to learn—or better yet, learn naturally through play. And so the glimmer of an idea began to form.

"**It is the simple details of everyday life—the clothing** our ancestors wore, **the furniture** they sat on, **the dishes** in their kitchens, **the decorations** in their parlors—that breathe life into history and inspire the imagination."

PLEASANT ROWLAND

In the 1970s, before starting Pleasant Company, Pleasant developed a curriculum for kindergarten called *Beginning to Read, Write, and Listen.* Later, she created materials for other grades and early readers, featuring characters called the Superkids.

Writing in the Woods

During the Christmas season of 1983, Pleasant was shopping for gifts for her nieces. She wanted to give them a really nice doll to remember their Aunt Pleasant by. But she didn't care for any of the dolls she found in stores. She thought, *I and my contemporaries are pushing against the glass ceiling, trying to redefine the roles of women, and yet what we are giving our daughters are . . . the same role models of teen queen and little mommy that they have always had. I can't be the only person this Christmas, an aunt or grandma or mom, looking for something more meaningful.*

That winter, Pleasant and her husband, Jerry, spent a weekend at their cabin in northern Wisconsin. Truly a little house in the big woods, the unwinterized cabin over a boathouse was heated with a wood-burning stove, and the outhouse used water pumped from the lake. Pleasant and Jerry enjoyed the simple, back-to-basics living conditions, which were not unlike the everyday experience of Americans in the eighteenth and nineteenth centuries. Inspired by Colonial Williamsburg, provoked by her frustrating doll search, and stirred by the simple, rustic setting that hearkened to times in America's past, Pleasant's ideas came together: "I just simply went into this cocoon of vision or creativity or whatever it was, and I wrote the business plan for Pleasant Company in one weekend. Everything: what the characters would be, what the products would be, that there would be a magazine for girls . . . eventually there would be a store that would have historical displays like little museums. The whole thing was like it was delivered to me. I just wrote and wrote and wrote. And it took fourteen years, but I did every single thing that I wrote that weekend in Minocqua."

When Pleasant left the cozy boathouse and began to ask people what they thought of her idea, none of them believed it would work. She spoke with many marketing professionals who couldn't believe she wanted to create a publishing company, a clothing company, a toy company, a direct-mail company, a theater, a magazine, and retail stores, all in one business. The standard response was, "Are you kidding?"

> "I just simply went into this cocoon of vision or creativity or whatever it was, and **I wrote the business plan for Pleasant Company in one weekend.**"
>
> PLEASANT ROWLAND

An excerpt from The Addison-Wesley Reading Program

UT— An idea: 12/2/83

“Jill the Pill”
“Rebecca's Story”
“Meg-in-the-Middle”
+ “1 new one”

A series of books (Sunshine Books!) “for girls about girls”. Revise for about 3rd grade readability + take out phonetic controls. Package in box for counterdisplay. Put paper back cover + 4 color illustration. (Good illustration) Sell for $1.95 each. What do you think? “Sunshine Mag” is moving along. xx

P.T.R.

The Addison-Wesley Reading Program
It works.

Valerie Tripp
Hilton Head
South Carolina

Pleasant wrote this postcard to author Valerie Tripp in December 1983. The idea for a series of books “for girls and about girls” was the beginning of Pleasant Company.

This *V* postcard is an illustration from *Dictopedia*, the third-grade reader Valerie and Pleasant created as part of the *Beginning to Read, Write, and Listen* curriculum.

Pleasant celebrating her eighth birthday

The Child Within

As a young girl, Pleasant delighted in organizing all manner of performances with the kids in her neighborhood. She put together plays, pageants, circuses, and parades: "Having been the little eight-year-old entrepreneur, I thought you could think big like that."

When people heard about her plans to create dolls and books rooted in history, they asked Pleasant, "How are you going to make these dolls?" "Are very many people really interested in history?" "Do you even have a fax machine?" The answers were: "I don't know," "I believe so," and "I don't know what that is."

8400 Fairway Place
Middleton, WI 53562 0998
Telephone 608 836 4848

March 21, 1990

Dear Penny:

What an amazing connection! I am, indeed, the Pleasant Thiele standing next to you in the 5th grade class picture of Clissold School in 1951. I can't believe that you could put your hands on that relic from our past. How absolutely beautiful you were back then, and I bet still are today. I loved your recollection about "standing room only" performances in my basement. I guess those of you who knew me long ago probably did see early seeds of Cecile B. Director! Building Pleasant Company has been a wonderful adventure. One of the best parts of sending ten million catalogues out each year is that sooner or later they land in the mailbox of just about everyone I ever knew. Your letter is living proof of it.

In 1990, a former fifth-grade classmate of Pleasant's reached out to her to see whether Pleasant was indeed the girl she remembered from their childhood school and neighborhood.

Sketching a Plan

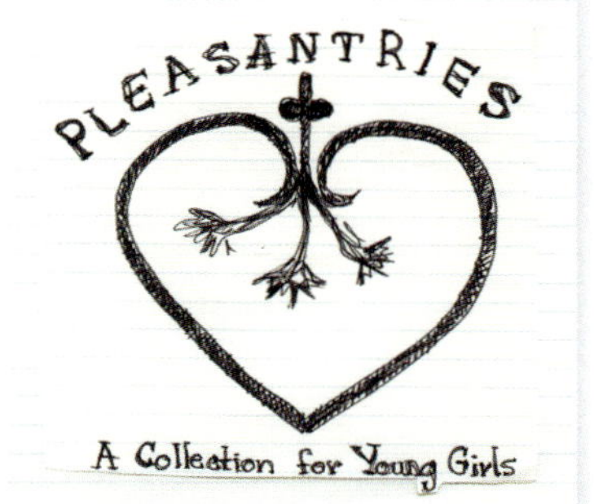

Pleasant's hand-drawn sketches from 1984 show early plans for the product line, then with the working name "Pleasantries." She highlighted three characters who lived in different times in American history:

- **Rebecca**, a Norwegian immigrant in 1865 (who later became Kirsten, from Sweden)
- **Samantha**, a girl growing up in 1905
- **Megan**, a girl growing up in 1945 (who later became Molly)

Pleasant's concept sketches also noted "Books, Dolls, Dresses & Other Delights," including doll furniture, play environments, paper goods, and party supplies. She also included the first known sketch of the doll box, which was square-shaped and had a window so girls could see the doll sitting inside.

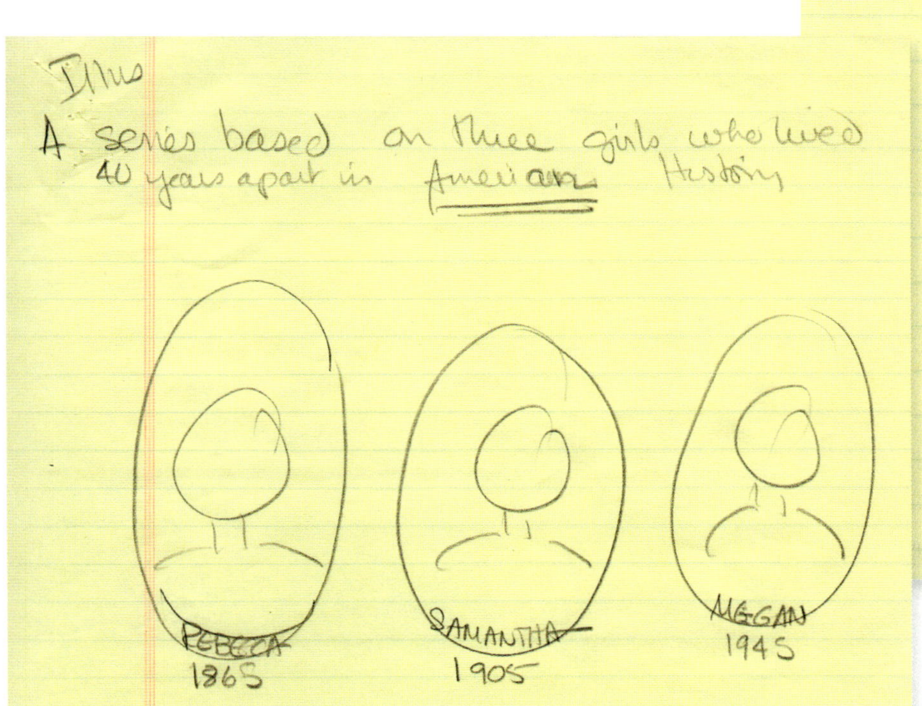

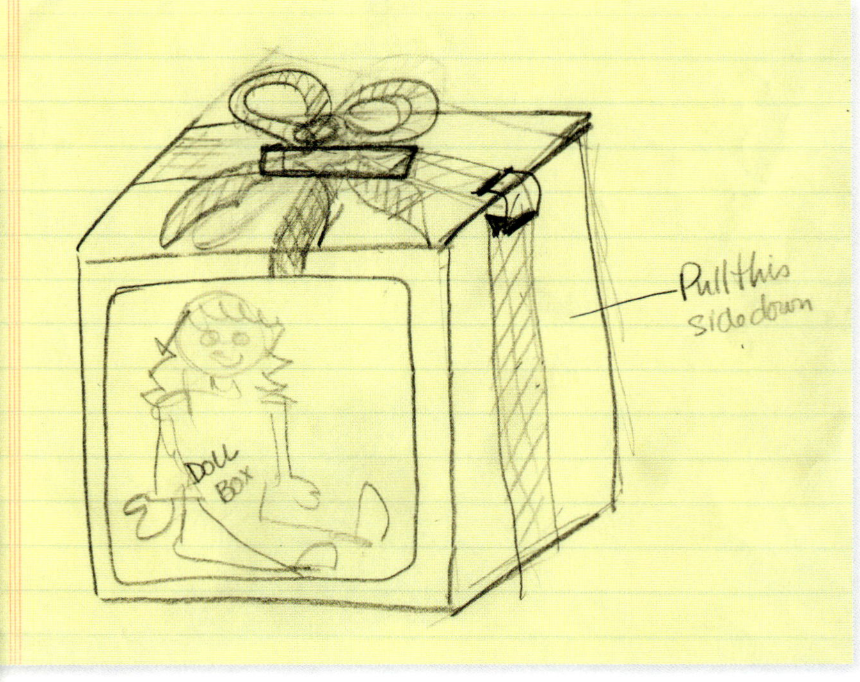

> "What I didn't know didn't stop me. I simply knew **I had a good idea,** and somehow, **I would figure out how to get it done.**"
>
> PLEASANT ROWLAND

PLEASANT RIGS
A COLLECTION FOR YOUNG GIRLS
BOOKS DOLLS DRESSES + OTHER DELIGHTS
© 1984 Pleasant T Rowland

REBECCA + HER WORLD
REBECCA
FATHER
NORWEGIAN IMMIGRANTS IN THE MIDWEST
HER FAVORITE PET
NEIGHBOR FARM
HER ROOM
2

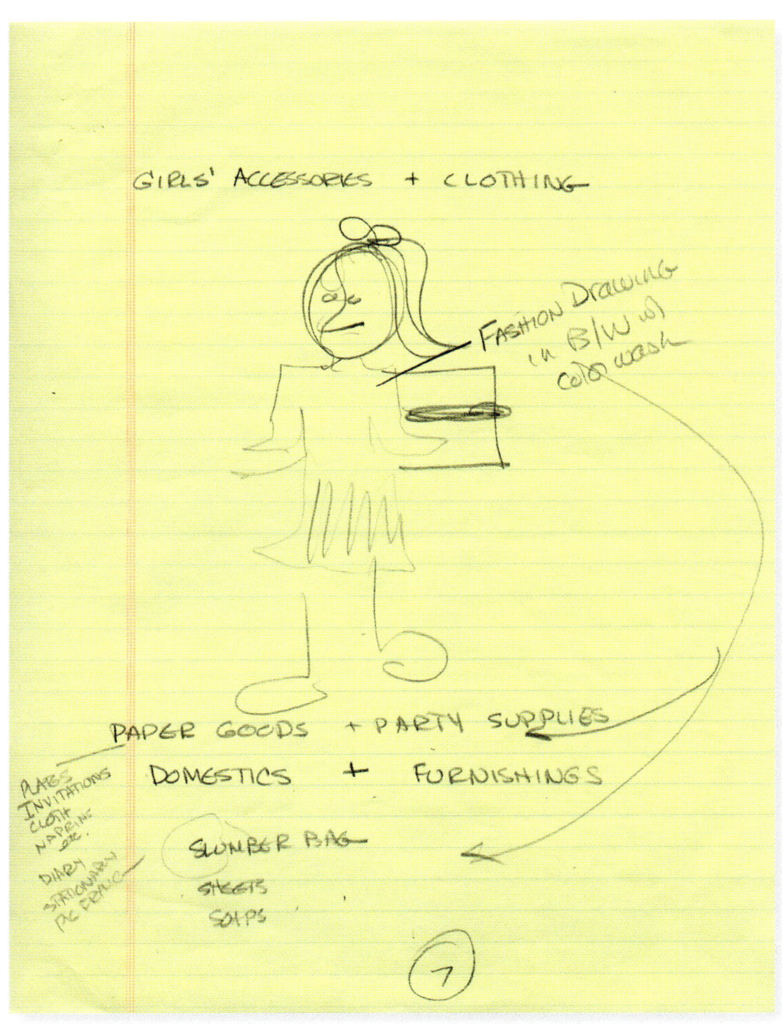
GIRLS' ACCESSORIES + CLOTHING
FASHION DRAWING IN B/W W/ COLOR WASH
PAPER GOODS + PARTY SUPPLIES
DOMESTICS + FURNISHINGS
SLUMBER BAG
SHEETS
7

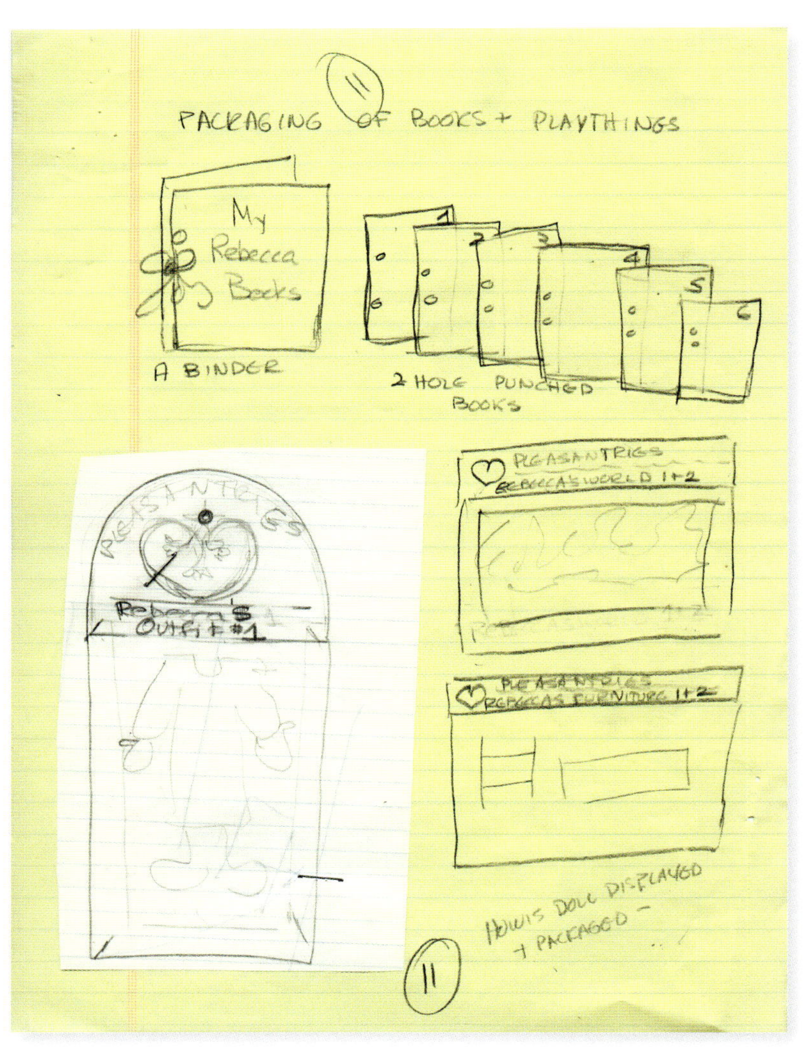
PACKAGING OF BOOKS + PLAYTHINGS
My Rebecca Books
A BINDER
2 HOLE PUNCHED BOOKS
PLEASANT RIGS
REBECCA'S WORLD 1+2
PLEASANT RIGS
REBECCA'S FURNITURE 1+2
HOW IS DOLL DISPLAYED + PACKAGED -
11

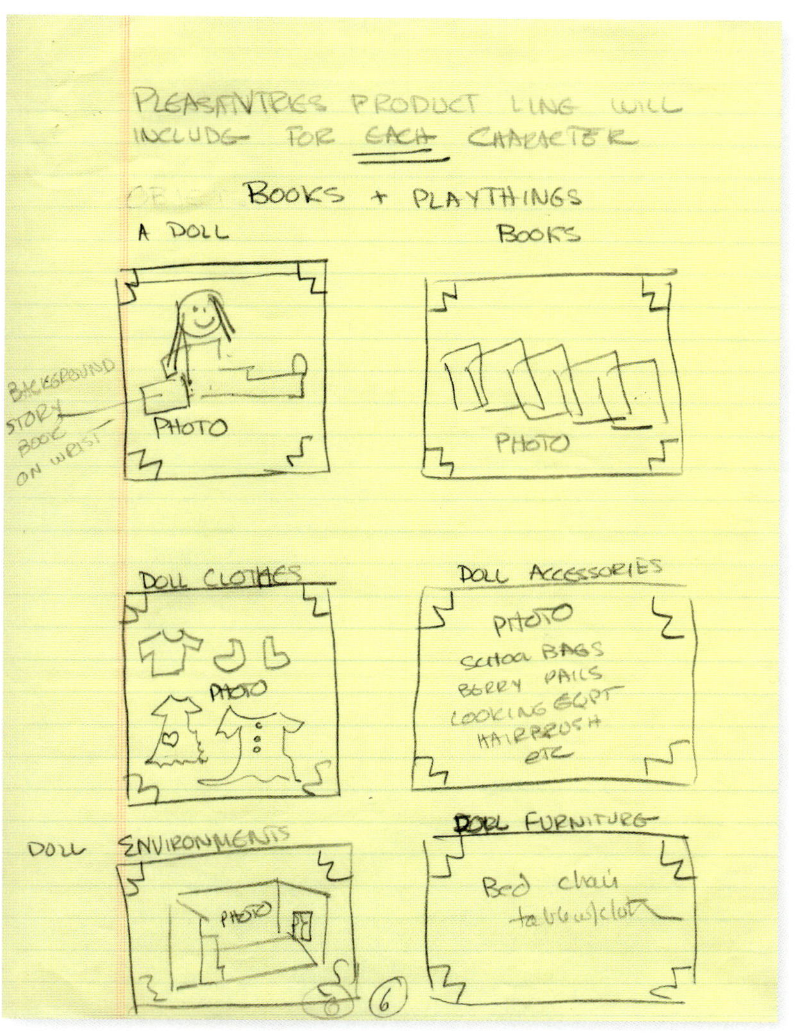
PLEASANTRIES PRODUCT LINE WILL
INCLUDE FOR EACH CHARACTER
BOOKS + PLAYTHINGS
A DOLL
BOOKS
BACKGROUND STORY BOOK ON WRIST
PHOTO
PHOTO
DOLL CLOTHES
DOLL ACCESSORIES
PHOTO
PHOTO
SCHOOL BAGS
BERRY PAILS
COOKING EQPT
HAIRBRUSH
ETC
DOLL ENVIRONMENTS
FURNITURE
PHOTO
Bed chair
table w/cloth
6

FOR INSTANCE:
Exploded illus of cover
REBECCA GOES TO BED
1
Illus from inside book
Cover on book
PHOTO OF DOLL IN ENVIRONMENT W/ DOLL FURNITURE BED TOWEL
PHOTO
DOLL
FASHION SKETCH
CURTAINS
BED
NIGHTIE
DUST RUFFLE

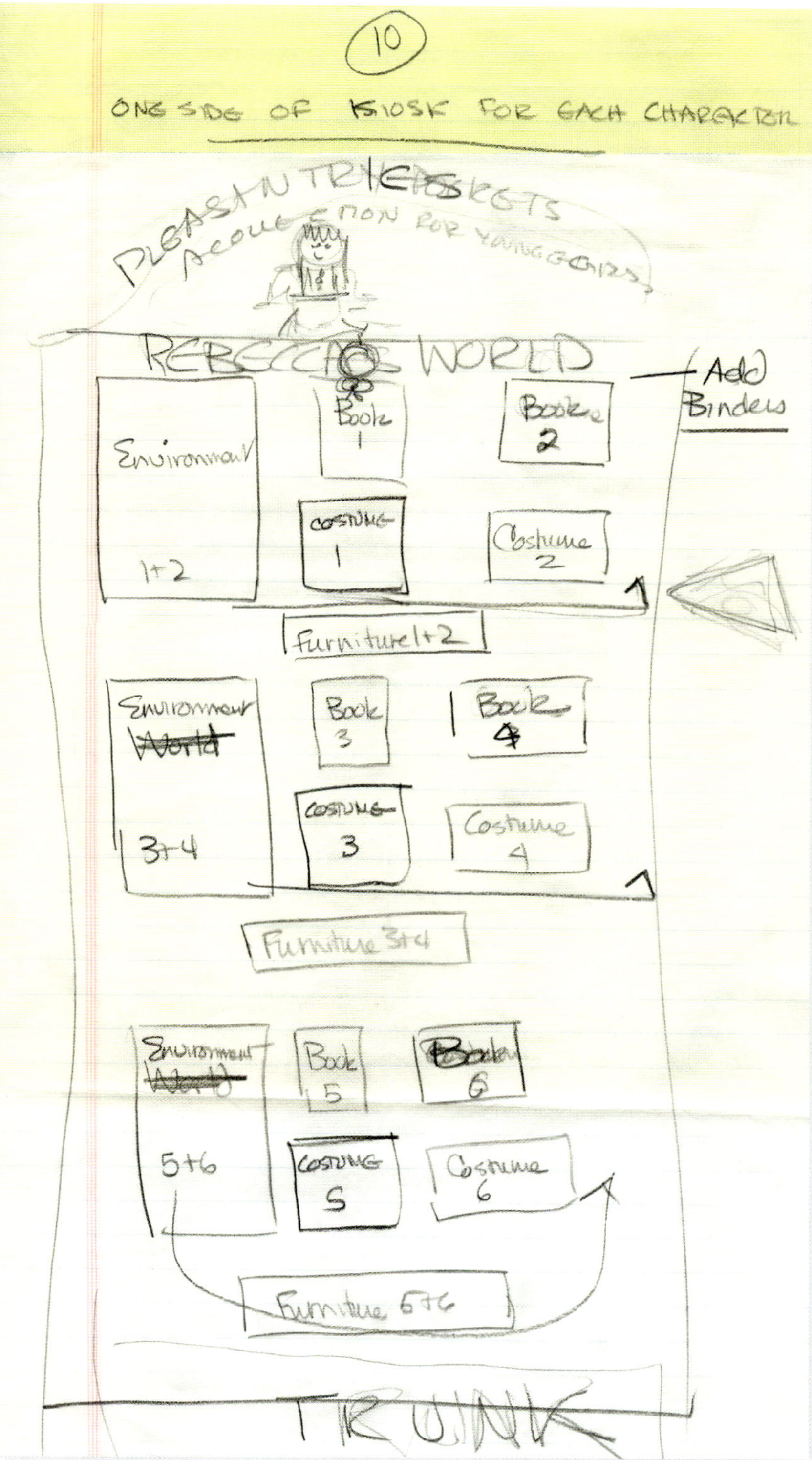
10
ONE SIDE OF KIOSK FOR EACH CHARACTER
REBECCA'S WORLD
Add Binders
Environment
1+2
Book 1
Book 2
COSTUME 1
Costume 2
Furniture 1+2
Environment
World
3+4
Book 3
Book 4
COSTUME 3
Costume 4
Furniture 3+4
Environment
World
5+6
Book 5
Book 6
COSTUME 5
Costume 6
Furniture 5+6
TRUNK

The Seeds of Stories

Pleasant has always been a storyteller at heart, since those early days of putting on plays and pageants. She adored school, loved to read, and dreamed of becoming a teacher. She wanted to serve children and to make the world a better place for them. These deeply held passions and a sense of higher purpose guided Pleasant no matter what she endeavored to do. Characters and stories were the heart of the idea that grew into The American Girls Collection, inspired by remembrances handed down by the women in Pleasant's own family: "When I looked back at my ancestors and all the women who had come before, I saw that so much of what I thought was important in my own life had been important all through their lives as well. What I think American Girl really did was give mothers and daughters and grandmothers a chance to connect, as my mother and grandmother had with me in a simpler time of childhood."

To this day, each of the American Girl characters represents what Pleasant thought of as a "small-s" story about one girl growing up in one particular time and place, living one particular life. Together, all these stories form the real "Story," with a capital S, that tells more broadly what it means to be a girl in America.

> "That capital 'S' Story, broad in scope and told in many ways through books, products, and experiences, is Pleasant Company's most unique and valuable asset, for **no other corporation is so singularly committed to or so strongly identified with 'educating and entertaining' young girls in all aspects of their lives.**"
>
> PLEASANT ROWLAND

Jeanne – Excellent points. I accept the sub-titles. Please tell Julie + Shelley + be sure Renée gets this right on presentation product boards. I'm still not happy w/ main heads – Surprise + Secret are too close. "___'s Secret" + "A Surprise for ___" work a bit better. Use them for time being & will keep thinking – We have a contest in both Molly + Samantha's school story – does that go anywhere? Share this memo w/ Shelley + Julie

PTR

To Pleasant

From Jeanne

I thought more about book covers this afternoon. I think that using either Victorian or War-Time will be a mistake.

I am still troubled by the question of accuracy. But the more important question, it seems to me, is this one: Will Victorian mean anything more to a third grader than the date 1903 will? I don't think so. I think it will be the illustration that carries the message of how long ago Samantha's (or Kirsten's or Molly's) story is set.

War-time, for me, evokes the Second World War because my father fought in it. But our readers' fathers' war was Vietnam; her parents are the peace generation; and, if the news and women's magazines are right, her own very vivid fears are of nuclear holocaust. A War-Time Story might easily discourage sales because of any of these things.

Finally, you made a point about strengthening the message that these are American stories. Why not, then, the following?

Meet Kirsten
An American Girl
1854

Meet Samantha
An American Girl
1904

Meet Molly
An American Girl
1944

Kirsten's Secret
A School Story
1854

Kirsten's Surprise
A Christmas Story
1854

In Pleasant's handwritten notes to her editor, Jeanne Thieme, she changed the characters' years so they all end in fours. Pleasant felt that the consistent numbering would make the dates easier for young readers to recall.

Early concept sketches for Samantha's first three stories. Note that her school story initially centered around a spelling bee, which later became a speaking contest in the published book.

Guiding the Illustrations

KATIE BROWN
ART DIRECTOR

Katie Brown was Pleasant Company's first book art director. She worked closely with Pleasant to conceptualize illustrations for the books and guide the illustrators, always mindful of the high standards of historical accuracy Pleasant had set out in her vision. Katie had a deep love for children's literature and had collected an extensive library of her own, including many beautifully illustrated antique editions. She loved reading and acting out stories with her son. She found great joy in using her exceptional creative talents to bring the American Girls characters and story moments to life. Kirsten artist Renée Graef recalls,

> "Katie herself posed as Miss Winston in the Kirsten books—**it adds such a special touch to the series!**"

Miss Winston is seated second from right.

Note: Kirsten will be Swedish, not Norwegian. Her family will move to a Midwestern state, but it may not be Wisconsin.

Book 1: Meet Kirsten

Summary: Kirsten and her family emigrate from Norway to Wisconsin

When Kirsten's father gets a letter from his brother Olav inviting him to come to Wisconsin and share a farm, he decides that he and his family will go. Kirsten has mixed feelings of excitement, apprehension, regret, and curiosity. At her mother's insistence she packs up only her most essential belongings regretfully leaving behind some favorite possessions. At the last moment she secretly tucks in a few treasures. Finally the family leaves their pretty, familiar, comfortable house in Norway and heads off to the unknown, wild frontier in Wisconsin.

The journey is long and arduous. The Larson family sails from Bergen to New York, takes a steamer up the Hudson to Albany, takes a train to Buffalo, takes another steamer across three Great Lakes to Milwaukee. They run out of money and have to walk the last legs of the journey from Milwaukee to New Bergen. They leave their large trunk in Milwaukee to lighten the load. When at last they arrive in New Bergen, Uncle Olav, Aunt Inger and their daughters Lisbeth and Anna welcome them and make them comfortable.

Soon the Larsons move out to their own house on the farm, a small log building Uncle Olav no longer uses. Kirsten loves the

This early story description for *Meet Kirsten* was written by Valerie Tripp. The handwritten note at the top indicates that Kirsten's background would change from Norwegian to Swedish. The sample illustration was created in 1984.

Book 1: Meet Samantha and Jessie

Summary: Samantha leads her friend Phoebe on a midnight adventure to find out why Jessie, the seamstress, has left her job at Grandmary's house so unexpectedly.

Jessie is the tall, beautiful black woman who works in Grandmary's house as a seamstress and laundress. Samantha loves to sit in the laundry room and talk to Jessie while she washes, irons, and mends clothes. Jessie tells Samantha all about the places her husband, Lincoln, a railroad porter, has been. He brings Jessie postcards and gifts from far-off places like Chicago and New Orleans, which Samantha loves to see. Jessie's beauty, regal manner, and knowledge (through Lincoln) of distant places make her a romantic figure to Samantha.

When, one day after she has finished working, Jessie calmly rolls down her sleeves, puts on her hat, and goes to Grandmary to give her notice, everyone is surprised. Samantha is heartbroken and immediately begins to invent dramatic, extravagant reasons for Jessie's departure, which she explains to her friend Phoebe. One fantasy she has is that Jessie might be going to have a baby, but she is afraid to ask Grandmary if her suspicion is accurate.

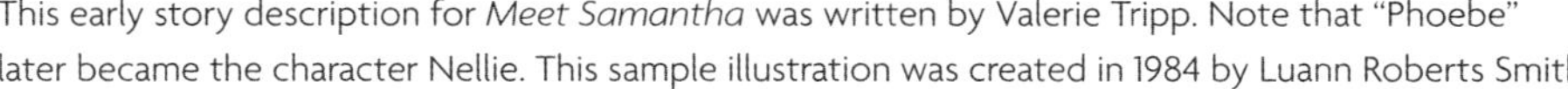

This early story description for *Meet Samantha* was written by Valerie Tripp. Note that "Phoebe" later became the character Nellie. This sample illustration was created in 1984 by Luann Roberts Smith.

Book 1: Molly's Room

Summary: Molly, Linda, and Susan have a sweet revenge on Ricky after he spoils their Halloween.

Molly, Linda, and Susan are sitting on the back stoop of Molly's house trying to decide what to be on Halloween. Cinderella and her two stepsisters? Needless to say, no one wants to be an ugly stepsister so they decide the only fair thing is to be three hula dancers. Ricky, Molly's older brother, has been listening to their conversation, imitating the girls, and scoffing at their vanity. When Jill's friend Dolores sweeps by, he quickly loses interest in taunting them. All at once Ricky turns into Mr. Cool and begins dribbling his basketball with elaborate footwork and making swooping shots at the basket. The girls immediately spot a crush. They tease Ricky to the point where he threatens to retaliate.

And Ricky does retaliate. On Halloween, as the three hula dancers come up Molly's front walk in costumes made from crepe paper, carrying paper bags bulging with treats, Ricky squirts them with the hose. The bags burst, the candy is ruined, the costumes fall apart, and the girls' Halloween fun has been destroyed. Ricky just laughs and chants, "I see London, I see France, I see Molly's underpants."

The girls are outraged: if this is Ricky's idea of retaliation, they will teach him a lesson. They spend the night at Molly's house and plot their revenge.

This early story description of *Meet Molly* was written by Valerie Tripp, and the sample illustration was created in 1984.

A True Friend

AUTHOR VALERIE TRIPP

Valerie Tripp is the award-winning author of dozens of American Girl books about Samantha, Molly, Felicity, Josefina, Kit, Maryellen, and more. But these weren't the first characters she and Pleasant had created together. Valerie first met Pleasant when Pleasant hired her right out of college to work on a reading program she was creating, featuring characters called the Superkids. For ten years, Valerie and Pleasant wrote stories, songs, and poems about this wonderful little group of characters. While they worked, they chatted about the books they had loved passionately when they were girls—*Anne of Green Gables*, *Little Women*, and *Beezus and Ramona*—stories where girls had the adventures and caused all the trouble.

They talked about the kinds of stories they wished existed for girls, where the girls solved the problems and saved the day and were the heroes of their own stories.

Several years later, Pleasant shared her ideas for creating stories about girls who lived in different eras of American history. She asked Valerie to work with her to write character descriptions and plot outlines. Valerie remembers sitting with Pleasant under a shady tree next to the capitol building in Madison, Wisconsin, dreaming up stories about who these girls would be and where they would live. They talked about the girls' families, their personalities, their failings, and their abilities. Valerie recalls,

> "It has been my life's honor, privilege, challenge, and delight to work with all the exceptional people at Pleasant Company over the past forty years. I am grateful that Pleasant trusted me—beginning more than forty years ago—to be the **first voice of American Girl** and the voice of so many characters."

Pleasant remembers fondly, "Valerie was the first person I ever talked to about the American Girl idea. She is a friend so trusted and true, so wise and principled, so quick and creative, that I turned to her frequently throughout the years for solace and inspiration, support and affirmation. Because she did not work at Pleasant Company and was not caught up in the daily crises and deadlines, her perspective was always fresh and her objectivity priceless."

PLEASANT ROWLAND

VALERIE TRIPP

The Role of Research

When Pleasant dreamed up the idea for The American Girls Collection in the early 1980s, there was little scholarship on the history of children—and even less on girls. Historical scholarship had traditionally concentrated on the experiences of adults and usually featured men and boys. In textbooks and reading materials for children, Pleasant also found few girls and women. Aside from classics such as the Little House series, girls weren't the stars of many children's stories. Most educators and publishers at the time believed that girls would read stories about boys, but not vice versa. Boys were their audience, and girls had no choice but to ride along.

Pleasant saw girls as her audience, and she knew that to provide them with historically accurate books and products, her team would need to conduct their own research. She referred to this careful balance between education and play as "vitamins in the chocolate cake." Pleasant was a pioneer in prioritizing the history of girls and women. She called on experts and brought advisory boards together to find the pockets of overlooked history necessary to bring her American Girl characters to life. She built a significant body of research devoted solely to girls—who they were, what their lives were like, and what has held meaning for them throughout time.

This painting of girls in fashionable dresses with open necklines, along with the historical dress at far right from the Wisconsin Historical Society, served as inspiration for Addy's Cape Island Dress (at right) in the short story "Addy's Summer Place."

From its earliest days, Pleasant Company forged a strong relationship with the Wisconsin Historical Society, which was just a few blocks from the company's original offices. The Wisconsin Historical Society library has one of the country's most extensive collections of materials on North American history, second only to the Library of Congress. Dresses from the Historical Society's collection, such as the ones seen on this page, inspired several outfits for The American Girls Collection, including Kirsten's Plaid Dress and Samantha's Talent Show Dress.

Painted trunks from the 1850s, like the one above, inspired Kirsten's Trunk, shown below.

Notice the unfinished prototype of Josefina's Chest on the workroom table, along with Josefina's doll-head mold and painted portraits by Jean-Paul Tibbles.

Trunks with pullout drawers for storing doll accessories, like the one above, were an inspiration for Samantha's Trunk (left).

Job Description: Research Assistant

It is the job of the research assistant to provide factual background information for use by the writers, illustrators, and product developers. The resource notebooks compiled by the research assistant will be continually updated as new stories are conceived and additional verification is needed. The research assistant should provide copies of photos or drawings that will help the writer or illustrator envision the period and lifestyle each character lived in. The researcher should always be alert to unusual or interesting information that could be woven into a story or even become an integral aspect of it. While such information may not seem immediately pertinent it can become the real "stuff" of creative inspiration. The research assistant will be the primary resource for the writer and illustrator and will be on call to them for verification of primary sources or reliable secondary resources. Since part of Pleasant Company's objective is to reproduce products from each period both as doll accessories and children's accessories, the researcher should be constantly on the lookout for period objects (or pictures of them) that are attractive and would be appropriate for reproduction or interpretation.

1/3/85
slr

Pleasant wrote a job description that emphasized the important and impactful role research would play in Pleasant Company's stories and products.

An Excellent Go-cart with Hood Cover.

The body of this cart is made with closely woven flat and round reeds of the very finest quality. Has a hood cover, full lined, with large roll in front, put on with clamps by which it can be adjusted to any position. Has our patent sleeper attachment by which the back and dash can be independently adjusted to any position desired. The body of the cart is finished in natural color, protected by a heavy coat of shellac. Has our very latest Automobile Comfort Gear, fully described on page 402, finished in Brewster green enamel, heavy cushion tire wheels, rubber hub caps, patent wheel fasteners and automatic foot brake. The handles form part of the gear so that it is easily controlled.

No. 25Y907 Without uholstering or hood. Price.............. $14.95

No. 25Y908 Upholstere[illegible] cushions of Bedford Cord, an[illegible] on seat, back, sides and dash. Price. ....$1[illegible]

This cart with regular ru[illegible] tired wheels for $1.00 less than above prices.

Images from catalogues served as inspiration for products like Samantha's Elegant Doll Pram.

Reproductions of Civil War–era publications, like *Harper's Weekly*, were used to line Addy's Trunk.

An Honorary Doctorate

In May 2004, Pleasant was awarded an honorary doctor of letters degree from the University of Wisconsin–Madison. Professor Dave Riley, from the School of Human Ecology, honored her with remarks that celebrated her achievements, especially her commitment to historical scholarship:

"When the picture in the chapter shows Kirsten's lunch pail, you can rest assured that the staff found, photographed, and dated an identical lunch pail in a museum somewhere in North America while researching the book. These books maintain a level of scholarship that we academics can respect, and it is a level that is simply unheard of in children's literature. What makes this commitment to costly research all the more surprising is that it ran so directly against the grain of American merchandising during the early years of the books' development. The advice of business consultants in those years was to reduce costs of products and services in every way possible. . . . Making a commitment to the costs of scholarly quality in her products must have made Ms. Rowland look very foolish and even naïve at the time. Of course, she has the last laugh now, but we should acknowledge that her commitment to historical scholarship certainly required an unusual degree of courage and conviction."

DAVE RILEY
UNIVERSITY OF WISCONSIN–MADISON
SCHOOL OF HUMAN ECOLOGY

Since Pleasant Company was founded, primary sources such as diaries, schoolbooks, magazines, and catalogues have served as invaluable references for editors, authors, illustrators, and product designers.

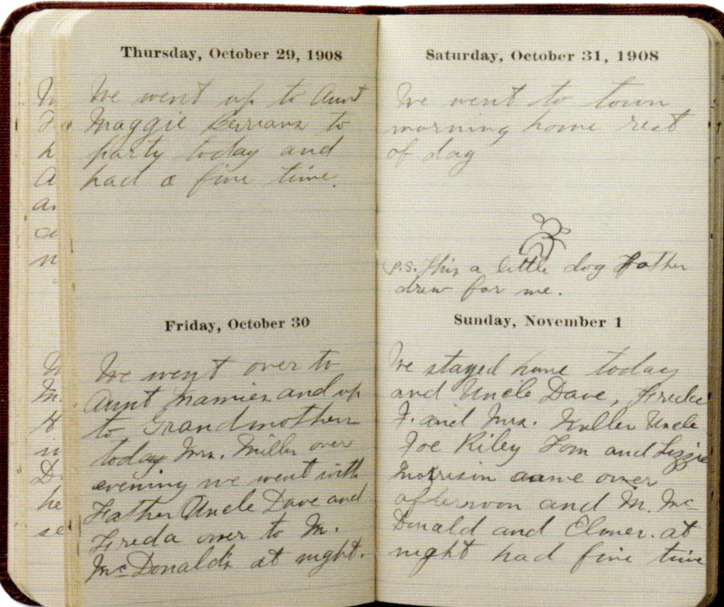
Thursday, October 29, 1908
Saturday, October 31, 1908
Friday, October 30
Sunday, November 1

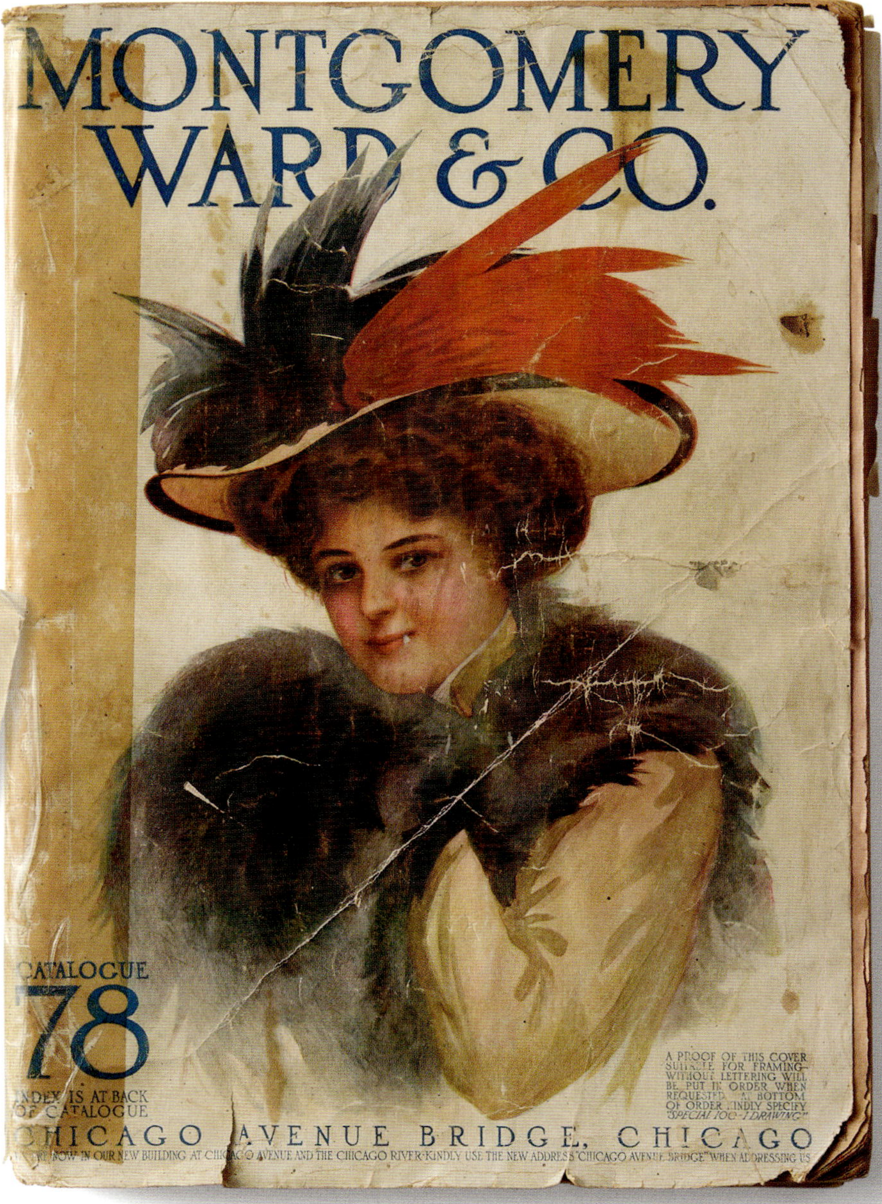
MONTGOMERY WARD & CO.
CATALOGUE
78
INDEX IS AT BACK OF CATALOGUE
CHICAGO AVENUE BRIDGE, CHICAGO

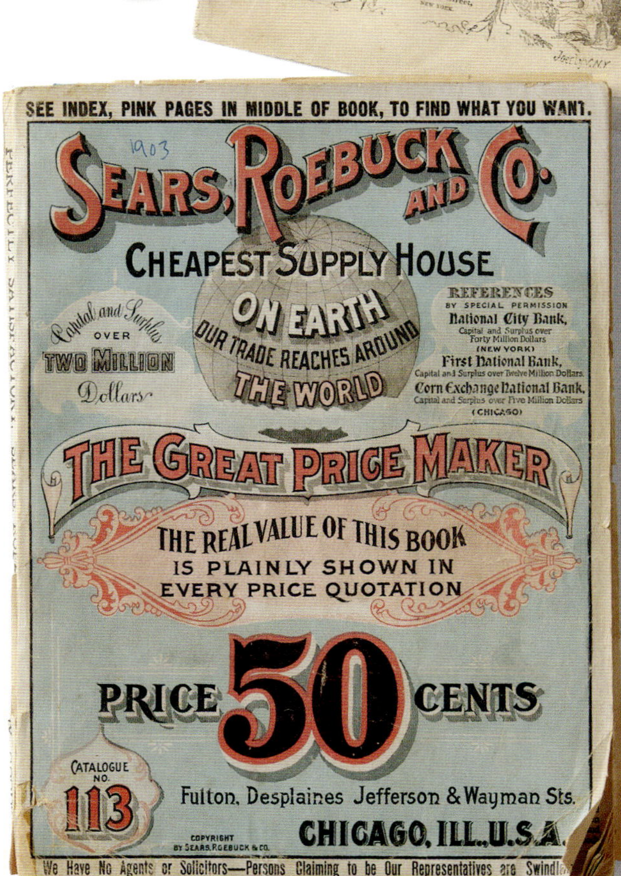
SEE INDEX, PINK PAGES IN MIDDLE OF BOOK, TO FIND WHAT YOU WANT.
SEARS, ROEBUCK AND CO.
CHEAPEST SUPPLY HOUSE
ON EARTH
OUR TRADE REACHES AROUND THE WORLD
Capital and Surplus over TWO MILLION Dollars
REFERENCES
BY SPECIAL PERMISSION
National City Bank,
First National Bank,
Corn Exchange National Bank,
THE GREAT PRICE MAKER
THE REAL VALUE OF THIS BOOK IS PLAINLY SHOWN IN EVERY PRICE QUOTATION
PRICE 50 CENTS
CATALOGUE NO. 113
Fulton, Desplaines Jefferson & Wayman Sts.
CHICAGO, ILL. U.S.A.

WALL PAPER
SEARS, ROEBUCK & CO. CHICAGO.

Designs Come to Life

Product design was a flurry of activity beginning in mid-1984. Pleasant's small team brainstormed and refined lists of potential product ideas, filled file after file with historical references, sketched many versions of dresses and accessories for dolls and girls, and stitched dress samples in plain muslin to start bringing designs to life in 3D. Worktables were awash in fabric swatches, ribbons, and trims. Slowly, the iconic colors, shapes, patterns, and textures of each of the first three characters' product worlds came into focus.

In January 1985, work began in earnest to create actual prototypes of outfits and accessories. Pleasant implemented a "policy of authenticity." Every item was verified for accuracy with at least one existing period item from a museum, pictures from reliable sources of items with attributable dates, or a sketch or description created by a respected expert. "The purpose of the prototype stage," said Pleasant, "is the same as that of a first draft of a manuscript: to give us all something to react to; to give manufacturers an idea of our needs; to give writers and illustrators a source for their work; to show investors what these products will look like."

Pleasant and prototype creator Susan Weston agreed that it would be impossible for the items in the collection to be exact reproductions of period items down to every detail. Instead, they would be authentic interpretations that took playability and wearability by modern girls into account, while still giving them the opportunity to learn through play about the material culture of each time period.

Pleasant did not want to create "shelf dolls" that looked pretty but gathered dust. She wanted her dolls and their enchanting outfits and accessories to be loved and played with for generations. "The products sprang from the stories," Valerie recalls, "and they were consistent across the first three characters' storylines. The product developers and Pleasant would choose certain items mentioned in the stories to be products, such as the box of presents and the radio for Molly. When they suggested a product to me, such as Molly's green velvet dress, I always loved incorporating those ideas into later versions of the stories."

> "We wanted readers to be able to **compare characters across time.** That is, what was school like for Molly, for Samantha, for Kirsten? **How was it the same? How was it different?**"
>
> VALERIE TRIPP

Pleasant Company's product design workroom in the 1990s. Outfits for Addy, Molly, and Felicity are in development. Notice the board with miniature food and lunch-box samples in the foreground, a prototype of Josefina's Chest on the back table, and paintings from the Scenes & Settings product on the high shelf at the back of the room.

Early sketches and swatches for girls' clothing from 1984

Women's magazines such as *Harper's Bazar* (later *Harper's Bazaar*), *Woman's Home Companion*, *The Delineator*, *Good Housekeeping*, and *Ladies' Home Journal* were rich sources of inspiration for the original dresses.

For easy reference, designers created sheets of fabric swatches for each character.

Kirsten Line Fabric (1 of 2)
KMA
KBAGR
KSO
KXO
KPO
KSAB - new slate bag fabric
94-95 production
KMO
KAO
Early Rendition of KSO
KNO
KCO
KMO
KSO
KAO
KWAU
KWO
KBO
KXO
KHOS
KDO
KBAG
KXOH

Felicity Line Fabric
Girl (Felicity) Line Fabric (2 of 2)
ECO
EC600
EXO
EA600
EM600
EA600
ES601 & ES602
(Jacket) (skirt)
EB600
EY600
EW600

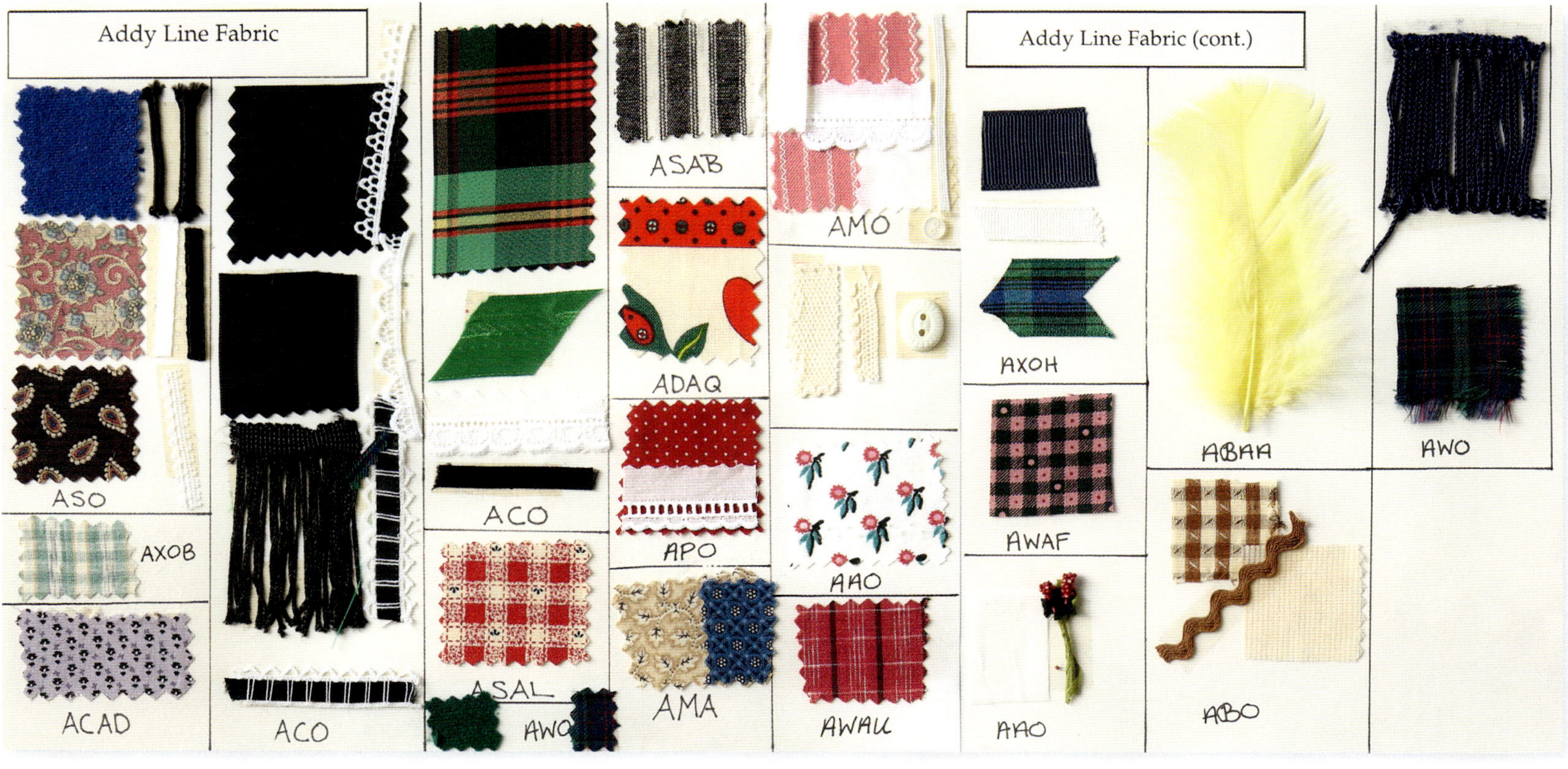
Addy Line Fabric
ASAB
AMO
Addy Line Fabric (cont.)
AXOH
ADAQ
ABAA
AWO
ASO
AXOB
ACO
APO
AWAF
AAO
ACAD
ACO
ASAL
AWO
AMA
AWAU
AAO
ABO

An Illustrator Gets Her Start

RENÉE GRAEF
ILLUSTRATOR

Renée Graef, who was later chosen to illustrate Kirsten's series, created early sketches and color illustrations for Kirsten's, Samantha's, and Molly's outfits and accessories. Here, Renée's early dress sketches for the characters show the delightful charm and personality her illustrations are known for. As Renée recalls,

"When I entered Pleasant's office, six or seven employees were gathered in the room. She reviewed my artwork, then asked them to leave the room before turning to me and asking when I could start sketching her idea for the company's dolls, historical fiction books, and related products.

I arrived the next day, and Pleasant led me to my desk at the end of the hallway from her office. She carried an armful of meticulously researched reference materials for Kirsten, Samantha, and Molly and explained her vision of Pleasant Company.

I created about ten boards for each character, thirty total. One board featured a placeholder sketch of each doll. The other boards depicted the Meet, School, and Holiday doll outfits for each character, and a separate illustration showed a modern-day girl wearing the same outfit.

Additional boards showcased the accessories designed for each ensemble. **The drawings closely reflected the products that were in development, planned by Pleasant, who had considered every detail.**"

Meet Kirsten
An American Girl
A Surprise for Samantha
A Christmas Story
Girls' Clothes
Kirsten's Secret
A School Story
Samantha's Secret
A School Story
Girls' Clothes
A Surprise for Kirsten
A Surprise for Molly
A Christmas Story
Girls' Clothes
© Copyright 1985 · Pleasant T.
Molly's Secret
A School Story
Girls' Clothes
Samantha's Secret
A School Story
$90.
Girls' Clothes

Defining the Look of Pleasant Company

MYLAND MCREVEY
CREATIVE DIRECTOR

In early 1984, Pleasant began working with nationally known designer and illustrator Myland McRevey. While visiting San Francisco, where Myland lived at the time, Pleasant saw a beautiful logo for a local bakery and could not get it out of her mind. She found the designer, Myland, and told him about her business plans. She asked if he would design her logo and move to Madison, Wisconsin, to create her entire brand identity, overseeing the design of her catalogue, packaging, and book covers. Myland agreed. His work shaped the look of Pleasant Company and continues to influence American Girl's brand today.

In one of Pleasant's early logo sketches, she tried out the company name "Pleasantries." This eventually became the name of Pleasant Company's employee newsletter.

Creating a Logo

When Pleasant first began work on Pleasant Company's original logo, she considered calling the company The Sunshine Collection. Then someone suggested that she include her name in the title: The Sunshine Collection by Pleasant Rowland. In a letter to creative director Myland McRevey in 1984, she wrote,

> "I am uncomfortable on one hand with this concept, and flattered on the other. Perhaps you might want to conceive an alternative using my name as well. . . . **My name at least has a cheery, wholesome sound, which fits with the concept.** (People would probably think I made it up!)"
>
> PLEASANT ROWLAND

While Pleasant mulled name options, she set out her thoughts about what the logo should look like. She wanted a silhouette logo showing a little girl reading a book with a doll near her. The silhouette had a historical feel, and it also suggested "girl" without depicting any specific girl. A little girl could imagine it was one of the characters in the books, or she could imagine it was herself reading with her doll. In November of 1984, Pleasant sent Myland "some scratchings" she had made to show this concept for the logo. These are the first sketches that show the name "Pleasant Company." Pleasant's sketches didn't include a doll (although she told Myland he needed to add one!), but they gave the "lost in a good book" feeling she was hoping for.

PLEASANT T. ROWLAND

7 NORTH PINCKNEY STREET · MADISON, WISCONSIN 53703 · 608-251-2222

March 8, 1984

Pleasant sent along these "scratchings" to show Myland the feeling she wanted in the logo—a little girl lost in a good book.

Dear Myland:

This letter is just to confirm the main points of our telephone discussion of Monday. I am delighted you are interested in participating in the design of The Sunshine Collection. I think it is an enormously exciting project with the ability to have a positive impact on lots of little girls and on the toy and merchandise industry that reaches them. I am setting out to put together a strong team of the brightest, most creative and talented individuals I can find so that we can realize all the potential of the idea.

We discussed the need for the primary product logo; perhaps a silhouette of an 8-year-old girl standing holding or reading a book. This logo would relate to the entire product line: The Sunshine Collection for All American Girls. (Note there is no hyphen between All and American.) Then we need some way to vary the logo, e.g., with color, background pattern, posture of silhouette, to relate to each of the four characters. The characters are:

- Rebecca who embodies the American Folk Art tradition and lives some time around 1880 in rural America.

- Victoria who embodies the "country Victorian" look and lives some time around 1910 in small town America.

- Megan who lives in suburban America in 1943-44.

Pleasant wrote this letter to Myland to share her early vision for the logo. Note that the characters' names and dates were still in flux.

When Pleasant received the first renderings of the logo from Myland, she asked "innocent bystanders" to stop and vote on the various versions. She took their comments into account as she spent hours studying the alternatives before selecting one:

Myland drew the original silhouette logo and designed the typography, which he named "Pleasant Palatino."

Pleasant loved the natural, involved pose Myland captured in the girl reading her book, the perky posture of the doll, and the playful way the girl's feet were posed. She loved how the girl's head, feet, and book broke the frame, bringing her visually closer to the viewer. Pleasant was not a fan of the big *P* in the typography, and she asked Myland to try a different type solution. She also thought the doll's curled toes felt too "elfin" and asked that the girl's hairstyle be given more life—especially the bangs, which she described as "a ledge." Before sending her comments back to Myland, she added a hair ribbon to the girl to reinforce the idea that girls could dress like their dolls.

Pleasant and Myland tried several versions of background patterns within the logo, which Pleasant liked because they resembled wallpaper and gave a cozy, room-like feel to the little scene. Ultimately, though, they were concerned that the patterns felt too reminiscent of the designer Laura Ashley and might distract viewers from the lovely moment between the girl, her doll, and a good book.

PLEASANT T. ROWLAND

7 NORTH PINCKNEY STREET · MADISON, WISCONSIN 53703 · 608-251-2222

June 7, 1985

Dear Myland:

Eeek! Help! A logo crisis!

Wednesday we did an informal "woman on the street" field test of the logo. The results are enclosed, and you will see that we have a problem. Only 50% of the respondents identified the doll as a doll. Other people thought it was a second, smaller girl or a baby. Clearly, our batting average has to improve on instant recognition.

I think two things could be done that would help the problem: (1) reduce the size of the doll, and (2) shorten her legs.

In scrutinizing the proportions of dolls, we have become aware that their legs are shorter than humans in relation to the rest of their bodies. So if you could reduce the length, I think this could help alleviate our problem. Could you send us a revision approximately 3 1/2" x 2 1/2" as well as in the letterhead size.

I am enclosing the copy of Valerie Tripp's manuscript you requested as well as some photo-copied pages from a book whose page trim size is 6" x 8 1/4" (with 3/8" taken up in the stitching of the binding). Its type size, leading, and margins seemed appropriate to our reader. I also like the illustration style and would like your reaction to it. This book is done completely in black-and-white. We will contact the illustrator to see if she has samples in color.

We look forward to seeing you on July 8. I do want to extend an invitation to you to stay in our guest house for a week or so while you look for housing in Madison. It is completely separate from our home and you may come and go as you please. Let me know when you expect to arrive in Madison so I don't plan on having other guests at the same time. Of course, if you would prefer to stay somewhere else, that is fine, too.

Please return the revised logo at your earliest opportunity. We really need to do another test to make sure that we are on target.

Sincerely,

Pleasant

Pleasant T. Rowland

PTR/mlc

Enclosures

"Eeek! Help! A logo crisis!"

Just as Pleasant and Myland were closing in on the final details, they found themselves in an unexpected "logo crisis," as the letter at left details. Thankfully, the crisis was narrowly averted. The final logo shows a smaller doll with shorter legs, longer hair, and a hairbow that more closely matches the girl's.

Packaged with Care

When a Pleasant Company package arrived on a customer's doorstep, there was no company logo or address on the shipping carton, just in case a girl might find the package. Pleasant wanted to make sure the special surprise wasn't spoiled. Inside, an elegant burgundy box with a creamy satin ribbon awaited.

Employees packed each box with care, gently wrapping the doll or accessory in pretty printed tissue paper, creased just so. They wore white gloves to avoid leaving fingerprints on the glossy packaging, and they placed each logo sticker by hand for a special finishing touch.

Outfits were hung on hangers with heart-shaped cutouts and placed in specially printed garment bags.

Pleasant chose a rectangular doll box both to showcase the doll's full outfit and to place the book front and center. Because these boxes were not going to be on toy shelves, she didn't need to include the window from her earlier concepts. She wanted a girl to open the doll box the way she would open a present—excitedly removing the ribbon and lifting the lid to find out what was inside!

A Catalogue That Tells a Story

III. <u>Product Presentation and Merchandising</u>

The merchandise of Pleasant Company does not lend itself to traditional marketing techniques--particularly those used so extensively by licensees of children's characters. Since the images of the three characters will never appear on any of the merchandise it will be difficult for any individual product to retain its identity away from the whole. The merchandising concept--in fact, the very justification for the product--is lost if the collection is distributed throughout a large store where the dolls would be placed in the toy department, sheets in the linen department and dresses in the children's clothing department. A single, focused presentation of such diverse merchandise is necessary if the product synergy is to take effect for the whole of Pleasant Company is greater than the sum of its parts.

That single, focused presentation can take place in two forms:

- through a direct mail catalog devoted exclusively to Pleasant Company merchandise
- through a Pleasant Company store or leased boutique within a larger retail establishment.

A direct mail catalog is an extremely appropriate vehicle for this merchandise since it allows us the opportunity to "romance" our product, and to tell our story thoroughly. The catalog can emphasize the product relationship. At a glance the catalog shopper can see an illustration from the book of a doll dressed and accessorized to match and then a live model dressed and accessorized in an appropriate period setting styled like the illustration. It is possible to include excerpts from the books themselves so the catalog gives the child some enjoyable reading material while she browses through its pictures of products.

A mini-catalog will be created for each book featuring only the products that relate to that episode. It will be bound into the back of each book but will be perforated so it can be torn out. Since the books will be distributed through traditional bookstore outlets we can be assured that every girl who reads one of the stories also knows that there is other merchandise available--a passive direct marketing technique that saves postage!

Pleasant updated her business plan in 1985 and included the reasoning behind her choice of a direct-mail catalogue. Later in the document, she also explained why future retail stores were an important part of her plan.

One of the first questions Pleasant had to answer when she was planning Pleasant Company was how she was going to reach her audience—primarily girls and their mothers and grandmothers. She didn't have the money to buy shelf space at retail. Besides, what fueled retail for kids' products in the late 1980s was Saturday morning TV. That was expensive, too, and more importantly, Pleasant had a much subtler story to tell. It needed to be told in a softer voice. So Pleasant learned all she could about direct mail, and she began to create a catalogue that told a story.

The first catalogue cover was inspired by a famous painting by Jessie Willcox Smith, originally used in a 1905 edition of Robert Louis Stevenson's *A Child's Garden of Verses.*

Some of Pleasant's early catalogue concepts

Early Catalogue Development

Before there were glossy photographs of professionally styled dolls, before there was delightful catalogue copy that read like a story (Pleasant wrote every word herself), before there were beautiful book covers illustrated in full color, and before some product prototypes were even available, Pleasant and Myland worked out the designs for each spread, using whatever props, sketches, and early prototypes they had. These next pages offer a peek behind the curtain at the early ideas that became the beloved catalogue that girls still tuck under their pillows.

Above, Pleasant looks in on the photo shoot for the first catalogue cover. At right, a mock-up of the first catalogue cover that used the inspiration art as a placeholder beneath a vellum overlay.

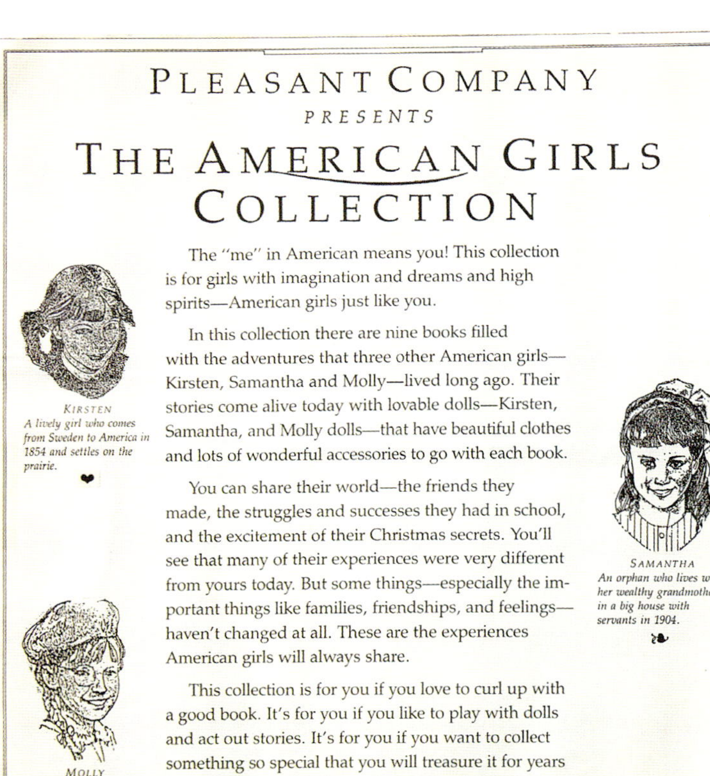

PLEASANT COMPANY
PRESENTS
THE AMERICAN GIRLS COLLECTION

The "me" in American means you! This collection is for girls with imagination and dreams and high spirits—American girls just like you.

In this collection there are nine books filled with the adventures that three other American girls—Kirsten, Samantha and Molly—lived long ago. Their stories come alive today with lovable dolls—Kirsten, Samantha, and Molly dolls—that have beautiful clothes and lots of wonderful accessories to go with each book.

You can share their world—the friends they made, the struggles and successes they had in school, and the excitement of their Christmas secrets. You'll see that many of their experiences were very different from yours today. But some things—especially the important things like families, friendships, and feelings—haven't changed at all. These are the experiences American girls will always share.

This collection is for you if you love to curl up with a good book. It's for you if you like to play with dolls and act out stories. It's for you if you want to collect something so special that you will treasure it for years to come—a keepsake to remind you of the pleasant company you had with Kirsten, Samantha, and Molly.

The American Girls Collection:
An Experience to Treasure

KIRSTEN
A lively girl who comes from Sweden to America in 1854 and settles on the prairie.

SAMANTHA
An orphan who lives with her wealthy grandmother in a big house with servants in 1904.

MOLLY
The middle child in a large family whose father is off at war in England during World War II.

MEET KIRSTEN

Offnen sich die mau zaunen und trotzen. Die form eines plakes verschieden nach dem samen, au Beide wurzeln im fuchtbaren bord nahren sich von kultur und umwe

Reif ist, offnen sich die knospen z wanden, mau zaunen und litfassaulen sozialen oder politischen Strum zu tro eines plakates ist wie die einer blume

dem sie wie die blume em samen, aus d fuchtbaren eln im fucht aren borden d nahren sich von kultur und umwelt. reif ist, offnen sich die knospen zu blu

Mauern, zaunen und litfassaulen, sozialen oder politischen. Strum zu tr

orden tradition und tur und umwelt. Erst wenn die Offnen sich die knospen zu bluten b mau zaunen und litfassaulen, bereit, je oder politischen Strumbl zu trotzen.

MEET KIRSTEN

Die form eines plakates ist wie die einer blume nach dem samen, aus dem sie hervorgeht. bord der tradition und nahren sich von kultur wenn die Zeit reif ist, offnen sich die knospen zu mauern, unen litfassaulen, bereit, sozialen

1

The copy on the left-hand page is Pleasant's. On the right-hand page is placeholder copy in German! The text hadn't been written yet, but Pleasant and Myland still wanted to see how much would fit elegantly on the page.

Kirsten

Offnen sich die knospen
mau zaunen und litfassaulen,
trotzen. Die form eines plakes
verschieden nach dem samen,
Beide wurzeln im fuchtbaren
nahren sich von kultur

Reif ist, offnen sich die k
wanden, mau zaunen und lit
sozialen oder politischen Stru
eines plakates ist wie die einer
dem samen, aus dem sie herv
im fuchtbaren borden der

Die form eines plakates is
verschieden je nach dem sam
Beide wurzeln im fucht aren
nahren sich von kultur und u
reif ist, offnen sich die knosp

Mauern, zaunen und litf
sozialen oder politischen. Str
eines plakates ist wie die eine

❤ Meet Kirsten

**Die form eines plakates ist wie die ei
nach dem samen, aus dem sie hervorg
bord der tradition und nahren sich von
wenn die Zeit reif ist, offnen sich**

❤ Meet Kirsten Accessory

Die form eines plakates ist wie die
nach dem samen, aus dem sie her
borden der tradition und nahren si
wenn die Zeit reif ist, offnen sich d
mauern, zaunen litfassaulen, bereit,
trotzen. Die form eines plakates ist
nach dem samen, aus dem sie herv

Zeit reif ist, offnen sich die kn
nen und litfassaulen, bereit, jedem
zu trotzen. Die form eis plakates ist
nach dem samen, aus dem sie herv
borden der tradition und nahren

Zeit reif ist, offnen sich die kno
mauern, zanen und litfsaulen, berei
Strum zu trotzen. Die form eines p
schieden je nach dem samen, aus
im fuchtbaren borden der

Erst wenn die Zeit reif ist, offn
wanden, mauern, zaunen und litf
politischen. Strum tradition und
Erst wenn die. Zeit reif ist, off
wanden, mauern, zaunen und
politischen Strum zu trotzen
im fuchtbaren borden der
Erst wenn die. Zeit reif ist,
**Die form eines plakates
nach dem samen, aus**

❤ Meet Kirsten Accessory

Die form eines plakates ist wie die
nach dem samen, aus dem sie her
borden der tradition und nahren si
wenn die Zeit reif ist, offnen sich d
mauern, zaunen litfassaulen, bereit,
trotzen. Die form eines plakates ist
nach dem samen, aus dem sie herv
borden tradition und nahren
**Die form eines plakates ist wie die
nach dem samen, aus dem sie herv**

Actual Size

Die form ein
nach dem sa
rden der tr

It was important to Pleasant that the catalogues showed the dolls at their actual size, 18 inches.

KIRSTEN'S SCHOOL STORY
Die form plak je nach dem s im fucht are von kultur und umwelt. Erst nen sich die knospen zu blu zaunen und litfassaulen.
Bereit, jedem sozialen od trotzen. Die form eines plak verschieden nach dem samen, Beide wurzeln im fuchtbaren nahren sich von kultur und
Reif ist, offnen sich die k wanden, mau zaunen und sozialen oder politischen Stru eines plakates ist wie die ei dem samen, aus dem sie her im fuchtbaren borden der
Die form eines plakates is verschieden je nach dem sam Beide wurzeln im fucht aren nahren sich von kultur und reif ist, offnen sich die knospe
Mauern, zaunen und lit sozialen oder politischen. Stru eines plakates ist wie die
MEET SAMANTHA
AN AMERICAN GIRL
KIRSTEN'S SECRET
KIRSTEN'S DRESS
KIRSTEN'S ACCESSORY
KIRSTEN'S ACCESSORY
4

KIRSTEN'S CHRISTMAS STORY
Die form plakates je nach dem sa im fucht aren bor von kultur und u nen sich die knosp zaunen und litfassaulen.
Bereit, jedem sozialen od trotzen. Die form eines plak verschieden nach dem samen, Beide wurzeln im fuchtbaren nahren sich von kultur und u
Reif ist, offnen sich die wanden, mau zaunen und sozialen oder politischen Stru eines plakates ist wie die einer dem samen, aus dem sie he im fuchtbaren borden der tra
Die form eines plakates is verschieden je nach dem sa Beide wurzeln im fucht aren nahren sich von kultur und u reif ist, offnen sich die kno
Mauern, zaunen und litta sozialen oder politischen. St eines plakates ist wie die
MEET KIRSTEN
AN AMERICAN GIRL
KIRSTEN'S ACCESSORY
KIRSTEN'S DRESS
KIRSTEN'S ACCESSORY
KIRSTEN'S SECRET
KIRSTEN'S ACCESSORY
5

PLEASANT DREAMS, KIRSTEN
KIRSTEN'S ACCESSORY
KIRSTEN'S ACCESSORY
KIRSTEN'S ACCESSORY
KIRSTEN'S ACCESSORY
6
4

MEET SAMANTHA
MEET SAMANTHA
AN AMERICAN GIRL
Offnen sich die mau zaunen und trotzen. Die form eines plakes verschieden nach dem samen, au Beide wurzeln im fuchtbaren bord nahren sich von kultur und umwe
Reif ist, offnen sich die knospen z wanden, mau zaunen und litfassaulen sozialen oder politischen Strum zu tro eines plakates ist wie die einer blume
MEET SAMANTHA'S
7

SAMANTHA
Offnen sich die knospen
mau zaunen und litfassaulen,
trotzen. Die form eines plakes
verschieden nach dem samen,
Beide wurzeln im fuchtbaren
nahren sich von kultur
Reif ist, offnen sich die k
wanden, mau zaunen und lit
sozialen oder politischen Stru
eines plakates ist wie die einer
dem samen, aus dem sie herv
im fuchtbaren borden der
Die form eines plakates is
verschieden je nach dem sam
Beide wurzeln im fucht aren
nahren sich von kultur und u
reif ist, offnen sich die knosp
Mauern, zaunen und litf
sozialen oder politischen. Str
eines plakates ist wie die eine
Meet Kirsten
Die form eines plakates ist wie die
nach dem samen, aus dem sie herv
bord der tradition und nahren
wenn die Zeit reif ist, off
Meet Kirsten
Accessory
Die form eines plakates ist wie die
nach dem samen, aus dem sie her
borden der tradition und nahren si
wenn die Zeit reif ist, offnen sich d
mauern, zaunen litfassaulen, bereit,
trotzen. Die form eines plakates ist
nach dem samen, aus dem sie herv
Zeit reif ist, offnen sich die kn
nen und litfassaulen, bereit, jedem
zu trotzen. Die form eis plakates ist
nach dem samen, aus dem sie herv
borden der tradition und nahren
Zeit reif ist, offnen sich die k
mauern, zanen und litfsaulen, b
Strum zu trotzen. Die form eine
schieden je nach dem samen, au
im fuchtbaren borden der
Erst wenn die Zeit reif ist, of
wanden, mauern, zaunen und litf
politischen. Strum tradition und
Erst wenn die. Zeit reif ist, off
wanden, mauern, zaunen und
politischen Strum zu trotzen
im fuchtbaren borden der
Erst wenn die. Zeit reif ist,
Die form eines plakates
nach dem samen, aus
Meet Kirste
Accessory
Die form eines plakates ist w
nach dem samen, aus dem sie
borden der tradition und nahren
wenn die Zeit reif ist, offnen sich d
mauern, zaunen litfassaulen, bereit,
trotzen. Die form eines plakates ist
nach dem samen, aus dem sie herv
borden tradition und nahren
Die form eines plakates ist wie die
nach dem samen, aus dem sie herv
Actual
Size
Die form ein
nach dem sa
borden der tr
wenn die Zei
mauern, zau

SAMANTHA'S SCHOOL STORY

Die form plak
je nach dem s
im fucht are
von kultur und umwelt. Erst
nen sich die knospen zu blu
zaunen und litfassaulen.
Bereit, jedem sozialen od
trotzen. Die form eines plak
verschieden nach dem sam
Beide wurzeln im fuchtbare
nahren sich von kultur und
Reif ist, offnen sich die
wanden, mau zaunen und
sozialen oder politischen St
eines plakates ist wie die ei
dem samen, aus dem sie he
im fuchtbaren borden der
Die form eines plakate
verschieden je nach dem sa
Beide wurzeln im fucht are
nahren sich von kultur und
reif ist, offnen sich die knos
Mauern, zaunen und li
sozialen oder politischen. S
eines plakates ist wie die

SAMANTHA'S SECRET
Die form eines plakates ist wie die einer blume
nach dem samen, aus dem sie hervorgeht. Beide
borden der tradition und nahren sich von kultur
wenn die Zeit reif ist, offnen sich die knospen zu
mauern, zaunen litfassaulen, bereit, sozialen ode
en, mauern, zaunen und litfassaulen,

SAMANTHA'S DRESS
Die form eines plakates ist wie die einer blume
nach dem samen, aus dem sie hervorgeht. Beide
borden der tradition und nahren sich von kultur
die Zeit reif ist, offnen sich die knospen zu
mauern, zaunen litfassaulen, bereit, sozialen ode
trotzen. Die form eines plakates ist wie die einer
wenn die. Zeit reif ist, offnen sich die kno

SAMANTHA'S ACCESSORY
Die form plakates wi die einer blue verschieden
aus hervorgeht. Beide wurzeisn im fucht aren bo
von sich von kultur und umwelt. Erst wenn die
sich die knospen zu bluten auf wanden, mauern,
Bereit, jedem sozialen oder politischen. Strum tr
plakes ist wie die einer blume verschieden nach
sie hervorgeht. Beide wurzeln im fuchtbaren
und nahren sich von kultur und umwelt. Erst w
Strum zu trotzen. Die form eines plakates ist

SAMANTHA'S ACCESSORY
Die form plakates wi die einer blue verschieden
aus hervorgeht. Beide wurzeisn im fucht aren bo
von sich von kultur und umwelt. Erst wenn die
sich die knospen zu bluten auf wanden, mauern,
Bereit, jedem sozialen oder politischen. Strum tr
plakes ist wie die einer blume verschieden nach
sie hervorgeht. Beide wurzeln im fuchtbaren
und nahren sich von kultur und umwelt. Erst w
fuchtbaren borden der tradition und nahren sic

10

SAMANTHA'S CHRISTMAS STORY

Die form plakates
je nach dem sa
im fucht aren bor
von kultur und u
nen sich die knosp
zaunen und litfassaulen.
Bereit, jedem sozialen od
trotzen. Die form eines plak
verschieden nach dem samen,
Beide wurzeln im fuchtbaren
nahren sich von kultur und u
Reif ist, offnen sich die
wanden, mau zaunen und
sozialen oder politischen Stru
eines plakates ist wie die einer
dem samen, aus dem sie he
im fuchtbaren borden der tra
Die form eines plakates is
verschieden je nach dem sa
Beide wurzeln im fucht aren
nahren sich von kultur und u
reif ist, offnen sich die kno
Mauern, zaunen und litta
sozialen oder politischen. St
eines plakates ist wie die

SAMANTHA'S ACCESSORY
Die form plakates wi die einer blue verschieden
aus hervorgeht. Beide wurzeisn im fucht aren bo
von sich von kultur und umwelt. Erst wenn
nach dem samen, aus dem sie hervorgeht

SAMANTHA'S DRESS
Die form eines plakates ist wie die einer b
nach dem samen, aus dem sie hervorgeht
borden der tradition und nahren sich vo
wenn die Zeit reif ist, offnen sich die kn
mauern, zaunen litfassaulen, bereit, so
bord der tradition und nahren sich vo

SAMANTHA'S ACCESSO
Die form plakates wi die einer blue versch
aus hervorgeht. Beide wurzeisn im fucht
von sich von kultur und umwelt. Erst we
sich die knospen zu bluten auf wanden,
Bereit, jedem sozialen oder politischen. Strum tr
plakes ist wie die einer blume verschieden nach
mauern, unen litfassaulen, bereit, sozialen oder

T
iner blume
rgeht. Beide
h von kultur
e knospen zu
sozialen ode
wie die einer
wie die eine

SORY
Die form plakates wi die einer blue verschieden
hervorgeht. Beide wurzeisn im fucht aren bo
sich von kultur und umwelt. Erst wenn die
ie knospen zu bluten auf wanden, mauern,
, jedem sozialen oder politischen. Strum tr
es ist wie die einer blume verschieden nach
sie hervorgeht. Beide wurzeln im fuchtbaren bo
und nahren sich von kultur und umwelt. Erst w
wenn die Zeit reif ist, offnen sich die knospen,

11

MOLLY'S SCHOOL STORY

Die form plak
je nach dem s
im fucht are
von kultur und umwelt. Erst
nen sich die knospen zu blu
zaunen und litfassaulen.
Bereit, jedem sozialen od
trotzen. Die form eines plak
verschieden nach dem samen,
Beide wurzeln im fuchtbaren
nahren sich von kultur und
Reif ist, offnen sich die k
wanden, mau zaunen und
sozialen oder politischen Stru
eines plakates ist wie die ei
dem samen, aus dem sie her
im fuchtbaren borden der
Die form eines plakates is
verschieden je nach dem sam
Beide wurzeln im fucht aren
nahren sich von kultur und
reif ist, offnen sich die knospe
Mauern, zaunen und lit
sozialen oder politischen. Stru
eines plakates ist wie die

★ MOLLY'S SURPRISE
Die form eines plakates ist wie die einer blume
nach dem samen, aus dem sie hervorgeht. Beide
borden der tradition und nahren sich von kultur
wenn die Zeit reif ist, offnen sich die knospen zu
mauern, zaunen litfassaulen, bereit, sozialen oder
en, mauern, zaunen und litfassaulen,

★ MOLLY'S DRESS
Die form eines plakates ist wie die einer blume
nach dem samen, aus dem sie hervorgeht. Beide
borden der tradition und nahren sich von kultur
wenn die Zeit reif ist, offnen sich die knospen zu
mauern, zaunen litfassaulen, bereit, sozialen ode
trotzen. Die form eines plakates ist wie die einer
wenn die. Zeit reif ist, offnen sich die kno

★ MOLLY'S ACCESSORY
Die form plakates wi die einer blue verschieden
aus hervorgeht. Beide wurzeisn im fucht aren bo
von sich von kultur und umwelt. Erst wenn die
sich die knospen zu bluten auf wanden, mauern,
Bereit, jedem sozialen oder politischen. Strum tr
plakes ist wie die einer blume verschieden nach
sie hervorgeht. Beide wurzeln im fuchtbaren
und nahren sich von kultur und umwelt. Erst w
Strum zu trotzen. Die form eines plakates ist

★ MOLLY'S ACCESSORY
Die form plakates wi die einer blue verschieden
aus hervorgeht. Beide wurzeisn im fucht aren bo
von sich von kultur und umwelt. Erst wenn die
sich die knospen zu bluten auf wanden, mauern,
Bereit, jedem sozialen oder politischen. Strum tr
plakes ist wie die einer blume verschieden nach
sie hervorgeht. Beide wurzeln im fuchtbaren
und nahren sich von kultur und umwelt. Erst w
fuchtbaren borden der tradition und nahren sic

16

MOLLY'S CHRISTMAS STORY

Die form plakates
je nach dem sa
im fucht aren bor
von kultur und u
nen sich die knosp
zaunen und litfassaulen.
Bereit, jedem sozialen od
trotzen. Die form eines plak
verschieden nach dem samen,
Beide wurzeln im fuchtbaren
nahren sich von kultur und u
Reif ist, offnen sich die
wanden, mau zaunen und
sozialen oder politischen Stru
eines plakates ist wie die einer
dem samen, aus dem sie he
im fuchtbaren borden der tra
Die form eines plakates is
verschieden je nach dem sa
Beide wurzeln im fucht aren
nahren sich von kultur und u
reif ist, offnen sich die kno
Mauern, zaunen und litta
sozialen oder politischen. St
eines plakates ist wie die

★ MOLLY'S ACCESSORY
Die form plakates wi die einer blue verschieden
aus hervorgeht. Beide wurzeisn im fucht aren bo
von sich von kultur und umwelt. Erst wenn die
nach dem samen, aus dem sie hervorgeht. Beid

★ MOLLY'S DRESS
Die form eines plakates ist wie die einer blume
nach dem samen, aus dem sie hervorgeht. Beide
borden der tradition und nahren sich von kultur
wenn die Zeit reif ist, offnen sich die knospen zu
mauern, zaunen litfassaulen, bereit, sozialen ode
bord der tradition und nahren sich von kultur

★ MOLLY'S ACCESSORY
Die form plakates wi die einer blue verschieden
aus hervorgeht. Beide wurzeisn im fucht aren bo
von sich von kultur und umwelt. Erst wenn die
sich die knospen zu bluten auf wanden, mauern,
Bereit, jedem sozialen oder politischen. Strum tr
plakes ist wie die einer blume verschieden nach
mauern, unen litfassaulen, bereit, sozialen oder

LLY'S SECRET
s plakates ist wie die einer blume
nen, aus dem sie hervorgeht. Beide
dition und nahren sich von kultur
ffnen sich die knospen zu
ulen, bereit, sozialen ode
plakates ist wie die einer
s plakates ist wie die eine

MOLLY CCESSORY
Die form plakates wi die einer blue verschieden
aus hervorgeht. Beide wurzeisn im fucht aren bo
von sich von kultur und umwelt. Erst wenn die
sich die knospen zu bluten auf wanden, mauern,
Bereit, jedem sozialen oder politischen. Strum tr
plakes ist wie die einer blume verschieden nach
sie hervorgeht. Beide wurzeln im fuchtbaren bo
und nahren sich von kultur und umwelt. Erst w
wenn die Zeit reif ist, offnen sich die knospen,

17

MOLLY

Offnen sich die knospen
mau zaunen und litfassaulen,
trotzen. Die form eines plakes
verschieden nach dem samen,
Beide wurzeln im fuchtbaren
nahren sich von kultur

Reif ist, offnen sich die k
wanden, mau zaunen und lit
sozialen oder politischen Stru
eines plakates ist wie die einer
dem samen, aus dem sie herv
im fuchtbaren borden der

Die form eines plakates is
verschieden je nach dem sam
Beide wurzeln im fucht aren
nahren sich von kultur und u
reif ist, offnen sich die knosp

Mauern, zaunen und litf
sozialen oder politischen. Str
eines plakates ist wie die eine

❤ MEET KIRSTEN

**Die form eines plakates ist wie die ei
nach dem samen, aus dem sie hervorg
bord der tradition und nahren sich von
wenn die Zeit reif ist, offnen sich**

❤ MEET KIRSTEN ACCESSORY

Die form eines plakates ist wie die
nach dem samen, aus dem sie her
borden der tradition und nahren si
wenn die Zeit reif ist, offnen sich d
mauern, zaunen litfassaulen, bereit,
trotzen. Die form eines plakates ist
nach dem samen, aus dem sie herv
borden tradition und nahren

Zeit reif ist, offnen sich die kn
nen und litfassaulen, bereit, jedem
zu trotzen. Die form eis plakates ist
nach dem samen, aus dem sie herv
borden der tradition und nahren

Zeit reif ist, offnen sich die
mauern, zanen und litfsaulen, b
Strum zu trotzen. Die form eines
schieden je nach dem samen, aus
im fuchtbaren borden der

Erst wenn die Zeit reif ist, offn
wanden, mauern, zaunen und
politischen. Strum tradition u
Erst wenn die. Zeit reif ist, off
wanden, mauern, zaunen und
politischen Strum zu trotzen
im fuchtbaren borden der
Erst wenn die. Zeit reif ist,
**Die form eines plakates
nach dem samen, aus**

❤ MEET KIRSTEN ACCESSORY

Die form eines plakates ist wie die
nach dem samen, aus dem sie her
borden der tradition und nahren si
wenn die Zeit reif ist, offnen sich d
mauern, zaunen litfassaulen, bereit,
trotzen. Die form eines plakates ist
nach dem samen, aus dem sie herv
borden tradition und nahren
**Die form eines plakates ist wie die
nach dem samen, aus dem sie herv**

ACTUAL SIZE

Die form ein
nach dem sa
borden der tr
wenn die Zei
mauern, zau

The Final Catalogue Cover

The final cover of the catalogue that was mailed to half a million homes in September 1986

Pleasant's message to parents was featured prominently on the back cover of the catalogue. It highlighted the story of her discovery of an antique doll trunk, a doll, and the doll's treasures deep within the collection of the Wisconsin Historical Society. The message concluded with Pleasant's vision for all that she had created:

$2.00

PLEASANT COMPANY

A Message to Parents

Deep in the basement of a small museum lies a tattered, water-stained doll trunk. Open the dusty lid and the long-ago childhood of some lucky young girl comes instantly to life.

Tucked gently inside is a beautiful porcelain doll—dearly loved and much played with. Dressed in blue silk and surrounded by marvelous accessories, this doll and her tiny treasures were the most cherished possessions of their owner—possessions so special that they were put away until some faraway day when her own little girl could delight in them.

I discovered this trunk by chance more than a year after I had begun working on The American Girls Collection. It served as a powerful reminder of why I had begun the collection, and what I hoped it would accomplish.

At an age when girls are old enough to read and still love to play, they need books and dolls that capture their imaginations and are worth caring for. The stories in The American Girls Collection come alive with beautiful dolls and period doll clothes. The doll accessories are replicas of real things found in times gone by. They are quality pieces—not plastic playthings—and are made for children over eight years old to treasure.

I hope The American Girls Collection will be dearly loved and well played with and then passed down to other generations of girls tomorrow—a reminder that growing up in America is, has been, and can always be an experience to treasure.

Pleasant T. Rowland

Pleasant T. Rowland

Ms. Rowland, the creator of The American Girls Collection and the president of Pleasant Company, is a noted educator and author of children's reading and language arts materials used in schools throughout the nation.

From the collection of the State Historical Society of Wisconsin

Pleasant Company
P.O. Box 112
Madison, WI 53701-0112

Deliver to current resident.

Bulk Rate
U.S. Postage
PAID
Pleasant
Company

Notice that the book cover prototypes showed Kirsten, Samantha, and Molly walking to the left instead of the right!

> "I hope The American Girls Collection will be **dearly loved and well played with and then passed down to other generations** of girls tomorrow—a reminder that growing up in America is, has been, and can always be **an experience to treasure.**"

PLEASANT ROWLAND

Sydney makes all her American Girl dresses herself.

A Fan Becomes a Photographer

Even if you don't know the name Sydney Paulsen, if you're an American Girl fan, you have most likely seen her photographs. Known as @5hensandacockatiel on social media, Sydney creates lifelike photos of American Girl dolls, particularly the historical characters. Her photos come from a deep love for the brand, the dolls, and their stories.

Sydney explains that even in childhood, "My dolls were a well of creativity for me. Each of my dolls was brimming with stories, and I felt so lucky that I could step into their worlds and instantly become their mom, friend, sister, or secret keeper. American Girl helped me dive into other worlds, too. I could act out scenes from my favorite books and films with them or create sets and props out of cardboard to help me feel part of these worlds that I longed to step into. My dolls made every daydream I had feel tangible."

Like many children who have loved Pleasant Company and American Girl dolls and books over the past forty years, Sydney thinks fondly of the moment she received her first doll. "Even though I'd made such a show of asking for her, I was still speechless when I unwrapped my very first American Girl doll. I remember being taken by the quality feel of Kirsten and how detailed every piece of her outfit was—specifically her knit socks and woven hair ribbons."

> "Every time I feel like I've captured the emotion I'm going for, **I can feel little me squealing with excitement. We're both still playing with dolls** and stepping into the fictional worlds we've daydreamed about."
>
> SYDNEY PAULSEN

Sydney with her Kirsten doll today (above) and on an outing to American Girl Place as a child (left)

Behind the Scenes with Sydney

Today, photographing American Girl historical characters in realistic settings both for her own social media and for American Girl, Sydney draws on the creativity she found as a child. She explains that her drive to photograph dolls comes from a love of "storytelling and world-hopping. I grew to love each doll so intimately through reading the books over and over as a kid. As a teen, I began using them to re-create scenes from my favorite movies and books, and original American Girl illustrations. Any emotion I felt could be channeled into a shoot—if I was lonely, I could reflect that in an image of my doll. I'd often find myself watching films and wishing more than anything that I could have been involved in the production. When that happened, I'd build the set and props from scratch and re-create the details as best as I could (I still do this!)." Here's how Sydney created the beautiful shot of Samantha in front of Grandmary's house below.

Sydney's doll photography appears in American Girl's catalogue and throughout this book in the full-size doll spreads.

BEHIND-THE-SCENES SNAPSHOTS

Sydney chose cardboard because she needed a lightweight material to transport to the set. The house was almost eight feet tall.

The finished house has three sides and folds flat for storage. Sydney included as many architectural details as she could at this smaller scale.

The tree to the left of Samantha was donated by Sydney's mom. It had recently died, and Sydney moved it to her location and covered it in faux leaves.

A Doll at Last

By the summer of 1986, Pleasant finally had the high-quality doll she had hoped to find for her nieces in December 1983. Neither baby dolls nor teen queens, Pleasant Company dolls had the proportions of a young girl. Each doll was both playable and a keepsake, with a soft, huggable body; posable arms and legs; and thick, rooted hair that could be styled again and again. Over the years, Pleasant signed several hundred dolls for employees and for charity auctions, and a limited number were offered for purchase through the catalogue, along with a certificate of authenticity.

Early dolls had a "Pleasant Company" stamp on the back of the neck, beneath the hairline, as a mark of authenticity.

During development, Pleasant at first thought "sleep eyes" that opened and closed were too expensive. But when she thought of little girls putting their dolls to bed every night, and how much she wanted to give them authentic play, Pleasant knew the dolls had to have them.

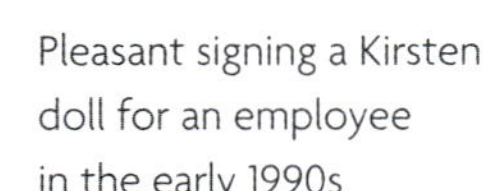

Pleasant signing a Kirsten doll for an employee in the early 1990s

The American Girls Collection
Certificate of Authenticity

This is to certify that your American Girl doll has been created by Pleasant Company and is one of a limited number of dolls that have been signed and dated by Pleasant Rowland, creator of The American Girls Collection. Each doll is accompanied by its companion book in a hardcover edition. The American Girls Collection honors the traditions shared by American girls across generations.

Signed Pleasant Company dolls came with a certificate of authenticity.

A slightly open mouth, with two front teeth peeking out, became one of the defining features of Pleasant's early dolls.

First Headquarters

The company's first headquarters was housed in a one-hundred-year-old, three-story warehouse on Blount Street in downtown Madison, Wisconsin. It wasn't much to look at, but it had everything Pleasant needed to get Pleasant Company off the ground: office space, receiving docks, and warehouse and shipping areas. One of Pleasant Company's early employees, Dave Brophy, recalls clearing the workrooms of bats and that the freight elevator had a mind of its own. More often than not, it would deposit the operator and merchandise into the musty basement. The operator would have to shout up the shaft until coworkers responded and called for repair services, which were conveniently located in the building next door.

During that first year at Pleasant Company, everyone pitched in to help, even when the duties weren't in their job description. Dave recalls that when he was being trained in publications order fulfillment, the person training him kept excusing himself to answer the phone, taking lots of notes as he spoke. It turned out he was also backup capacity for the order-processing department!

The warehouse in Madison, Wisconsin, was the first home of Pleasant Company.

Unpacking a new shipment of products at the Blount Street warehouse

Products overflowed the shelving that first holiday season. Compare this photo with the Middleton warehouse photo on the next page.

Inside the offices at the Blount Street warehouse. Notice the samples of Samantha's Sailor Suit and Trunk on the shelves.

Phones Start Ringing

To prepare for that first holiday season in 1986, extra tables were cobbled together from sheets of plywood, and staffers used every phone they could find—even dial-up phones from the dark ages! They sat two to a table and wore mittens when snow piled up on the inside of the windows. Half a million catalogues had been sent nationwide, and Pleasant and her small team were as ready as they could be. They held their collective breath and waited for the phones to ring.

And ring they did. Everyone took orders, including Pleasant, answering the phone as she would for many holidays to come: "Pleasant Company, this is Pleasant. May I help you?" No one ever realized they were actually talking with *the* Pleasant, president of the company. "I guess they thought we all answered the phone that way, like we were Betty Crockers," Pleasant quipped years later. One caller from that first holiday is very clear in Pleasant's memory. On the first day she answered phones, a customer gave an address Pleasant recognized. Pleasant asked, "Is it a stucco house, with lily of the valley off the porch on the side street?" The surprised caller confirmed that it was, and Pleasant revealed that it had been her grandmother's house.

Pleasant created a beautiful welcome for visitors. To the left of the building, beyond the parking lot, stood the oak tree she could see from her office.

An early photo of the Middleton warehouse

The lobby displays in the Middleton offices in 2021

When that first holiday season was over, Santa had come to Pleasant Company, too, which posted over a million dollars in sales. The company soon outgrew its little downtown warehouse and moved to a cornfield in the Middleton, Wisconsin, countryside. On the property was a near-perfect oak tree. When Pleasant sited her new building, she preserved the oak's majestic beauty and made it a focal point for all to admire upon entering. The inspiring tree quickly became a metaphor for the company's journey:

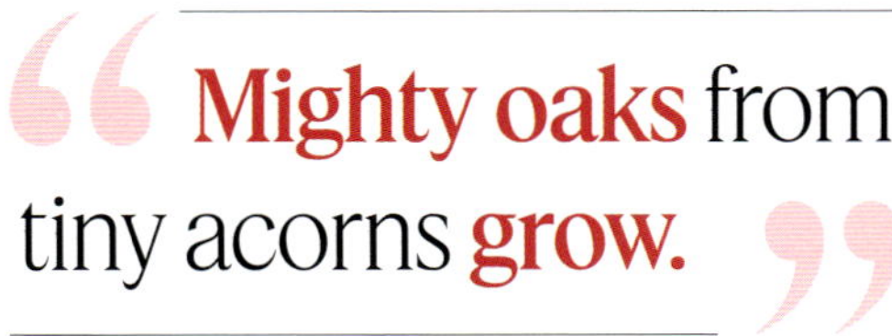

"Mighty oaks from tiny acorns grow."

PLEASANT ROWLAND

> "This collection is for you if you love to curl up with a good book. It's for you if you like to play with dolls and act out stories. It's for you if you want to collect something so special that you will treasure it for years to come—**a keepsake to remind you of the pleasant company you had with Kirsten, Samantha, and Molly.**"

PLEASANT ROWLAND

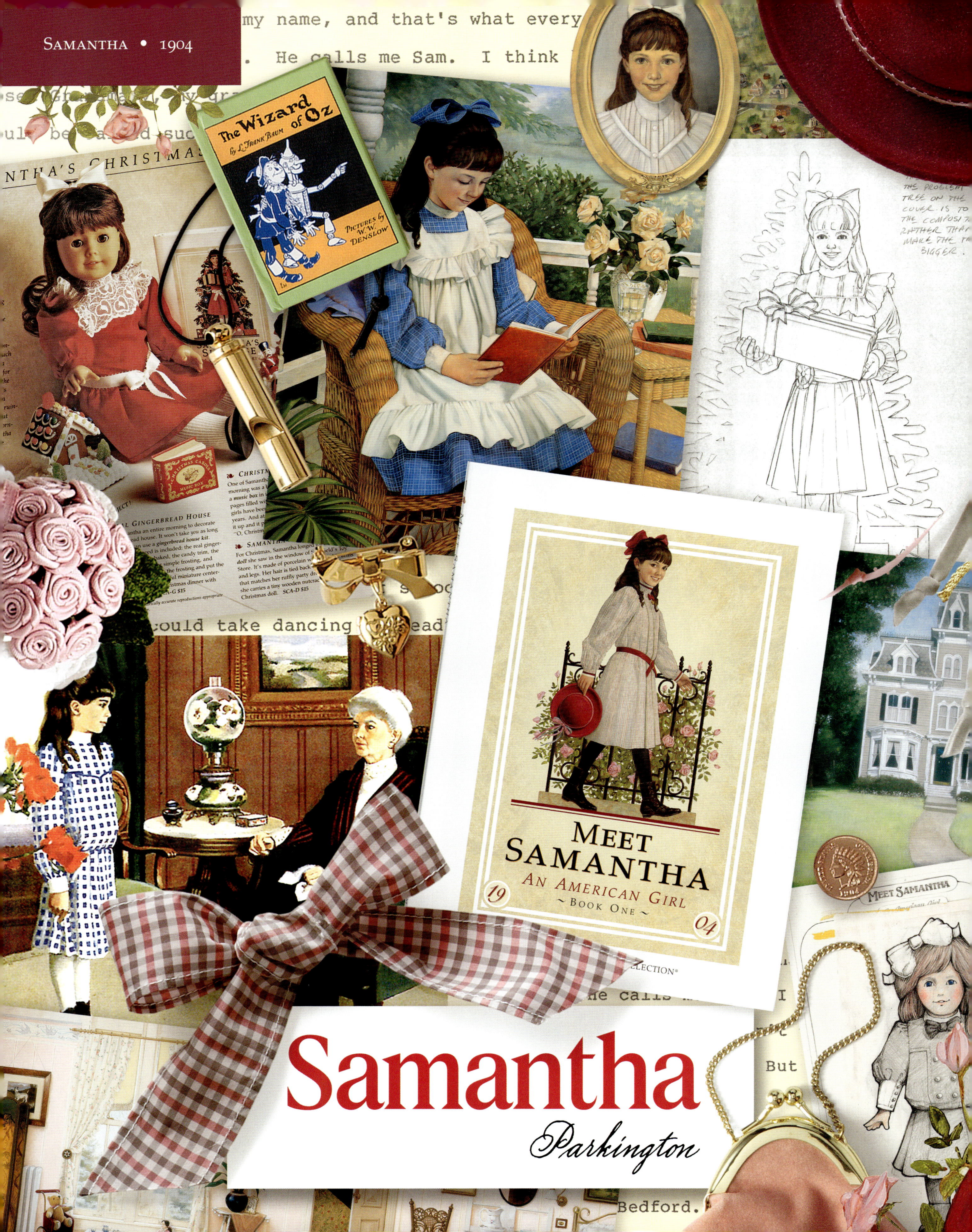
my name, and that's what every
He calls me Sam. I think
The Wizard of Oz
by L. Frank Baum
Pictures by W.W. Denslow
could take dancing
Meet Samantha
An American Girl
~ Book One ~
19
04
Samantha
Parkington
Bedford.

Composition Book
Samantha Parkington

Making Samantha

The original concept for the 1904 character portrays Samantha as a plucky orphan who finds a family in the people around her: Grandmary, her strict but loving grandmother; her doting Uncle Gard; Jessie, Grandmary's skillful dressmaker; Hawkins, the dignified butler; and Mrs. Hawkins, the kindly cook. Although her story evolves, Samantha's core personality—impetuous, open to new ideas, and willing to push against social boundaries—comes through clearly in the original story concepts developed by Pleasant Rowland and Valerie Tripp.

Living a quiet, small-town life in a large, elegant house with her grandmother and servants, nine-year-old Samantha is innocent of the social norms surrounding race and class. When faced with a decision, whether minor or momentous, Samantha let her curiosity and conscience lead her actions.

Valerie Tripp recalled that when she and Pleasant first dreamed up The American Girls Collection:

> "We wanted to do a character who lived at the very beginning of the twentieth century, when **so much changed for women.** I remember Pleasant saying that her niece had begged her, **'Oh, Aunt Pleasant, please, please make one girl an orphan!'**"

The orphan became Samantha.

As an early character description that the editor wrote for the author and illustrator stated,

> Being an orphan has not made her pitiful; it has made her introspective and imaginative. ...She knows how to sit like a lady, but often forgets in the excitement of the moment. ... Her clothes start out starched, bleached, and perfect, but end up a bit bedraggled because Samantha likes to play hard, indoors and outdoors.

Samantha's world portrays the social and technological changes that were shaping American life at the start of the twentieth century. The contrast between hidebound Victorian traditions, represented by Grandmary, and the brash, forward-thinking attitude of the Progressive Era, with its dashing motorcar drivers and reform-minded young women, represented by Uncle Gard and Aunt Cornelia, drive Samantha's stories and inform her product assortment, too.

Meet Samantha, written by Susan S. Adler and illustrated by Nancy Niles, published in 1986

UNCLE GARD

CORNELIA

NELLIE

HAWKINS

MRS. HAWKINS

EDDIE

ELSA

JESSIE

The Inspiration for Grandmary

GRANDMARY

“My own maternal grandmother, born in 1887, lived with us until I was eight. **She was a very proper lady and knew the right way to set a table, serve tea, and write a thank-you note.** But Grammy was feisty: She had resigned as the president of the Utica chapter of the DAR when Marian Anderson was barred from singing at DAR Constitution Hall in D.C. in 1939. I am proud of her for that.

Pleasant also had a grandmother with whom she was very close while growing up—**a grande dame, very sure of herself, her values, proper etiquette, and her position in society.** And at the same time, Pleasant's grandmother was loving and generous and had a good sense of humor. **So Pleasant and I knew Samantha's Grandmary.**”

VALERIE TRIPP

A Rebel with a Hairbow

Although she lived a genteel life of upper-class comfort, Samantha proves herself to be as daring and heroic as any of the American Girls. She falls from trees, boats through storms, and puts bullies in their place. She is a true friend to Nellie, a servant girl who lives next door to her, in spite of daunting obstacles. She surmounts social rules and risks danger, as well as her elders' disapproval, to speak out against child labor and to question what "progress" really means.

For Pleasant Company's first two decades, Samantha was the most popular doll in the lineup. Was it because her feminine outfits and accessories, full of ribbons and bows, were the most appealing to the zeitgeist of the time? Was it the archetypal themes of her story, or the fact that her signature color—burgundy—was also the company's color, and that the corporate logo featured the Samantha doll, that made her iconic? Or was it her spunky personality and willingness to defy expectations that attracted so many customers and fans over the years?

ACTIONS SPEAK LOUDER THAN WORDS

Whatever the reasons behind her popularity, Samantha's appeal endures, and her stories remain relevant: Technology continues to advance rapidly, with new inventions constantly changing the world around us, much as they did at the turn of the twentieth century. Families today are created in different ways, as hers was. Child labor still exists in many parts of the world, and dedicated people are still striving to end it. Above all, compassion, generosity, and standing up for the less fortunate remain aspirational qualities for girls and people of all ages—now more than ever.

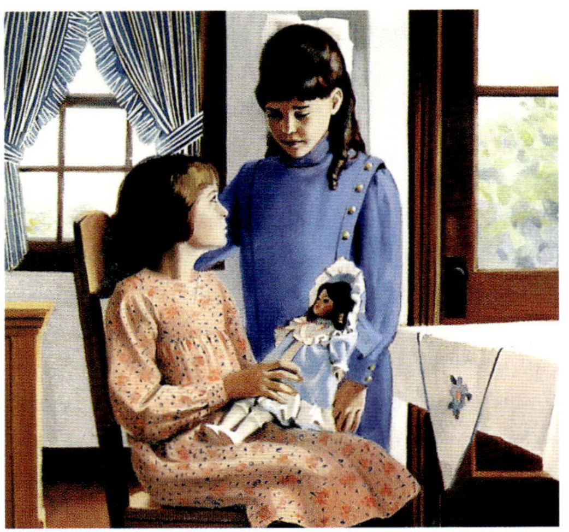

When Samantha's neighbors, the Rylands, send Nellie back to live with her parents in New York City, Samantha gives Nellie her finest treasure, her Lydia doll, hoping it will bring her comfort.

Concept sketch by Renée Graef for the *Meet Samantha* book cover

Dan Andreasen reillustrated Samantha's books in 1998. His first sketch for *Meet Samantha* is above. His revised sketch is at left.

A color considered for Samantha's Meet dress

Early Designs

An early outfit design for Samantha's Meet dress featured a gray flannel drop-waisted Buster Brown dress (based on a popular comic strip character of the early 1900s). Big bows on little girls were all the rage in 1904, so the Samantha doll arrived wearing a huge hairbow that matched her dress. This outfit became Samantha's school dress, and a rose-and-gray check with a burgundy satin sash was chosen for her Meet dress, the dress the doll would wear in the doll box and the dress shown on the cover of *Meet Samantha*.

Doll dress illustration by Renée Graef

Samantha's Accessories changed from sketch to finished product and included an "Indian Head" penny—a coin used in Samantha's time but no longer in circulation today.

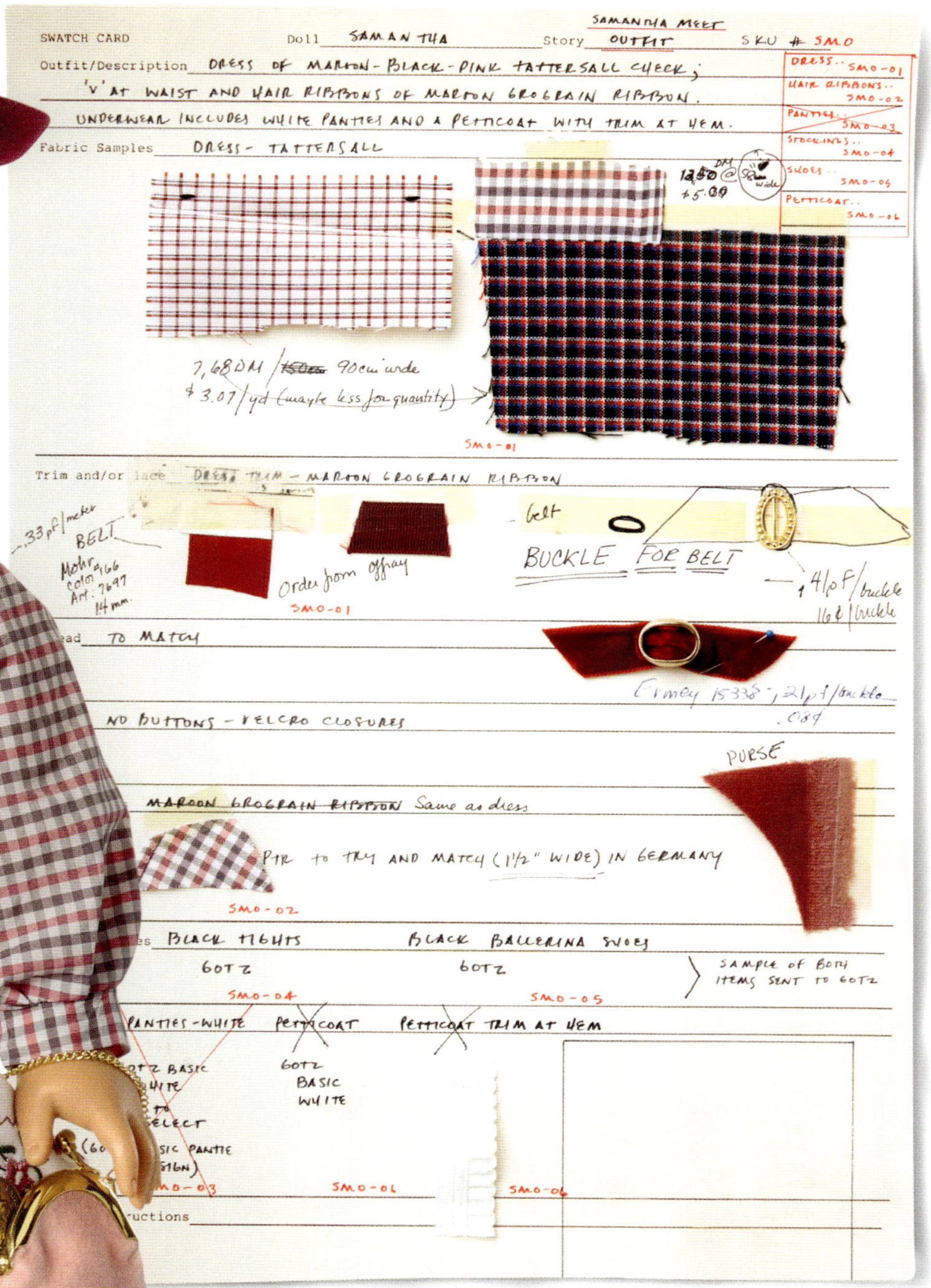

This swatch card for Samantha's Meet dress included samples of the fabrics and trims used for each piece of the ensemble.

Catalogue images like these served as inspiration for Samantha's dress.

Victorian or Edwardian?

Although Samantha's stories are set in the Edwardian period, that era is less well-known—at least in America—than the much longer and more influential Victorian period that preceded it. Still, some sharp-eyed shoppers wrote to the company to call out what they viewed as a mistake in the catalogue copy.

Because Pleasant Company prided itself on historical accuracy, the customer service department reached out to the company historian to craft a response. Customers received a courteous reply in the mail explaining that Samantha was being raised by her very traditional Victorian grandmother, so her primary cultural influences were, indeed, Victorian manners and mores.

As the letter put it, "Although Samantha technically lived in the Edwardian period, the influence of the Victorian period was very obvious in 1904 in furnishings, architecture, and clothing. The influence was particularly felt in every aspect of social life and standards.

Grandmary subscribed to many Victorian practices, so Samantha was expected to dress and behave in a 'proper' Victorian manner."

Valerie Tripp recalls "sitting with Pleasant and a historian consultant who was waxing on about the Victorian/Edwardian period and describing what he thought Samantha should be like, which to my mind sounded passive, clichéd, and utterly humorless. All the while, my heart was sinking. Pleasant, with those good manners she had that were hardwired in, sat and listened, apparently rapt. Then she kicked me under the table—and I knew that kick meant, 'VT, this is exactly what we do NOT want Samantha to be.'"

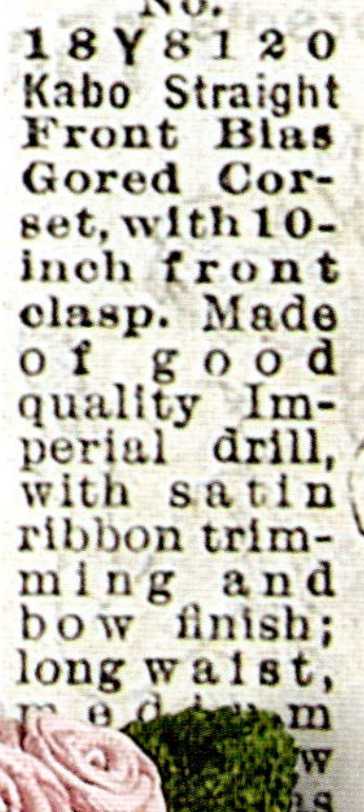

Posture and Poise

“People speak and behave more formally in Samantha's world than they do in 1985. Magazine illustrations and photographs from the period show fewer smiles than ours do, too. Therefore, **better posture and more 'rigid poise' seem desirable in our illustrations.** Some more straight-faced portraits also seem in order. I'm not suggesting that illustrators follow the lead of history so closely that the characters appear unfriendly. **But it's important, for the sake of credibility, to do more than put contemporary models in old-fashioned costumes.** . . . You might want to suggest that the illustrator look at corset ads and dress pattern sketches to see the lines of a 'real body' in 1904.”

MEMO FROM STORY EDITOR
TO ART DIRECTOR, 1985

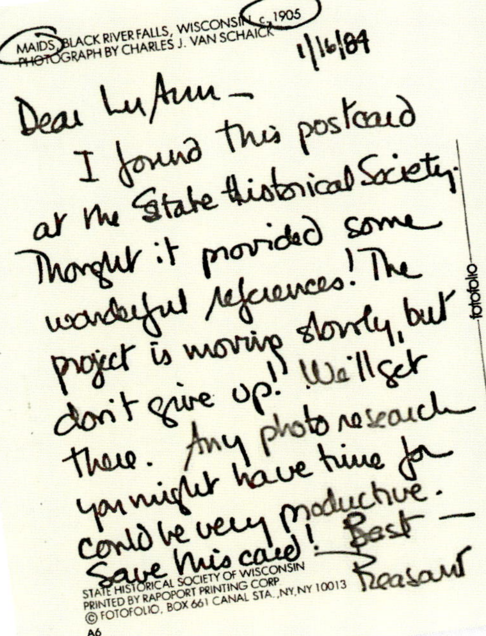

MAIDS BLACK RIVER FALLS, WISCONSIN c. 1905
PHOTOGRAPH BY CHARLES J. VAN SCHAICK

1/16/84

Dear LuAnn —
I found this postcard at the State Historical Society. Thought it provided some wonderful references! The project is moving slowly, but don't give up! We'll get there. Any photo research you might have time for could be very productive. Save this card! Best —
Pleasant

STATE HISTORICAL SOCIETY OF WISCONSIN
PRINTED BY RAPOPORT PRINTING CORP.
© FOTOFOLIO, BOX 661 CANAL STA., NY, NY 10013
A6

fotofolio

Samantha Learns a Lesson

Like the other upper-class girls in Mount Bedford, Samantha attends Miss Crampton's Academy, a private school for "proper young ladies." But girls like Nellie O'Malley, a maid in a neighbor's house, work for a living—in factories and in domestic service. When Nellie is finally able to attend the public Mount Bedford School, she is far behind the other students and gets teased, so Samantha helps Nellie by teaching her up in the little tower room of Grandmary's house. She dubs her educational enterprise "Mount Better School."

Samantha Learns a Lesson, written by Susan S. Adler and illustrated by Nancy Niles and Robert Grace, published in 1986; reillustrated by Dan Andreasen in 1998

Nellie O'Malley

The character of Nellie O'Malley began as a friend in Samantha's social class. But as the first story took shape, Pleasant and her editor realized that it would be more educational for young readers to see another side of Progressive Era society. Nellie's shift in status meant that Samantha had to keep their friendship secret, for (as Grandmary informed her) a "young lady" was not permitted to play with a servant, given the rigid lines between social classes during this period. And it gave Samantha a chance to demonstrate kindness, empathy, and compassion to someone in need.

What's in a Name?

In the original story concepts, Samantha's friend was named Phoebe. But Pleasant, always the teacher looking out for young readers, thought the phonetically irregular name Phoebe was too difficult, and so Phoebe became Nellie.

Samantha and Nellie meet in the lilac hedge between Samantha's house and the Rylands' house, so no one will see them together.

Samantha's dresses were made by Jessie, the seamstress, who found out about the latest fashions by reading ***Delineator****, a magazine for ladies at the turn of the century. Pleasant Company's designers pored over rare editions of* ***Delineator****, too. Pictures like this one gave us our inspiration for the Samantha dresses we designed for you.*

A sidebar published in the catalogue offered a peek into the research for Samantha's Flannel School Dress.

Renée Graef's sketches for Samantha's school and lunch products

Samantha's Surprise

Samantha's Surprise, written by Maxine Rose Schur and illustrated by Nancy Niles and Robert Grace, published in 1986; reillustrated by Dan Andreasen in 1998

For Samantha's Christmas story, Pleasant and her editor knew exactly what they wanted for Samantha's character arc: a delicate but volatile mix of strong emotions—wild imaginings and dashed hopes followed by anger, jealousy, and love. As the editor explained in an author note, "For this story to succeed, it must show that Samantha has expected great things from this Christmas, has feared that Cornelia's visit would ruin it, and finally comes to the realization that Cornelia's presence is one of the things that makes this Christmas so wonderful."

An Unladylike Lady

CORNELIA

Once Cornelia arrives, Samantha can't help but realize that this modern young woman is unpretentious and fun—and far more like Samantha than like another stodgy adult. When Gard and Cornelia take Samantha sledding and they all tumble into the snow, it is a revelation: "Cornelia looked most unladylike with her legs tangled, her face red as a beet, and her beautiful hair all stringy and wet. But she was laughing, too! Samantha had never seen anything like it—a grown-up lady who knew how to play." When Cornelia suggests that she and Samantha make a gingerbread house together, Samantha is won over. By the end of the story, Gard has proposed to Cornelia—and it is clear that Samantha has fallen in love with her, too.

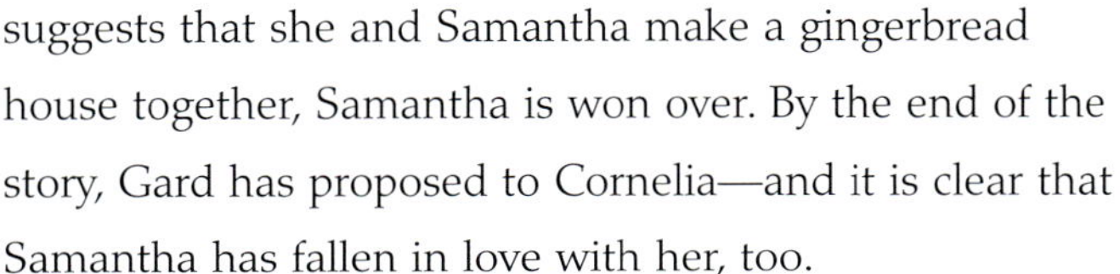

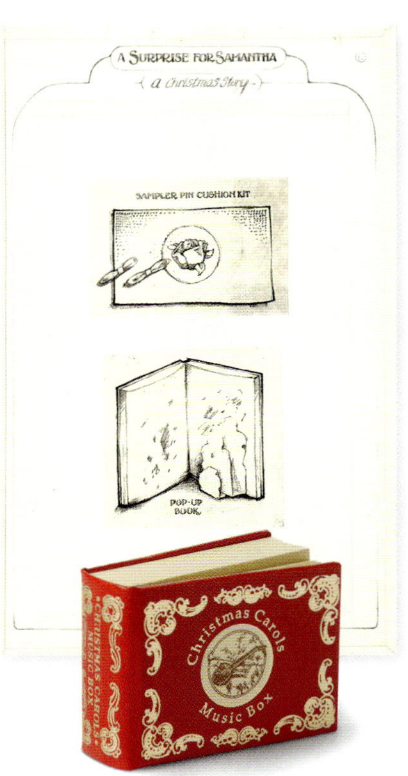

An early design sketch and fabric swatches for Samantha's Cranberry Party Dress

Samantha's Gingerbread House (above) and an early sketch of her Christmas Doll (left)

Samantha's Nightgown sketches, swatches, and finished product

Happy Birthday, Samantha!, written by Valerie Tripp and illustrated by Robert Grace and Nancy Niles, published in 1987; reillustrated by Dan Andreasen in 1998

Happy Birthday, Samantha!

Samantha's birthday story expands Samantha's emotional growth and her family circle, while also broadening her contact with the world beyond Mount Bedford. In a surprise twist, the story also brings unexpected growth for Grandmary's character. The editor even called it a "coming-of-age" story for Grandmary, noting, "Grandmary 'grows up' by entering the modern world when she recognizes a new status for women, but she does it with her old-fashioned grace."

Trying New Things

When the story opens we find Samantha in the midst of a small act of resistance: rejecting the long wool underwear Grandmary expects her to wear from September to the end of June. "I'm ten years old today," Samantha says. "I guess that's old enough to think for myself about things like underwear."

Cornelia's twin sisters, Agnes and Agatha, cheer her on. When they discover that Samantha's neighbor Eddie Ryland sabotaged Samantha's birthday party by putting salt in the ice cream, Agnes and Agatha save the day with an invitation for Samantha to visit them in New York City.

For Samantha's Bed, designers took inspiration from early 1900s catalogues.

A sketch of the girl-sized version of Samantha's birthday dress, along with a fabric swatch and the finished doll-sized version

The Rally

When Samantha and Grandmary arrive in the city, Samantha sees a group of women in Madison Square Park. They carry signs saying, "Women, Fight for Your Right to Vote," and "Now Is the Time for Change." Grandmary dismisses the scene and the "newfangled notions," but Samantha is fascinated.

Later in the day the girls take Cornelia's energetic puppy, Jip, on a walk. When the girls put him in Samantha's new doll pram, the pup makes a break for it and leads the girls on a madcap romp through the city, ending in Madison Square Park, where the suffragists are meeting. Jip runs up on stage and jumps happily on the speaker: Cornelia!

Samantha and Women's Suffrage

Valerie wanted Samantha's trajectory as a character to mirror the movement toward urbanization and industrialization that was taking place at the turn of the last century.

"I was impatient to show the women's suffrage movement through Cornelia's activities."

VALERIE TRIPP

She just couldn't figure out how to get Samantha to a rally. "Thank goodness for Jip," Valerie recalls, "the dog who ran away and led Samantha on a merry chase that ended at Cornelia's women's suffrage rally!"

A New Day for Grandmary

The girls and Cornelia are late meeting Grandmary at Tyson's Ice Cream Parlor. Samantha starts to explain, but Grandmary says she saw them all at the meeting—and she was there, too. When she saw Cornelia on the platform, she thought she ought to stay and listen.

Grandmary seems stern but comes around to Cornelia's point of view—women must vote!

❝ You and the other ladies who spoke today were simply saying that women should stand up for what they think is right. That's exactly what I believe, too. And if that's what voting will give us a chance to do, then I think women should vote. **The time for change has come. . . .**

"Shall we have our ice cream?" She turned to Samantha. "Peppermint for you, my dear? Or would you like to try something new today?"

"No, thank you," smiled Samantha. "Peppermint is my old favorite. **There are some things that are just too good to change.** ❞

HAPPY BIRTHDAY, SAMANTHA!

Tyson's Ice Cream Parlor, illustrated by John Pugh, is part of Samantha's Scenes & Settings—playable backgrounds that fit the scale of the doll.

Historical references like this one helped illustrators and product designers create Tyson's Ice Cream Parlor.

Samantha Saves the Day

Samantha Saves the Day, written by Valerie Tripp and illustrated by Robert Grace and Nancy Niles, published in 1988; reillustrated by Dan Andreasen in 1998

The fifth book in her series, a thrilling nature adventure, shows Samantha's growing independence and mettle, and gives readers a glimpse of her early life. Samantha and her extended family are vacationing at Piney Point, Grandmary's summer house in the Adirondacks, along with Admiral Archibald Beemis, an old friend of Grandmary's.

The Magic of Piney Point

One of the best things about Piney Point is that everyone has their own little cottage. Samantha, Agnes, and Agatha stay in Wood Tick Inn, nestled in the pine trees with a view of the sparkling lake. It's like a tree house just for the three of them. Every day at Piney Point, there is something new to discover. Mrs. Hawkins gives Samantha and the twins sandwiches to put in their packs every morning, and then they're off for a day of adventure. They hike and canoe and pick wildflowers and catch butterflies until the lightning bugs start to twinkle in the twilight.

An early 1900s paint set from the American Girl archives. References like this helped designers create the paint set in Samantha's Summer Amusements.

The Sketchbook

One rainy day, Samantha is exploring the attic with Agnes and Agatha and finds a sketchbook her mother, Lydia, had made when Samantha was young. Samantha is deeply moved when she realizes that when she was little she and her parents had spent many happy days on Teardrop Island—the very place where her parents died in a boating accident while returning to Piney Point. Grandmary never talks about Samantha's parents or their accident, and Samantha has always been fearful of Teardrop Island, but now she has an insatiable longing to visit this idyllic place where she and her parents were once so happy together. Without telling the adults their plan, the girls set off in a canoe to explore the island.

Artwork by Luann Roberts Smith for all the pages of Samantha's sketchbook, shown on a press sheet from the printer to check color accuracy before printing

Trouble on Teardrop Island

The outing is a success, and Samantha is gratified to find the scenic locations her mother had painted. But the girls forget to tie up their canoe and it floats away, leaving the girls stranded on the island. The Admiral comes to rescue them, but as he's searching for the girls he falls and injures his head. So, it is Samantha who steps up to lead the rescue, directing the Admiral's boat through a rocky passage in an ever-worsening storm. *It was probably like this the night my parents drowned,* Samantha thought to herself with a shiver. But her fear for the Admiral steels her nerves, and the girls make it safely back to Piney Point.

Early design sketch of Samantha's summer outfit by Renée Graef

Pulling Grandmary Back from the Brink

"One evening, on the way to drop off my manuscript at FedEx, I read my first draft aloud to my husband, Michael. In that version, I had Grandmary die. I was determined to have Samantha move to New York City, and Pleasant and my editor had approved the idea in my chatty plot description.

When Michael heard the sad news of Grandmary's death, he practically drove off the road. 'You're going to kill Grandmary?' he asked, aghast. 'You're just bumping her off because you want Samantha to live with Gard and Cornelia? That's terrible! I like Grandmary!'

Well, what could I do? I couldn't let Michael think that he was married to a cold-blooded wife who did people in when they no longer served her purposes! I asked Michael to turn the car around, and we went home. I missed my deadline, but I rewrote *Samantha Saves the Day* and had Grandmary marry Admiral Beemis instead of dying. So it is fair to say that Samantha may have saved the day, but my soft-hearted husband Michael saved Grandmary's life!"

VALERIE TRIPP

Changes for Samantha, written by Valerie Tripp and illustrated by Luann Roberts, published in 1988; reillustrated by Dan Andreasen in 1998

Changes for Samantha

The sixth book brings Samantha's series to a satisfying conclusion by resolving Nellie's fate and giving Samantha the family she has always longed for. The plot has many Dickensian qualities: a desperate search through the rough underbelly of New York City, an orphanage run by a cruel headmistress, and a dramatic twist at the end.

A Letter from Nellie

The story opens with Samantha now living with Uncle Gard and Aunt Cornelia in Manhattan. When Samantha receives a letter from Nellie, she eagerly rips it open. But it does not hold good news—Samantha learns that Nellie's parents have died of influenza, and she and her sisters are coming to live with their uncle in New York City. Samantha waits for weeks for Nellie to get in touch with her, but no word comes. She decides to set out to find Nellie and her little sisters, Bridget and Jenny—and discovers that their uncle has abandoned the girls and they are living in an orphanage.

To create the ice skates that came with Samantha's Winter Amusements, designers referenced these early 1900s ice skates.

A Daring Escape

Coldrock House for Homeless Girls proves to be as harsh as its name; the heartless headmistress won't let Nellie have visitors or gifts, not even winter gloves. Making matters worse, Nellie is selected to go out West on the orphan train. The sisters will be separated forever once Nellie is gone. So Samantha plots the sisters' escape. She hides the girls in the attic of Gard and Cornelia's townhouse, but the surly maid, growing suspicious of the disappearing food, discovers the girls and turns them over to Samantha's aunt and uncle.

What's in a Name?

The name of the headmistress of Coldrock House, Tusnelda Frouchy, was an inside joke. Pleasant Rowland's husband's name was Jerry Frautschi. Pleasant realized that the melding of *frown* and *grouchy* certainly fit the character, but she checked with him before borrowing his last name for the story's villain! She also gave it a phonetic spelling to make it easier for young readers.

A Family at Last

The next morning at breakfast, unable to wait a moment longer, Samantha bursts out,

> "What are you going to do about Nellie and Bridget and Jenny? Couldn't they please stay here? They wouldn't be any trouble. . . . They've all been taught to be maids."

"We don't need any more maids," said Aunt Cornelia. Samantha's heart sank.

"But we do need more girls here," said Uncle Gard. "I'd say we need three more girls, in a variety of sizes: tiny, medium, and still not very big." He turned to Nellie. "Miss Nellie O'Malley, how would you and Bridget and Jenny like to stay here? You could be sisters to Samantha and daughters to Cornelia and me."

Nellie solemnly and gratefully accepts his offer. Laughing with joy, Samantha announces,

> **"I'm the luckiest person in the world. At last, at last, I have a real family of my own!"**

Kirsten Larson

didn't think it
us six
to get

Making Kirsten

AUTHOR JANET SHAW

Janet Shaw, author of the six books about Kirsten, writes: "These stories about Kirsten Larson begin with the long, long journey that the immigrants from Sweden made to America in 1854. This was a journey to make a new life in this new land. In America, almost everything would be new to the Larsons, and it would take both sacrifices and hard work to make a home here."

Kirsten's books tell a bittersweet story of sorrow and joy. They are filled with adventure, courage, and hope. "Some of us are afraid of new things," Janet shares, thinking back on creating Kirsten's character. "Some of us prefer things—and places—to be safely familiar, with no surprises. Kirsten and her family are optimists who hope that things will turn out well. You wouldn't leave everything you've ever known, and those you love, if you didn't hope for the best."

Kirsten's stories help young readers understand both the rural and the immigrant experience. In a letter, story editor Jeanne Thieme writes, "Life on the farm is not easy—the work is hard, there is illness and death in the community—but there is a sense of unlimited opportunity as well. . . . Between Kirsten and her mother there is a special understanding because their reaction to the move—partly regret, partly exhilaration, partly confusion—is so similar."

> "Most of us here in America have ancestors from another country. **I think immigrants, then and now, are incredibly brave to leave their homeland for an unknown future.**"
>
> JANET SHAW

Kirsten Larsdotter

According to Swedish naming traditions, Kirsten's last name would have been Larsdotter, while her brothers would have had the surname Larsson. However, the editorial team decided that the family would all use an Americanized last name, as many Scandinavian immigrants chose to do when they came to the United States. In the stories, Kirsten is referred to as Kirsten Larson only after the family has immigrated.

An 1850s trunk and early sketches of Kirsten's Trunk by Renée Graef

This calico dress from the Wisconsin Historical Society helped inspire Kirsten's dress design. The daguerreotype (above right) shows a girl dressed in a similar fashion to Kirsten.

Early Designs

Kirsten's first American outfit is a gift given to her by Aunt Inger. It is a hand-me-down from Lisbeth, Kirsten's cousin and new friend. The outfit prepares Kirsten for the hard work she'll do on the farm: ankle boots, an apron, and a sunbonnet to protect her face from the sun and wind. Her dress of printed cotton has a "grow stripe"—a pleat at the hem that can be let down as Kirsten grows taller.

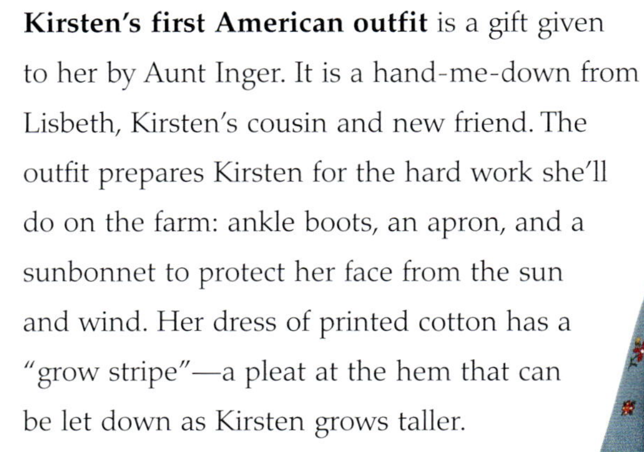

Early sketches for Kirsten's spoon bag

A color considered for Kirsten's Meet dress

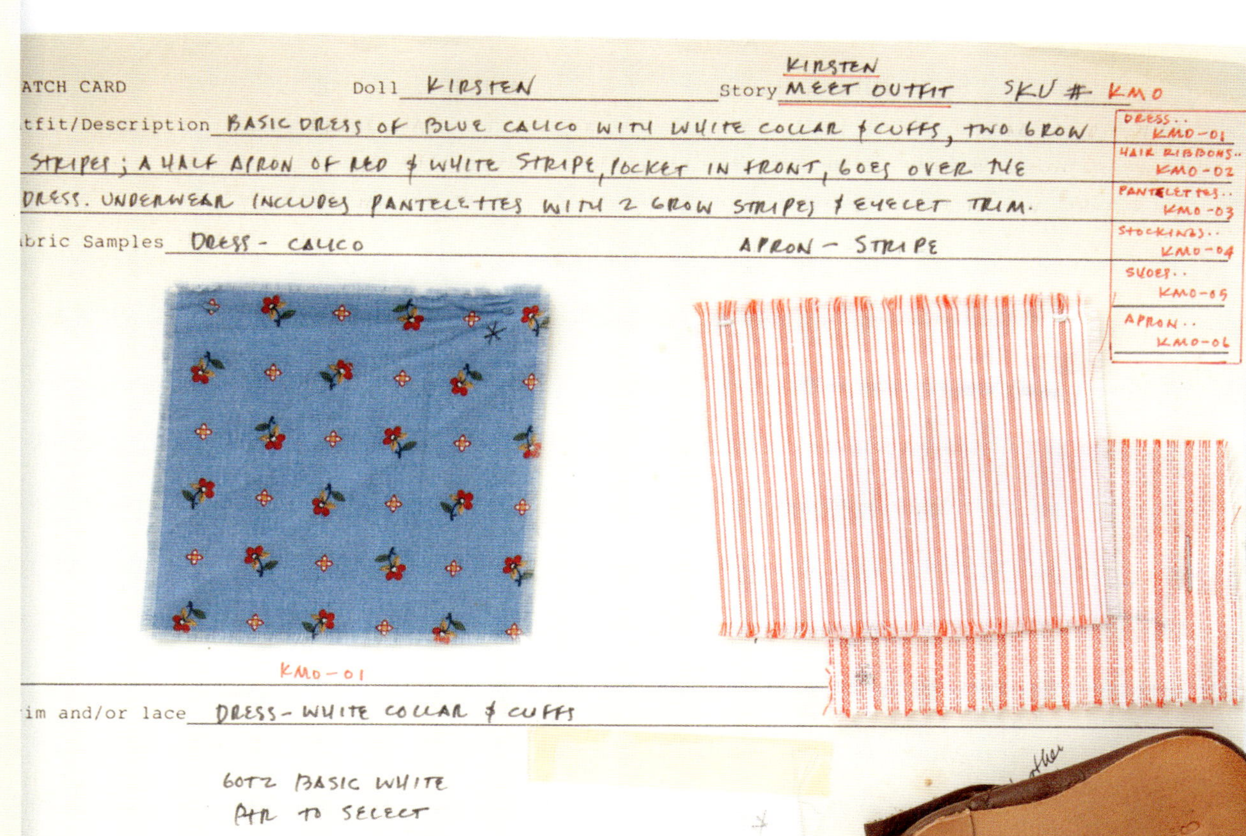

MEET KIRSTEN
An American Girl
PANTONE®
544 U
DOLL IN ARRIVAL OUTFIT

Illustrator Renée Graef drew the dress design (above) and accessory designs (below), while Pleasant Company staff researched and sourced materials for this important outfit.

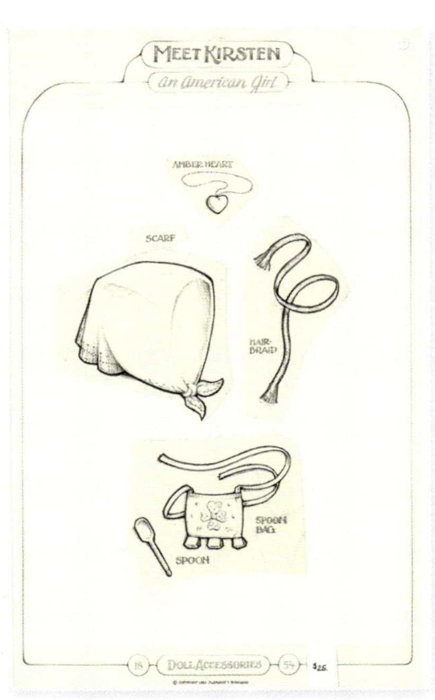

Meet Kirsten, written by Janet Shaw and illustrated by Renée Graef, published in 1986

Meet Kirsten

***Meet Kirsten* is the story of** the Larsons' difficult, dangerous, and long journey—by steamship across the Atlantic, and then by train and riverboat, and finally on foot—from their home in Sweden to America. Imagine how heartbreaking it was for Kirsten to say good-bye forever to her family in Sweden, and how happy she must have felt to reach Uncle Olav's homestead in Minnesota Territory, her family's new home.

Through the Storm

The story opens with Kirsten spotting land. "That's America!" she cries. For more than two months, twenty Swedish families have been cramped together in a small room below deck. By now, their food is stale, and they long to breathe fresh air and walk on solid ground.

But suddenly, violent storm waves wash across the deck and prevent the ship from reaching shore. Kirsten's heart sinks. America is so close and yet so far.

Immigrants traveled in a dark, stuffy area called steerage in the lower level of the ship. They tried to get as much fresh air and sunlight as they could, even in rough weather.

A family in Sweden reads a letter from relatives in America.

Kirsten loses sight of Papa in the crowded New York streets.

Kirsten wears a Swedish dirndl and kerchief on the journey from Sweden to Minnesota. Immigrant families carried clothing, food, and other supplies for the journey in carpetbags, baskets, boxes, trunks, and sometimes even bundled in bedsheets.

> “**When I'm writing about Kirsten, I am Kirsten.** What would I be thinking? What would I be seeing? Kirsten's fears are my fears, and I feel her joys because **I'm trying to be in her mind and in her experience when I'm writing.**”
>
> JANET SHAW

An 1887 illustration capturing the hope of immigrants arriving in the United States

Have Heart

Mormor, Kirsten's maternal grandmother in Sweden, gives Kirsten an amber heart necklace to remind her to always "have heart" on her long journey to find a new life in Minnesota. Kirsten needs to "have heart" many times on her journey: through storms at sea, when she gets lost in New York City, and on the hot, smoky train ride to Chicago. Kirsten also needs to "have heart" as she bids farewell to Sari, the beloved doll she brings all the way from Sweden, when the Larsons have to leave their trunks in Riverton and continue their journey on foot.

But the loss that is most heartrending, for Kirsten and for many readers, is the tragic death of Kirsten's friend Marta, who dies suddenly of cholera on the riverboat to Minnesota.

Images of riverboats, like the one above, informed Kirsten's story and illustrations.

"She can't be dead!" Kirsten cries. "She can't be!" Kirsten feels as though her heart is ripped in two.

Thousands of immigrants died of cholera and other maladies on their journey to America. Still, it was an upsetting topic for some parents and children to encounter in Kirsten's story. Senior editor Tamara England helped craft a response for parents who wrote in: "Although some of these incidents are difficult to read, they are important to the stories they tell. Our books do not reflect a perfect world—they can't, because they reflect history, and history is often gritty and hard. But they do blend fact and fiction in a way that leaves young readers hopeful that even difficult times can turn out well and life can get better."

> "Our books do not reflect a perfect world—they can't, because **they reflect history, and history is often gritty and hard.**"
>
> SENIOR EDITOR TAMARA ENGLAND

Illustrating Kirsten

RENÉE GRAEF
ILLUSTRATOR

Before Pleasant Company launched, illustrator Renée Graef had initially joined the small startup team to sketch Pleasant's ideas for the characters and to create some of the spot art. She almost became the Molly illustrator, but another artist was chosen for Molly instead. Renée recalls,

"Fortunately, Pleasant had remembered my sample illustrations when she decided to hire me as the illustrator for Kirsten. I came into the process late in the schedule, and I was initially concerned about how much time it would take to find models. However, Pleasant had already anticipated this. The very next day, she drove me to meet her friends, who would model for the reference photos for the illustrations."

Renée went on to illustrate the Little House picture books for HarperCollins.

An early drawing of Kirsten's Meet dress for girls by Renée Graef

Scenes & Settings illustration by Barb Fisher and Laura Chappel

Kirsten's American Home

The arc of Kirsten's series is both a literal and metaphorical journey toward feeling at home in America. Indeed, the title of an early concept for her first book was *Kirsten's American Home.* When she finally meets her cousins in Minnesota for the first time, Kirsten feels suddenly shy and shrinks back behind Mama.

> "Then she heard her own name above the shouts and laughter. **"Kirsten? You must be Kirsten!**"
>
> *MEET KIRSTEN*

The next morning, Kirsten wakes up in her very own bed, in a cozy log cabin filled with the smell of fresh-cut wood and the sound of birdsong. Outside the one tiny window, Kirsten sees a maple tree like the one outside her house in Sweden. She thinks to herself, *I'm home.*

Scenes & Settings sketch of the interior of the Larsons' cabin by Valerie Hodgson. Holiday scene illustrated by Mike Wimmer.

A Kirsten Fan

As a young girl, Megan Wagner Lloyd was a big fan of Kirsten. She grew up to become the award-winning and critically acclaimed author of *Allergic, Squished,* and *Winging It.*

The books were a big part of making her Kirsten doll—and history—feel real.

> "**Reading the Kirsten books as a kid helped me connect with the idea that the girls who had gone before me lived lives both extraordinarily different from my own and also very much the same.** I loved feeling this sense of community with girls from history—all of us from different time periods, with different families and circumstances, but all of us also rising to meet our own specific challenges with a shared strength."

When Lloyd became a mother, she shared her love of American Girl with her children, making her not just a lifelong fan of American Girl but also the mother of American Girl fans. "My three kids all loved American Girl dolls, but my oldest daughter, Izzy, was always especially enthusiastic. It was so rewarding to see how the dolls really fostered so much creativity in her. Izzy did everything from designing and sewing clothes for her dolls to making tiny books for them to photographing them. She even made up a storyline and planned outfits for her own historical doll, using a Truly Me doll. I loved that I was able to pass along not just a toy, but a shared experience through American Girl."

Author Megan Wagner Lloyd (right) with her daughter, Izzy, and the Kirsten doll from Megan's childhood that she later shared with Izzy

Kirsten Learns a Lesson, written by Janet Shaw and illustrated by Renée Graef, published in 1986

Renée's early concept sketch of Kirsten's school story included the working title *Kirsten's Secret*.

Kirsten Learns a Lesson

As the Larsons settle into their little log cabin, Kirsten finds herself pining for Sweden and struggling in school. Not only does she have to catch up with her classmates, but she must also learn to speak English. The teacher, Miss Winston, is stern and quick to correct her students' speech and writing, and Kirsten feels intimidated and ill at ease. However, Kirsten also discovers that language is no barrier to friendship when she makes a new friend, Singing Bird, outside of school.

Firm Hand, Soft Heart

Miss Winston is young and new to the school, but when a big boy in the one-room class laughs at Kirsten's heavy Swedish accent on the first day of school, Miss Winston wastes no time establishing her authority: "Then Miss Winston whirled around, raised her ruler over her head, and brought it smashing down on the top of the iron stove. The crack went through the room like the shot of a rifle. 'My father could not be a ship's captain if he weren't in charge of his crew. I couldn't be a teacher if I weren't in charge of my students.'"

When Kirsten finds out that Miss Winston is coming to board round, or live with Kirsten's family for a while, her spirits sink. She is having such a hard time at school—Kirsten doesn't want lessons at home, too! But seeing Kirsten more often gives Miss Winston just the insight she needs to help Kirsten memorize and recite a poem. When Miss Winston shows the Larson family the model of her father's ship inside a bottle, Kirsten is captivated, and all her memories of her long journey to America come out in a rush—in English! Miss Winston gives Kirsten a new poem to memorize, and Kirsten is able to recite it flawlessly and with feeling:

> "Swiftly, swiftly flew the ship
> Yet she sailed softly too:
> Sweetly, sweetly blew the breeze—
> On me alone it blew."
>
> *KIRSTEN LEARNS A LESSON*

The original artwork for Kirsten's Rewards of Merit, shown above and at the top of the page

Evolving Storyline

When Kirsten was first being developed, the editorial and research staff recognized that they didn't have the knowledge to present Singing Bird's Dakota culture and background in depth. The development team decided to limit Singing Bird's backstory and cultural depiction and to focus on scenes that the author could imagine, such as how a European girl and a Native American girl might meet and spend time together. As the company grew, it became the practice for staff to convene advisory boards when developing characters in an effort to more fully depict different cultures and historical contexts.

In 2025, American Girl rereleased *Kirsten Learns a Lesson* with some important updates to the way Singing Bird's story is told. Dakota advisers Dr. Amber Annis, Cheyanne St. John, and Šišóka Dúta guided the way Singing Bird and her people were presented in the narrative and the "Looking Back" essay and provided Dakota language to include in the story. The revised version includes Singing Bird's name in her own language, as well as a glossary of Dakota words. It is important to American Girl, as it was important in the early days of Pleasant Company, to regularly evolve how the company presents American history and the experiences of all American girls.

Kirsten and her new friend, Singing Bird, communicate through gestures and objects. They don't speak the same language, but that doesn't prevent their friendship from growing.

A girl Singing Bird's age would have sewn soft buckskin moccasins like these herself. She might have added decorations, such as tiny glass beads called "seed beads," with a bone needle and sinew thread.

Zitkádaŋ Dowáŋ Wíŋ
SINGING BIRD

Glossary of Dakota Words

Haȟ'áŋna *(ha-KH'AHN-nah)*—morning

Haȟ'áŋna kiŋháŋ *(ha-KH'AHN-nah keen-HAHN)*—tomorrow

Háŋ *(hahn)*—hello (all genders)

Pšithó *(p-shee-TOH)*—beads

Taŋyáŋ yahí *(tahn-YAHN yah-HEE)*—welcome

Waštédaŋ *(wah-SHTAY-dahn)*—pretty

Zitkádaŋ Dowáŋ Wíŋ *(Zeet-KAH-dahn Doh-WAHN Ween)*—Singing Bird

> When I was a kid, I was definitely a tomboy. My best friend, Mary, and I went every day to explore the creeks and woods near my house. When I wrote about Kirsten's friendship with Singing Bird, **I knew how special it is to share the creeks and meadows with a friend.**
>
> JANET SHAW

A New Friend

One morning, while fetching water from the stream, Kirsten sees a Dakota girl. Startled when Kirsten says hello, the girl runs off. But soon, the two begin leaving small gifts for each other—a bead, a pretty feather, a little doll, a piece of leather—and quietly become friends. When they finally meet face-to-face, they communicate by drawing pictures in the sand beside the stream. Before long, they are exploring the woods and streambanks together. Kirsten finds a comfort and freedom with Singing Bird that she doesn't feel at school or even with her cousins.

When Singing Bird invites Kirsten to visit her village, Kirsten jumps at the chance to escape her troubles at school. At the village, she is welcomed by Singing Bird's parents, and Singing Bird shows Kirsten her treasures: a leather pouch, a knife, and a buckskin doll stuffed with grass.

Later, Kirsten learns that Singing Bird and her people are leaving to go west because there is not enough game on the restricted area of land the U.S. government has made them live on. The government had promised them food and money, too, but there isn't enough of that either. Kirsten remembers the pain of hunger back in Sweden, so she is not only heartbroken to lose her new friend, but morally disturbed, too. In this poignant moment, she comes to understand two things: where her home is now—and what that means for the people who were here before her.

This intricate leather Dakota bag is decorated with beads, quills, fringe, and feathers. It features designs inspired by woodland plants and flowers.

Dakota grandmothers, mothers, and girls made exquisitely beaded and quilled doll dresses and adornments. Notice the tiny choker, belt, and knife sheath that accessorize this doll.

Singing Bird invites Kirsten to her village and shows Kirsten her treasured belongings.

Kirsten's Surprise, written by Janet Shaw and illustrated by Renée Graef, published in 1986

Kirsten's Surprise

With Christmas approaching, Kirsten and her family miss their Swedish holiday traditions, and this longing drives the plot of *Kirsten's Surprise*. Kirsten pesters Papa to go to town—a half-day's wagon ride—to fetch their trunks, but he is too busy preparing the farm for winter.

> When I was writing Kirsten's stories, I imagined adventures that I wished I could have had myself. **I would have loved to save my father in a snowstorm.**
>
> JANET SHAW

Finally, Kirsten and Papa set out to Maryville to retrieve their trunks. On the way home, they are caught in a ferocious blizzard. When Papa twists his knee, Kirsten bravely leads the horse through the blinding wind and snow, fighting back panic. She has heard stories of people who lost their way in snowstorms and unwittingly wandered in circles until they fell down.

She and Papa have to find shelter, and fast. Suddenly, Kirsten recognizes the cliffs where she used to play with Singing Bird, and she leads the horse to a small cave. Once they are safely inside the cave, they find dried grass and sticks left there by a Dakota hunting party. The hunting party's knowledge and resources prove to be essential to Kirsten and Papa's survival. After they have started a lifesaving fire, Papa smiles at Kirsten and says, "I'm glad you found this cave. Do you think you can find your way back to the farm from here?"

"I think so, Papa," Kirsten replies.

Images of nineteenth-century snowstorms like this one inspired Kirsten's story and illustrations.

The bird's-eye view of the blizzard is unusual but effectively conveys the feeling of being very small and lost on the vast prairie in the midst of a snowstorm. Illustrator Renée Graef says she worked very closely with the art director, "carefully considering the best perspectives to bring the stories to life."

Saint Lucia's Day

Kirsten and Papa finally make it home in the middle of the night. Kirsten realizes that it is now December 13, which is Saint Lucia's Day—the beginning of the Christmas season in Swedish tradition. While her family is busy unpacking, Kirsten sees her chance and slips away with a white nightgown and red sash from the trunk. Her cousins help her quickly dress as Saint Lucia to surprise everyone.

Kirsten dresses as Saint Lucia, bringing light to the dark days of winter. She carries a tray of coffee and Saint Lucia buns rolled into their distinctive pattern.

"Before I worked on the Kirsten books, I'd written only for adults. **I learned to respect the intelligence and savvy of young readers.** One student corrected the number of candles on the Saint Lucia crown. **These readers are sharp editors already.**"

JANET SHAW

For just a moment, the room is still. Then the commotion begins. Everyone calls out "Merry Christmas!" and "What a wonderful surprise!"

When Lisbeth asks Kirsten if this is what it was like last Christmas in Sweden, she replies, "It's almost the same, but this year I think it's even better. . . . I think it's the best one of all."

Happy Birthday, Kirsten!

Happy Birthday, Kirsten!, written by Janet Shaw and illustrated by Renée Graef, published in 1987

Farm children like Kirsten had serious responsibilities. They were expected to work hard and to put chores before fun. But as *Happy Birthday, Kirsten!* makes clear, there are joys to be found in community and working together.

The Quilt

The story opens with a tornado twisting its way toward the Larsons' farm! Everyone takes shelter in the root cellar, including Miss Winston, her head covered with a quilt. Anna touches the corner of Miss Winston's quilt and asks if she's forgotten her cloak.

> "I never thought about my cloak! I just knew I had to save my quilt, so I took it and ran." Miss Winston sat up straight like a lady and smoothed the quilt in her lap. "Every time I look at my quilt, it's like getting a letter from home."
>
> *HAPPY BIRTHDAY, KIRSTEN!*

Kirsten comes up with the idea of making a quilt for Miss Winston so that when Miss Winston moves on to board with another family, as rural school-teachers often did, she will have something to remember them by.

Friendship quilts from the mid-1800s, like the one shown above, inspired Kirsten's Friendship Quilt.

Photographs like this one from the late 1800s helped the development team envision the exterior of the Larsons' cabin.

Babies

Soon there are several new babies on the Larsons' farm. Missy, the barn cat, has her kittens, and Mama safely delivers Kirsten's baby sister, Britta, after Kirsten's daring horseback ride to get help from Aunt Inger. Kirsten does most of Mama's kitchen and farm chores, and several times a day she also washes diapers and hangs them on the line to dry. With all her extra work, there is no time for Kirsten to go to school or help make the quilt with her friends. Kirsten feels very tired and very lonely. Mama lifts Kirsten's spirits when she tells her that all her friends will be at the Larsons' farm to help raise their new barn.

Kirsten's Mama Cat and Kitten set is based on the cats on the Larsons' farm in *Happy Birthday, Kirsten!* There have been a few versions of Kirsten's cats, such as these, released in 2000.

Kirsten's Work Dress was based on the dress Kirsten wears in some of the illustrations for *Happy Birthday, Kirsten!*

Kirsten's toy pottery was originally made by Rowe Pottery Works in Cambridge, Wisconsin.

> "My favorite Kirsten scene is when Mama knows the baby is coming soon, and she takes Kirsten's hand in hers and says, **'I remember the day you were born.'** She makes it a time between herself and Kirsten. It's very close, very reassuring for Kirsten. And then after the baby's born, Mama doesn't forget Kirsten—she makes a party for her."
>
> JANET SHAW

In Kirsten's time, quilting was a way for girls and women to spend time together while creating a warm coverlet that was both beautiful and useful.

Friends Come Round

On the day of the barn raising, Kirsten is happily reunited with her sewing circle. Now that she's with her friends, Kirsten feels more strongly how much she's missed them. When it's time for a break, Mama comes from the kitchen carrying a heart-shaped cake, and Kirsten's birthday party begins. Lisbeth places a wreath of daisies on Kirsten's head. Aunt Inger gives her new hair ribbons. Mama, with a little help from Miss Winston, has made Kirsten a pretty white apron with fancy trim. But the best surprise comes from Kirsten's friends. The quilt that Kirsten had thought they were making for Miss Winston turns out to be a friendship gift for Kirsten herself!

Historical images, like this one from the Wisconsin Historical Society, helped illustrators bring Kirsten's barn raising to life.

> "We're giving this quilt to you because you missed out on the fun of making it," Lisbeth explained. **"We want you to know we didn't forget you, even when you weren't with us."**

HAPPY BIRTHDAY, KIRSTEN!

> "As a girl, sometimes I'd find my mom and dad dancing to music on the radio. If I cut in, Dad would dance with me, too. **When Kirsten dances with her father, I remembered how special I felt when I got to dance with my dad.**"
>
> JANET SHAW

After dinner, lanterns are lit, and the men bring out their fiddles. Just when Kirsten thinks the day can't get any better, Papa taps her on the shoulder. "Come on, ten-year-old," Papa says in his deep voice. "This is your birthday dance with me."

Kirsten Saves the Day

Kirsten Saves the Day, written by Janet Shaw and illustrated by Renée Graef, published in 1988

More adventures abound in Kirsten's summer story. The woods around Kirsten's tiny log cabin are bountiful in summertime—berries grow in thick, brambly patches; streams are full of trout; and sometimes trees are full of honey. Kirsten has the freedom to roam, and we see in this story that she has grown in both her knowledge of and her confidence in her new American home. She strides off confidently to fill her bucket with berries or to catch a fish dinner for her whole family. The woods are full of dangers, too. Mama warns Kirsten to watch out for snakes, especially since Kirsten walks barefoot in the woods. And where there are berries, fish, and honey, there are also bears!

While Kirsten is trout fishing, her dog Caro gets stung by a bee. Kirsten comforts the poor pup and also sees an opportunity—there might be a bee tree nearby, filled with valuable honey and beeswax.

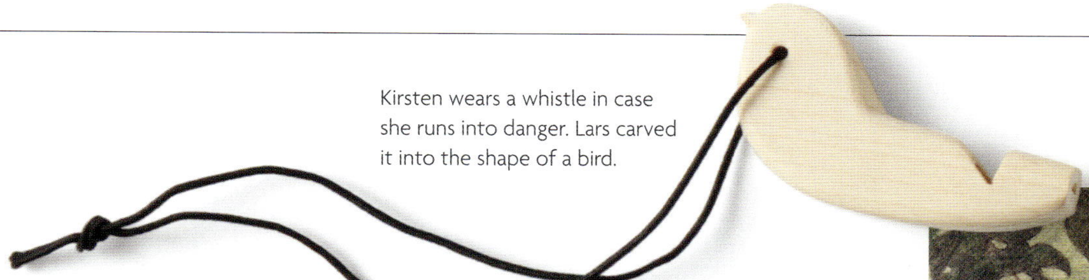

Kirsten wears a whistle in case she runs into danger. Lars carved it into the shape of a bird.

The Bee Tree

"Finding a bee tree is like finding a treasure," Kirsten says to her little brother, Peter. "If we bring Papa a whole tree full of honeycombs, he won't have to worry about money."

Kirsten is so excited by her find and by the thought of being a hero for her family that she becomes a little overconfident and a bit foolhardy. She sees deep gashes in the tree trunk made by bear claws and bears' pawprints on the ground, as well. But Kirsten ignores these clues to danger and instead allows a surprising competitiveness to drive her actions. This is *her* honey, not the bears'!

The Bears

Kirsten is determined to get the honey herself. Peter is a less-than-willing accomplice, and just as he fears, the adventure is a disaster. A curious bear cub tumbles out of the bushes, followed by an angry mother bear. Kirsten saves herself and her little brother by climbing a tree in the nick of time.

THE
MAGAZINE OF SCIENCE,
And School of Arts.

No. LXIV.] SATURDAY, JUNE 20, 1840. [PRICE 1½d.

1 2 3

4 6 5

PRACTICAL MANAGEMENT OF BEES.

IN the practical management of bees, the formation and due arrangement of the apiary is of some importance. The prime requisites are *shelter* from the extremes of heat and cold, and *quiet*. Facing southwards, the hives should be carefully screened from the north and north-east. A group of young trees, or a close-growing hedge, will answer the purpose well; or advantage may be taken of a range of buildings, or a garden wall. In availing ourselves, however, of the shelter of buildings, care must be taken to keep the hives at such a distance as to be clear of the rain-drops, and from the eddying winds caused by such a locality. A distance of not less than eight or ten feet should intervene between them and the screen; and of this space the half-breadth next the hives should be laid

VOL. II.

Historical references, such as this page from a scientific magazine of the time, helped the development team understand beekeeping.

Taking the Bees to Town

The next day, in an elaborate process involving a two-man saw, smoke, veils, and a special bee house, Papa collects the bees and the honey, and all is forgiven. On a hot Fourth of July day, the Larsons bring the honey to sell to Berkhoff's General Store in Maryville. Will it be enough to get them everything they need? Kirsten shows maturity in her understanding of the difference between needs and wants when she admires the straw hat she's been wishing for. She knows better than to ask for what they can't afford. "It's lucky I don't need a straw hat," she tells Papa, "because I'm sure this one wouldn't fit me."

> "You've earned a special treat today, Kirsten," Papa said. "I worried that we wouldn't have enough to sell for all the things we needed from Mr. Berkhoff. But when he saw that beeswax and tasted your honey, I knew we'd have enough and a little more besides."
>
> *Kirsten Saves the Day*

Changes for Kirsten, written by Janet Shaw and illustrated by Renée Graef, published in 1988

Changes for Kirsten

Kirsten's final story opens with Kirsten, her brother Lars, and their neighbor John Stewart on the trap line, where they discuss the trapping, killing, and skinning of animals, as well as the value of their fur pelts. Kirsten is utterly unsentimental about the whole process, knowing her family needs the money to buy a farm of their own. But when she discovers a live baby raccoon in the last trap, vulnerable and alone, her heart melts, and she decides to bring it home, just "until it's healthy again," despite her brother's warnings.

John Stewart thinks Kirsten should stay home with the women and children. But Kirsten is an excellent wildlife tracker, and John eventually admits he was wrong!

The baby raccoon is charming, but it climbs all over the cabin and refuses to be caught. When it knocks over an oil lamp, a fire starts—and quickly spreads. Nobody is hurt, and Kirsten manages to drag the big blue trunk they brought from Sweden outside, but the log cabin burns to the ground along with everything else they own. The setback puts a farm of their own out of reach.

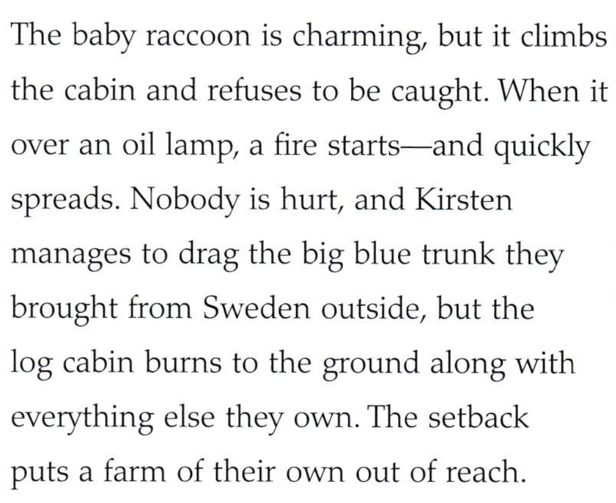

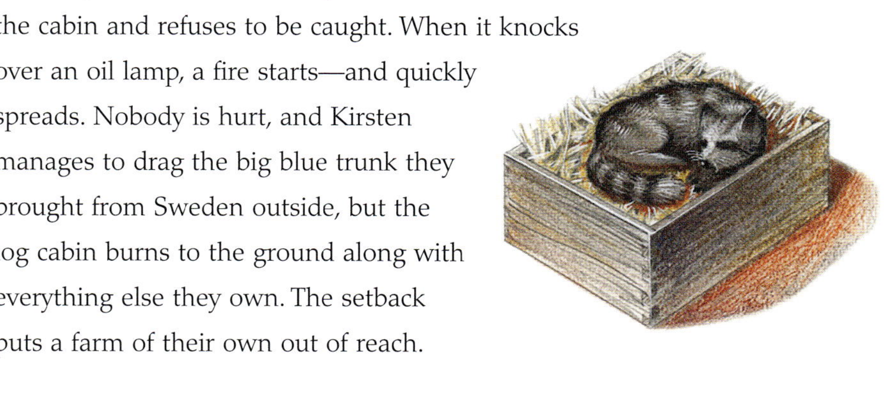

Old Jack

Kirsten and Lars go back out on the trap line. Even though her hands and feet tingle from the cold, Kirsten keeps working so they can set as many traps as possible. They need all the pelts they can get to sell for money to build a new home.

When an owl swoops overhead, Kirsten and Lars realize they've stayed out too late. Kirsten trembles as she recalls stories of people caught in the woods overnight. They could freeze to death, or a wolf might get them. As Kirsten and Lars trudge for home in their snowshoes, following the North Star as their guide, they come upon someone else's snowshoe tracks. They follow the tracks to a cave where a trapper named Old Jack lives, and there they make a grim discovery: the frozen body of the old trapper, along with piles of valuable furs—enough to buy a new house and farm. Kirsten is uncertain about the ethics of taking the furs, but Lars tells her,

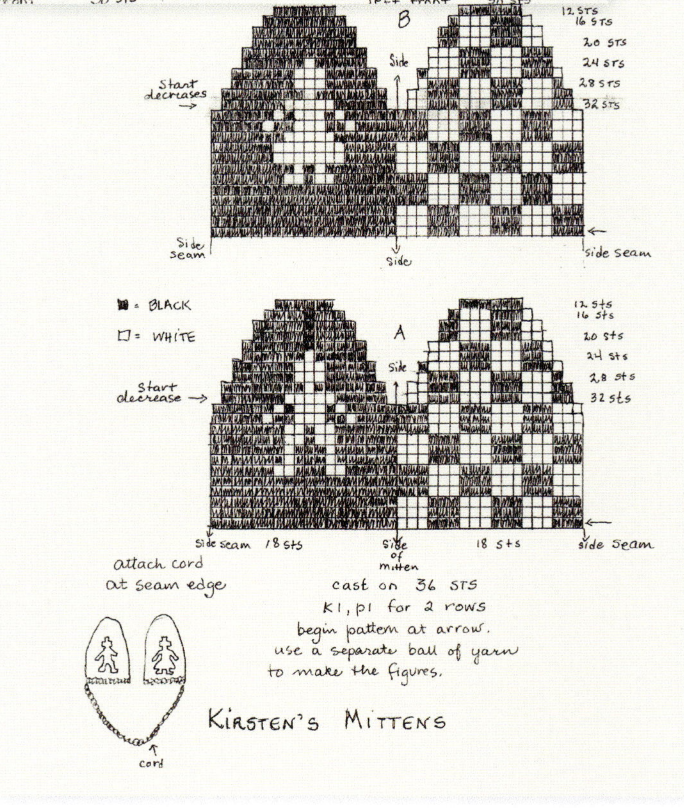

Knitting instructions designed by Gretchen W. Maring

> "If Old Jack were alive and we found something he'd lost, we would give it back to him. But he's dead and gone, so we can't give him back these furs. **We can't give him anything but a proper burial. He doesn't even have a family to do that.**"

CHANGES FOR KIRSTEN

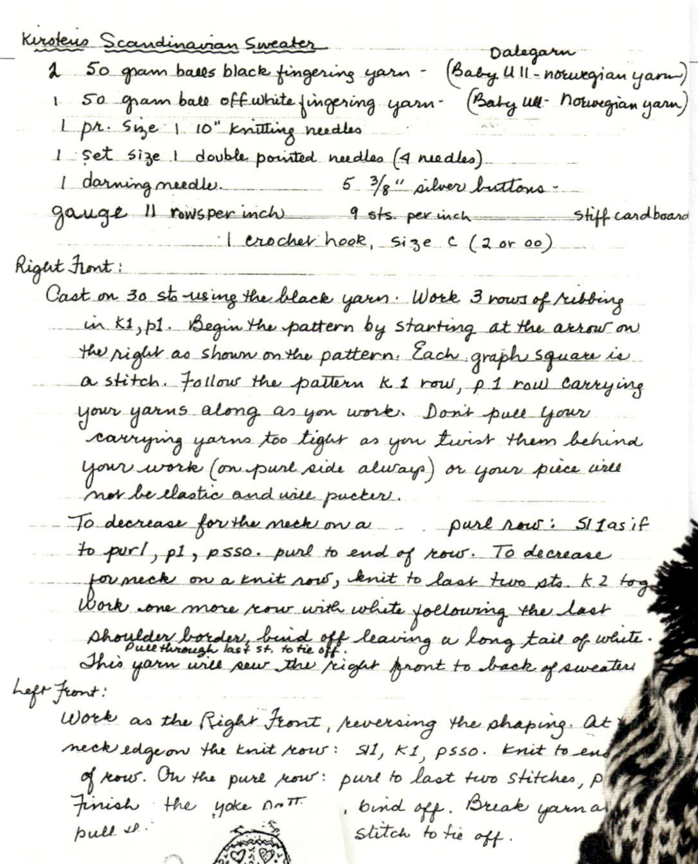

Kirsten's Scandinavian Sweater

2 50 gram balls black fingering yarn - (Dalegarn Baby U ll - norwegian yarn)
1 50 gram ball off white fingering yarn - (Baby Ull - Norwegian yarn)
1 pr. Size 1 10" knitting needles
1 set size 1 double pointed needles (4 needles)
1 darning needle 5 3/8" silver buttons
gauge 11 rows per inch 9 sts. per inch stiff cardboard
1 crochet hook, size C (2 or 00)

Right Front:

Cast on 30 sts using the black yarn. Work 3 rows of ribbing in K1, p1. Begin the pattern by starting at the arrow on the right as shown on the pattern. Each graph square is a stitch. Follow the pattern k 1 row, p 1 row carrying your yarns along as you work. Don't pull your carrying yarns too tight as you twist them behind your work (on purl side always) or your piece will not be elastic and will pucker.

To decrease for the neck on a purl row: Sl 1 as if to purl, p1, psso. purl to end of row. To decrease for neck on a knit row, knit to last two sts. k 2 tog. Work one more row with white following the last shoulder border, bind off leaving a long tail of white. Pull through last st. to tie off. This yarn will sew the right front to back of sweater.

Left Front:

Work as the Right Front, reversing the shaping. At neck edge on the knit row: Sl1, K1, psso. knit to end of row. On the purl row: purl to last two stitches, p... Finish the yoke ... , bind off. Break yarn a... pull ... stitch to tie off.

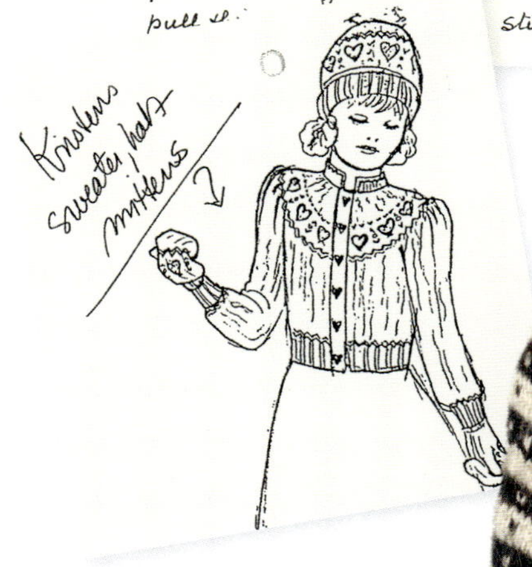

Kirsten's sweater, hat, mittens

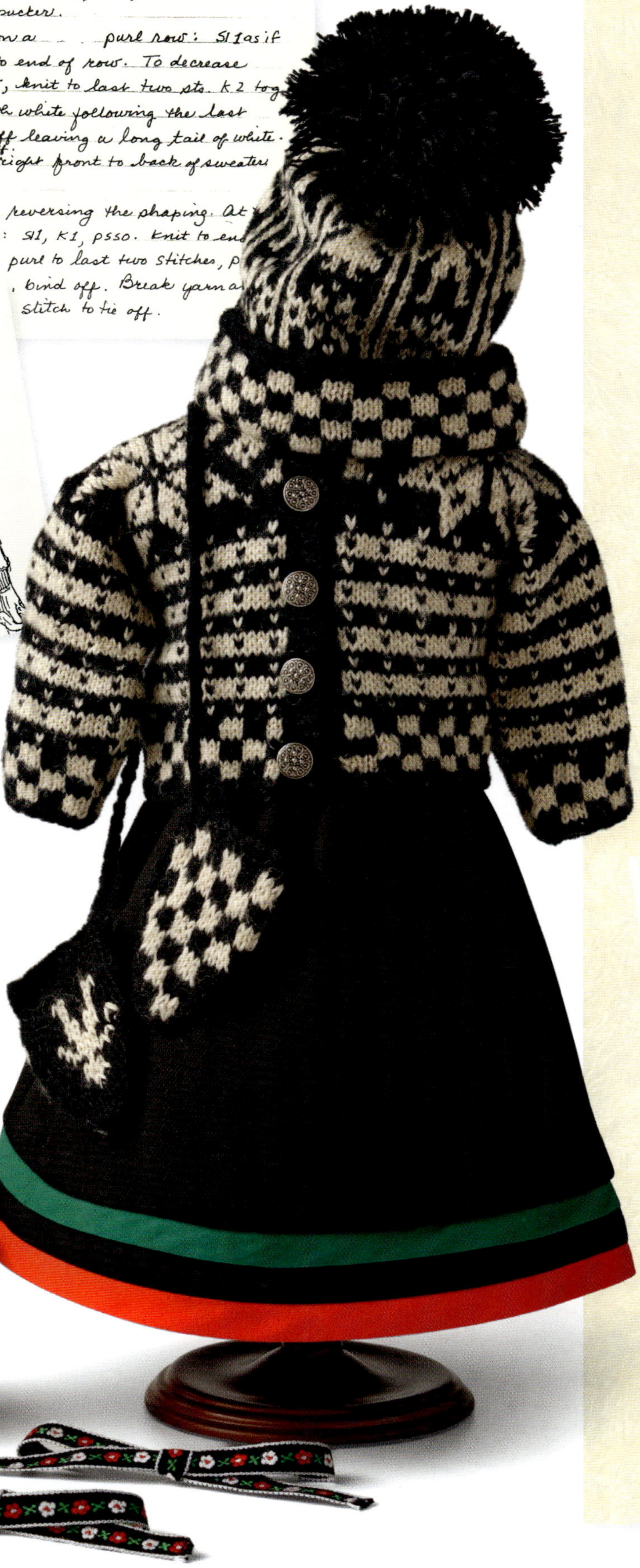

Home at Last

Thanks to Old Jack, the Larsons are able at last to buy a farm with a timber house on it. The former owners, Kirsten's friends John and Mary Stewart and their family, have gone west in a covered wagon. The wagon didn't hold very much, so luckily for the Larsons, the Stewarts left their furniture and some plates and cups behind. When Mama enters the house, she spreads her arms wide as she gazes around the kitchen: "When we sit at our table, we can look out the window and see that big maple tree." She sighs. "Oh, this is a real home, isn't it! This is the home your papa and I dreamed we'd have in America." Kirsten walks into the bedroom off the kitchen. Every night from now on, she will sleep on the soft mattress of her own trundle bed. As she looks out the window, Kirsten spies a bit of paper in the corner. She unfolds it to find a sweet surprise welcoming her to her new home.

Dear Kirsten,
Please be happy in your new house. The next time I write it will be from Oregon! Don't forget your loving friends,
Mary and John
P.S. John made the little toy for you!

A camera-ready paste-up of the letter from Mary that Kirsten finds in the window of her new home

Molly
Molly
McIntire
MEET MOLLY
AN AMERICAN GIRL
~ BOOK ONE ~
THE AMERICAN GIRLS COLLECTION®
CAMP GOWONAGIN
July 6, 1944
Dear Dad,
Here I am carrying the flag in the Camp Gowonagin Fourth of July parade. Do you think my face looks funny? Well, it does. I have poison ivy. Just about everyone at camp does. How did we get it? Well Dad, that's a long story.
MEET MOLLY
An American Girl
BLOUSE
UNDERPANTS
SADDLE SHOES
SOCKS

McIntire
Molly J.
Last Name
First Name and Initial
School
Elmwood
AMP GOWONAGIN

Making Molly

After Valerie Tripp wrote the character descriptions and plot outlines for Molly, Samantha, and Kirsten, Pleasant said to her, "So, VT, which character do you want to write about?" Valerie recalls with a laugh that she chose Molly because she felt sorry for her. Kirsten had thrilling, life-and-death adventures. Samantha had the excitement of new inventions and fighting for women's rights. Molly's stories, by contrast, were set right in the middle of a war and a dark time of loss for so many Americans.

> "I chose to write about Molly because it was scary to me—**I often like to step off cliffs, writing-wise.**"
>
> VALERIE TRIPP

As the plots developed, Pleasant and Valerie decided to set Molly's stories in fictional Jefferson, Illinois, which was based on Evanston, just outside of Chicago. They had both lived in the Chicago area at various points in their lives, and with Kirsten in Minnesota and Samantha in New York, they decided an Illinois location between the two other characters would be ideal. According to Valerie, "I changed the name to avoid people seeing the town as an important factor in the story, because it was not." After all, across the United States, many American families were experiencing the same rationing, calls to volunteer, and feelings of missing loved ones as the McIntire family, no matter where they lived.

From left: Renée Graef's concept sketch for *Meet Molly*; a fabric swatch and an early design for Molly's Meet dress for girls; and Molly's Accessories, underwear, and socks sketched by Renée Graef

A Father Far Away

Molly's father, James McIntire, and Valerie Tripp's father, Granger Tripp

Molly's story reflects how many Americans came together during World War II—showing resilience, making sacrifices, and supporting one another in their communities. While the war unified the country in some ways, it also exposed inequalities. Black Americans, for instance, contributed to the war effort both at home and abroad, yet continued to face discrimination and exclusion. Women stepped into factory jobs in place of men but were underpaid and undervalued. The U.S. government unjustly held many Japanese Americans against their will, far from their homes. These contradictions between unity and alienation shaped Americans' experience of the war and would continue to shape the postwar world.

Life Magazine

Life magazine was a prime research source during Molly's development. Its focus on photography and visual storytelling made the magazine an exceptional resource for illustrations and product design, especially clothing, hairstyles, accessories, and furniture.

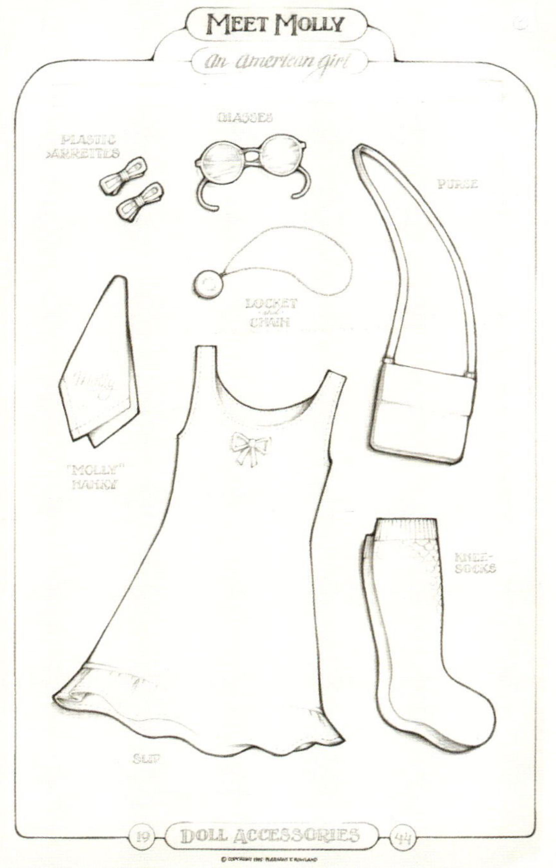

The character who would become Molly McIntire was, in part, inspired by Valerie's own family experiences. Valerie was born just six years after the war ended. She vividly recalls that her father's World War II footlocker, boots, and bedroll were kept on a shelf in the basement. Her father almost never spoke about his wartime experiences, but the war still felt very present to her. Valerie couldn't imagine anything scarier for a child than having a parent far away at war and in danger.

> "When I sat down to write about Molly, it was very clear what she wanted—**her father home safely**—and, poignantly, what she wanted but could not have, what none of us can have: **to return to the past.**"
>
> VALERIE TRIPP

Early Designs

Molly's Meet outfit separates were designed as mix-and-match, a practical and versatile choice during wartime, when fabric and clothing options were limited. The rounded Peter Pan collar trimmed in rickrack is a dickey, a piece that gives the look of a full shirt but is just a collar—a fabric-saving trick that still offers a fashionable appearance. In her shoulder bag, Molly keeps a 1943 steel penny that was used during the war, when copper was in short supply.

> "Pleasant and I loved talking about Molly and her appearance and her material culture. We enjoyed daydreaming about the accessories, clothing, and furniture it would be fun to make for her. **'Let's give her braids and glasses!'** I said. (I had always wanted braids and glasses when I was a schoolchild.)"
>
> VALERIE TRIPP

PANTONE® 281 U

A color considered for Molly's Meet outfit

Left: Renée Graef's early concept design for Molly's Meet outfit. Opposite page: Renée's early designs of Molly's Accessories

Molly always wears this sterling silver locket around her neck. Inside is a picture of Dad.

SWATCH CARD Doll MOLLY Story MOLLY MEET OUTFIT SKU # MMO

Outfit/Description NAVY BLUE WOOL A-LINE SKIRT WITH A SWEATER OF A NAVY BASE WITH RED-GREEN-NAVY ARGYLE PATTERN ACROSS FRONT WITH A WHITE DICKEY HAVING NAVY RICKRACK TRIM THE COLLAR. UNDERWEAR INCLUDES WHITE PANTIES.

SKIRT..	MMO-01
HAIR RIBBONS..	MMO-02
PANTIES..	MMO-03
SOX..	MMO-04
SHOES..	MMO-05
SWEATER..	MMO-06
DICKEY..	MMO-07
EYEGLASSES..	MMO-08

Fabric Samples SKIRT – NAVY BLUE WOOL DICKEY – WHITE

Webatex Art 5575 Color 1477 Price 16.42/DM Wide 148 cm

MMO-01 MMO-07

Trim and/or lace NAVY RICK-RACK ON DICKEY COLLAR

4.73/meter

.18pf/meter

will get lighter weight

MMO-07

Thread TO MATCH

NO BUTTONS – VELCRO CLOSURES

Ribbons Mohr – taffeta 15 mm / navy #034 .18pf/meter 5/8" width

TYPE OF RIBBON PREFERRED MMO-02

COLOR SAMPLE ONLY

Shoes WHITE ANKLETS

SELECT BOTH SENT SAMPLE OF BOTH TO GOTZ

-1-

Molly's Argyle Sweater

* 1 skein (1oz) Phildar yarn, blue – graph symbol X PRONOSTIC 229
* 1 skein (1oz) Phildar yarn, red – graph symbol • PRONOSTIC 229
* 1 skein (1oz) Phildar yarn, green · graph symbol ○ PRONOSTIC 229

1 pr. Size 1 10" needles 1 set double pointed needles Size 1

scrap yarn or stitchholders

Gauge: 9 st. per inch, 8 rows per inch

Front: Using the Blue yarn, cast on 50 St. K1, p1 for 1". On the last rib row increase 3 st, evenly spaced. Pearl the next row across. 53 St. on needle.

Begin knitting the argyle pattern by following the chart. When the entire piece measures 3" from the beginning, decrease for the raglan armhole shape as follows, always following the pattern on the graph: On the knit row: Sl 1, K1, psso Follow the graph to the last 2 sts. K 2 tog. On the plurl row, sl 1 as if to purl, p 1, psso. Purl to end of the row, following the pattern, p 2 tog. Continue decreasing at the beginning and end of each row, following the pattern, until 21 sts remain, ending with a purl row. There should be 4" of argyle pattern worked. The entire piece Should measure 5" including the ribbing.

Next row: Sl 1, K1, psso, K 5 sts. in pattern. Turn to purl side. Sl 1 as if to purl, p1, psso, p 2 sts. in pattern, p 2 tog.

next row: sl 1, K1, psso, K 2 tog. Turn to purl side, p 2 tog. Fasten yarn off by breaking it, leaving a 3" tail and pulling it through the remaining stitch.

Place the next 7 sts (center of sweater) on a holder or piece of scrap yarn. There will be 7 sts remaining on the needle. Proceed as follows: Leaving a 3" tail on the yarn, knit across 5 sts in

Knitting instructions designed by Gretchen W. Maring

Meet Molly

Meet Molly, written by Valerie Tripp. Originally published in 1986 with illustrations by C. F. Payne, reillustrated by Nick Backes in 1989

In the opening scene of *Meet Molly*, it's almost nine o'clock at night and Molly is still sitting at the dinner table, staring down at a plate of mashed turnips that her brother Ricky unhelpfully describes as "old, cold, moldy brains." Even though turnips are one of the only surviving vegetables from Mrs. Gilford's not-so-victorious Victory Garden, Molly will not eat a speck of them. But this isn't just a headstrong refusal to eat root vegetables. Molly is refusing to accept the massive changes that World War II has brought into her life: Her father is far away at war, her mother is busy working for the Red Cross, and the world around her is filled with ration books, blackout drills, and frightening news stories. The mashed turnips are simply the last straw. She fervently wishes, as she does throughout her series, that Dad will come home and her life can go back to the way it was before the war—safe, settled, and steady.

Meet Molly isn't just the first book in Molly's series—it's also the first American Girl book ever written, and Valerie knew it would serve as the model for all the American Girl books to come. As Valerie describes it, "I was flying without a net. I had no rules to follow. I was creating the paradigm, supplying the DNA. That was difficult, but exhilarating. Here's what I knew for sure: I wanted to write a story that would help readers become friends with my nine-going-on-ten-year-old heroine, Molly, and therefore want to learn about the U.S. home front during World War II."

DAD

MOM

JILL

RICKY

BRAD

LINDA

SUSAN

MRS. GILFORD

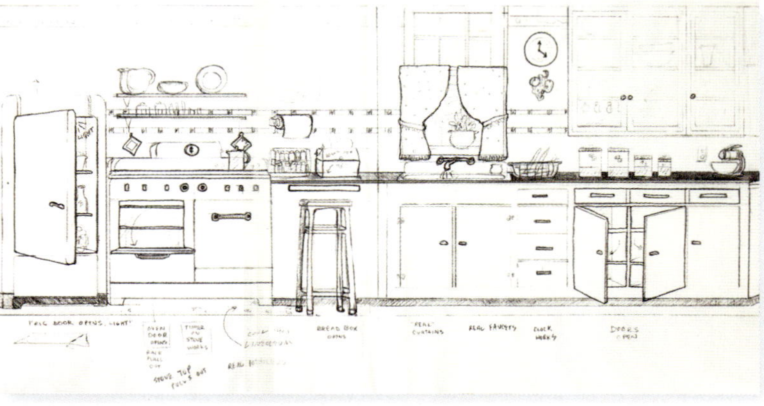

Molly's kitchen sketch by Valerie Hodgson and illustration by John Pugh and Lisa Pfeiffer, part of Molly's Scenes & Settings

Gladys Gilford, Home-Front Hero

The McIntires' housekeeper, Mrs. Gilford, has been a sure and steady presence in Molly's household since she was little. With both of Molly's parents serving in the war in their own ways, the McIntires need her more than ever. She keeps the household from spinning off its axis and brings the family stability and some measure of comfort during hard times. Because metal is needed for war supplies, canned vegetables are considered unpatriotic. Mrs. Gilford is undaunted: She sends away for a pamphlet called *Food Fights for Freedom* and plants a Victory Garden in the McIntires' backyard. She puzzles through the mysteries of the ration system, saving points and learning to cook with less butter, sugar, and flour so the family can have special treats like chocolate cake on Molly's birthday. Every week she tries a new bread recipe, and her Boston Brown Bread, baked in an old coffee tin with no butter or sugar, is a huge hit. Of all the changes Molly has had to endure, Mrs. Gilford's homemade bread is the only one Molly is happy to accept. A hearty salute to Mrs. Gilford, home-front hero!

World War II, Girl Sized

The day before Halloween, Molly, Linda, and Susan tease Ricky because he has a crush on Jill's friend Dolores. They embarrass him in front of Dolores, and Ricky vows that they will pay. On Halloween night, he makes good on his promise by dousing the girls with a water hose.

The girls plot their revenge. Molly really wants to embarrass him in front of somebody. That somebody is Dolores, and Molly has the perfect plan. Just as Jill and Dolores come out the back door, Molly executes a flawless strategic maneuver: dumping bags of Ricky's underwear on them, right in front of Ricky. Operation Mortification: complete.

Valerie has vivid memories of a boy named Stevie who turned a hose on her and her best friend, Bobby, one Halloween when they were dressed in then-popular hula costumes. When researching for *Meet Molly,* Valerie read that girls dressed as hula dancers in the 1940s, too. She got her revenge on Stevie by telling millions of readers what he did!

Love of All Things Hawaiian

In the 1940s, and especially following the attack on Pearl Harbor, Americans were fascinated with the island way of life in the U.S. territory of Hawai'i. Movies, music, and magazines often portrayed scenes like hula dancers in grass skirts swaying to drumbeats. Once the United States entered the war, roughly one million soldiers, sailors, and war workers spent time on the islands. They wrote home about sights like coconuts and palm trees, turquoise waters, and towering volcanoes, further fueling the national interest in Hawai'i. Across the country, Americans learned to play the ukulele, speak Hawaiian words, and dance hula wearing grass skirts and flower leis, especially at Halloween.

Both the storyline and costume reflect Molly's time and place, when grass skirts and leis were common at Hawaiian-themed parties. Today, however, wearing a hula costume just for fun is considered culturally inappropriate due to hula's deep cultural and spiritual significance in Hawaiian culture.

A student from Hālau Hula 'O Hokulani performs hula today.

Two of the most memorable scenes from *Meet Molly* bring World War II into girl size, in a way that's relatable across eras.

> "I guess I deserved it. Your trick was mean, but you know, it was funny too," he laughed. **"I guess it's better to be on your side than to be your enemy."**
>
> *MEET MOLLY*

Nick Backes

ILLUSTRATOR NICK BACKES

Nick Backes was a versatile illustrator who worked in the publishing, fashion, theater, advertising, and retail industries. After graduating from the Academy of Art in San Francisco, he landed a commission for three fashion seasons (1983–1985) with the House of Valentino in Rome. "It was thrilling to be in the Couture House with Audrey Hepburn in the next room, and to touch and feel Brooke Shields's dress," Backes said. "It was a whole new world; I was so innocent and had never traveled that far. But I got used to it pretty fast!"

Nick illustrated many books for children, including classics such as *Little Women* and *Lassie*, along with the *Alissa, Princess of Arcadia* series. His first book for Pleasant Company was *Molly Saves the Day*. Pleasant thought Nick's upbeat pencil-and-pastel illustrations captured Molly's energetic spirit, and he completed the rest of the series and then went back to reillustrate the first four books, which had originally been illustrated by C. F. Payne (*Meet Molly*, *Molly Learns a Lesson*, and *Molly's Surprise*) and David Gaadt (*Happy Birthday, Molly!*).

"I love what I do because I can do some things that a lot of people can't do," Backes said. "It's very nice to be born with something that can make you a living, and I feel very lucky." Nick continued to illustrate Molly in stories and activity books until his death in 2013.

Molly Learns a Lesson

Molly Learns a Lesson, written by Valerie Tripp. Originally published in 1986 with illustrations by C. F. Payne, reillustrated by Nick Backes in 1989

From the first morning song to the last dismissal bell, Molly's teacher, Miss Campbell, keeps her classroom marching along smoothly. Molly adores her and the energetic way she keeps her students on their toes. During geography, they study the places all over the world where the war is being fought. At the end of the day, Molly sometimes gets to lead her classmates as they march out of the building in orderly lines, just like soldiers.

> "School is your war duty," Miss Campbell reminded her class. "Being a good student is as important as being a good soldier."
>
> MOLLY LEARNS A LESSON

The design for Molly's school outfit changed from a green sweater and skirt (above) to a jumper and blouse based on Molly's originally planned Meet outfit (far right).

Lend a Hand

The roles of "being a good student" and "being a good soldier" converge when Miss Campbell announces that the class has been invited to participate in a schoolwide Lend-a-Hand Contest to help soldiers overseas. Molly tries to think of a spectacular project, one that is sure to get her noticed by Miss Campbell. While she daydreams about getting her photo in the newspaper with Miss Campbell—which Molly hopes will lead to Miss Campbell and her soldier fiancé asking her to be in their wedding—Molly misses her actual chance to lead a winning project. Molly's reverie is stopped cold when she hears Miss Campbell say, "What a wonderful idea, Alison!"

A classroom in the 1940s. Teachers explained why a war fought far away made some things scarce in America: Metal was needed for war supplies, and sugar and rubber came from countries where the fighting was happening.

Molly's Lunchbox, released in 1999, was a hand-me-down from her sister Jill.

Top Secret Agents

Alison Hargate suggests the third-grade girls knit socks for their Lend-a-Hand project. Molly knows that knitting socks is a terrible idea because Mrs. Gilford tried to teach her once, and it was both too hard and took forever. Molly didn't even finish one sock. She knows the third-grade girls will never win with this project, so she decides to go rogue.

Once again, Molly enlists Linda and Susan's help. Conspiring in their secret hideaway in the storage room above Molly's garage, they all agree that the girls are doomed unless they come up with a better project. When Susan jokingly suggests they become spies, Molly is instantly on board.

"Well," said Molly, "we're secret agents because nobody knows what we're doing, right? Just us three. And our mission is our project. Only instead of stealing information, we can collect something, something like—"

"Tops! Bottletops!" interrupted Linda. **"Get it? Top Secret. We'll be Top Secret Agents."**

MOLLY LEARNS A LESSON

25

"Ooooooh! Let me see," said Susan. She stood on tiptoe and leaned over Molly's shoulder.

Alison had printed:

You are invited to
A Knitting Bee
to work on your socks for the
Lend A Hand Contest
from nine o'clock to three o'clock
tomorrow
at Alison's house
Lunch and other refreshments, too!
Bring your own yarn and needles.

(yarn + needles)
(needles + knitting)
(basket of yarn)
(cat + yarn)
(letters made out of knitting needles)
(socks)
(cocoa)
(cookies)

Molly's hands were stiff and cold. Susan took the invitation from Molly and held it under the light. "Gee, I bet that will be fun," she said. "A knitting bee at Alison's house."

"Probably great refreshments, too," said Linda.

"Oh, I don't know," said Molly. "I don't think it will be fun. Just sitting and knitting, knitting and sitting all day. I think we'll have more fun."

Above, Valerie included a charming hand-drawn illustration of Alison Hargate's invitation with her draft manuscript of *Molly Learns a Lesson*, which inspired the illustration in the book (shown left).

Molly is first shown wearing her yellow slicker and hat in *Molly Learns a Lesson*, but the doll's version was released with other products from *Changes for Molly*, along with her red galoshes and umbrella.

Spies and Allies

On the morning of the knitting bee, Molly puts on her spy outfit: dark blue corduroy pants and a dark plaid shirt. It's a drippy, rainy day, so Molly also puts on her bright yellow slicker and hat. The girls set out to collect one hundred bottletops, but after hours of walking from door to door, they have cold hands, wet legs, tired feet, and only sixteen bottletops in Molly's school bag.

They realize they're on Alison Hargate's block and decide to peek in her window to see how the rest of the girls are faring. "WELL, what have we here?" booms a voice very nearby. Herded by Alison's mother, the Top Secret Agents trudge inside sheepishly and reluctantly to face their classmates. Just as Molly predicted, the sock knitting is not going well.

Suddenly, Grace Littlefield wails, "I just can't! . . . It was hard enough with the two needles, but three is impossible! Every stitch I knit comes undone. I'll never make a whole sock, never!"

"Socks are hard, Grace," Molly says. "But you know, you have a nice square here. If we—I mean, if *you*—all put your squares together, you could make a really nice blanket. I saw Mrs. Gilford do it once. See, you just lay out the squares . . ."

Molly discovers that it's more fun—and more effective—to cooperate with her classmates for the contest, which is another girl-sized interpretation of the larger conflict of World War II.

Headline → FOURTH GRADE GIRLS WIN CONTEST

sign on wall behind girls → LEND A HAND CONTEST WINNERS

ART: Newspaper-type photo of Miss Campbell and the girls-- probably only those named below are fully visible, others are heads in background. They stand behind a table holding the blanket up forthe camera. On the front of the table, there is a sign saying"4th Grade Girls". Letters are made out of bottletops stuck on cardboard. Howie Munson has stuck his head and hand in to the side of the photo. He is holding a baseball-sized ball of foil, and he is grinning.

photo caption → Miss Campbell and the 4th grade girls stand behind their two prize-winning projects. The girls knitted a large blanket and collected one hundred bottletops for scrap metal. L to R: Miss Campbell, Molly McIntire, Linda Silliman, Alison Hargate, Grace Littlefie[...] Also pictured, Howie Munson, holding his baseball-size ball of tin foil, collected by the four[...]

newspaper type → WILLOW STREET SCHOOL The ten girls in Miss Charlotte Campbell's fourth grade class at the Willow Street School demonstrated that they know the true meaning of allied effort this weekend. The girls spent Saturday working on not one but TWO projects for the school-wide Lend A Hand Contest. All students in the school were challenged to devote the weekend to a project to help the war effort. Miss Campbell's girls won first prize for their projects. They made a large, multi-colored blanket out of knitted squares. The blanket was presented along with an ingenious sign made out of one hundred bottletops the girls collected, also on Saturday. "Both projects were a surprise to me," said their teacher. "I don't know how the girls finished the blanket and collected all those bottletops, all in one day. I am very, very proud of every one of the girls." At a school-wide assembly today, each girl was given a blue ribbon[...] received a [...] from their [...] The blanke[...] will be se[...] St. Mary'[...] England w[...] one of t[...] McIntire[...] the US. [...] The bott[...] to the [...] metal drive.

Valerie tried to knit socks and found out how hard it was. She got the idea for the blanket from talking with her friend Beverly, who was ten during World War II. Beverly and her classmates (pictured above) knit squares and stitched them together to make a blanket for soldiers.

JEFFERSON DAILY NEWS

Molly McIntire and her teacher, Miss Charlotte Campbell, with winning project.

THIRD GRADE GIRLS WIN LEND-A-HAND CONTEST

Ten students at Willow Street School showed the true meaning of allied effort this weekend. The third grade girls won first prize in the school's contest to help the war effort. They knitted a blanket and collected 100 bottletops, which they made into a sign saying "Lend A Hand."

"Both projects were a surprise to me," said their teacher. "I don't know how the girls managed to finish them in one day. I am very proud of every one of the girls." At a school assembly today, each girl was given a blue ribbon.

The blanket will be sent to a hospital in England, where Dr. James McIntire, the father of Molly McIntire, is working with the U.S. Army Medical Corps. The bottletops will be given to the Boy Scouts' scrap metal drive.

Molly's Surprise

***Molly's Surprise* opens with** an illustration of a heartfelt Christmas letter that Molly has written to Dad. In it, she writes that she hopes he will send presents, but her truest, deepest desire is just to hear from him, to know that he's okay. This opening scene touches lightly but powerfully on the hard emotional truths that generations of families separated by war have had to endure: love despite distance, strength despite despair, and hope with no guarantees.

Great literature has explored these themes for centuries. Another classic about wartime girlhood, *Little Women*, written by Louisa May Alcott, was a book that both Valerie and Pleasant dearly loved reading as girls. Like Molly, the March sisters in *Little Women* have a father away at war. They are often reminded by their mother to be thoughtful and generous during wartime, just as Mrs. McIntire reminds her children. And just as the March family finds ways to celebrate and support one another during the holidays, so too do the McIntires—including a big surprise from Dad that brings comfort and joy.

Molly's Surprise, written by Valerie Tripp. Originally published in 1986 with illustrations by C. F. Payne, reillustrated by Nick Backes in 1989

December 23, 1943

Dear Dad,

Merry Christmas! How are you? I am fine except I miss you. I wish you could somehow magically be home for Christmas. Do you have a Christmas tree in the hospital? I hope so. Gram and Granpa will bring our tree on Christmas Eve. I can't wait! Right now Mom is making a wreath for the front door. Mrs. Gilford is away. She is visiting her nephew at the Army Base. I wish you were close enough to visit. Ricky is and Brad are lying on the floor listening to a radio show about bomber planes. Pete is asleep. Jill is knitting a hat for Dolores for Christmas. I hope you got the presents we sent you. We haven't gotten any presents from you yet. Probably they will come soon. Well, Merry Christmas again. XOXO!

Valerie's handwritten note and Christmas tree drawing (left and above) inspired the letter art at right that opens *Molly's Surprise*.

Dear Dad, December 21

Merry Christmas! How are you? I am fine except I wish you could somehow magically be home for Christmas. Do you have a Christmas tree in the hospital? I hope so. Gram and Granpa are bringing our Christmas tree tomorrow. I hope it's a big one! Right now, Mom is making a wreath for the front door and Ricky and Brad are listening to the radio. Jill is knitting. I hope you got the presents we sent you. We haven't gotten any presents from you yet. Probably they will come soon. XOXOXOX

“As they gathered about the table, Mrs. March said, with a particularly happy face, ‘I've got a treat for you after supper!’

A quick, bright smile went around the room like a streak of sunshine. . . . ‘A letter! A letter! Three cheers for Father!”

“It hardly seems like Christmas without Dad here. And on top of that, there are no presents from him.”

“Yet,” corrected Molly. “No presents from Dad yet.”

These scenes, set almost a century apart, show that there's always hope, especially during the holidays, for families during wartime.

> “We [Pleasant and Valerie] both loved historical fiction. **In the books we loved most of all, girls caused the mischief and trouble; girls were not timid sidekicks; girls were the agents of change.** We felt as though we were the heroines of our own stories, so we loved books like *Little Women*, *Anne of Green Gables*, and *Understood Betsy*. **We liked heroines who were headstrong because WE were headstrong. (Don't you love that word?)**”
>
> VALERIE TRIPP

A Realistic Christmas

When Gram and Granpa can't come for Christmas, the McIntire children fear there won't be a Christmas tree this year. Eldest child Jill shows a willingness to sacrifice during wartime by using her money so the kids can buy a tree and surprise Mom and Brad. In this, Jill models for Molly that it is just as satisfying and magical to make and give surprises at Christmas as it is to receive them. As the two sisters work together, readers see Molly move forward in the journey to cooperation and maturity she takes across her six books.

A Box Filled with Hope

Hope arrives on the McIntires' doorstep two days before Christmas, in the form of an unassuming, brown paper–wrapped box. It's from Dad, and on it he wrote, "Keep hidden until Christmas day!" Molly and Jill find the box and take Dad at his word. They hide it in the storage room above the garage, vowing to keep Dad's secret until Christmas morning. This shared secret between Molly and Jill is a refreshing shift from Jill's relentlessly "realistic" view of Christmas—that it's childish to hope for surprises. When the girls finish covering the box with an old blanket, Jill says, "I sort of don't want to go away and leave it. I'm afraid it's a dream and the box will be gone when we come back."

She nudges the box with the toe of her boot. "Good old Dad."

Christmas Eve

By Christmas Eve, Molly is exhausted—secret-keeping is hard work! At last, it's time to get ready for the Christmas Eve service at church. As she sits holding her small white candle, Molly remembers Dad's deep voice singing "Silent Night." She hopes Christmas truly will bring peace on earth—so he can come home.

> "**Maybe next Christmas Dad will be here with us,** thought Molly."
>
> *MOLLY'S SURPRISE*

A happy soldier receives his Christmas package from home.

The 6888th Central Postal Directory Battalion, known as the "Six Triple Eight," was composed entirely of women of color. They created a tracking system that allowed them to process around 65,000 pieces of mail every eight hours. In just three months, they cleared a six-month backlog of mail, despite segregated workspaces and living quarters that were unsanitary, unheated, and poorly lit. They lived by their motto, "no mail, low morale," and they worked tirelessly so troops and their families could be comforted by letters and care packages from their loved ones.

The Best Present of All

After church, the McIntires have their traditional Christmas Eve supper of scrambled eggs, bacon, hot chocolate, and cinnamon toast. They hang their stockings, and Mom reads *'Twas the Night Before Christmas* aloud just as Dad always did. It's usually hard to fall asleep on Christmas Eve, but this Christmas Eve it's even harder. At midnight, Jill and Molly creep out of the house, carry the box from Dad inside, and place it under the Christmas tree.

The next morning, their secret-keeping is rewarded when everyone—even Mom!—is wonderfully surprised by the presents from Dad. The house is filled with squeals of delight as they open more presents while listening to holiday programs on the radio. But Dad's best present is yet to come. The scratchy voice of the radio announcer tells listeners he is broadcasting from the USO Christmas party in England. Suddenly, Molly hears a voice she recognizes! It's Dad!

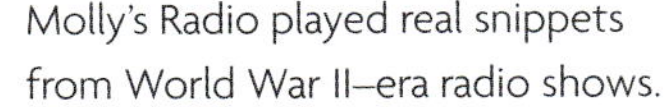

Molly's Radio played real snippets from World War II–era radio shows.

Early designs for what would become Molly's Christmas Box and Stocking, and Molly's Pajamas for Girls

"I'm Captain James McIntire. . . . **I'd like to say Merry Christmas to all the merry McIntires—Jill, Ricky, Molly, Brad, and my wife, Helen.** . . . I miss you all very much. And I hope you have a wonderful Christmas full of happy surprises."

MOLLY'S SURPRISE

Happy Birthday, Molly!, written by Valerie Tripp. Originally published in 1987 with illustrations by David Gaadt, reillustrated by Nick Backes in 1989

Happy Birthday, Molly!

Molly's birthday story begins with an exciting announcement: An English girl is coming to live at the McIntire house! This causes endless speculation among Molly and her friends. What will she be like? What has she been through? Most of all, Molly is excited to welcome her, make her feel at home, and share her birthday celebration with a new friend.

When Molly finally meets the English girl, she is not at all as Molly expected. Emily Bennett is shy and hardly lifts her gaze from the floor. She speaks very little, and when she does, it's barely above a whisper. Fun-loving Molly has a hard time understanding why Emily doesn't seem to want to be friends. But a blackout drill shortly after Emily comes to stay helps Molly see just how different the two girls' war experiences have been.

Emily Bennett

As Emily and Molly get to know each other, Emily opens up about what she experienced back in England. There, the fighting was a common part of everyday life—especially in places like London, where Emily lived. The government enacted rules, such as blackouts at night, to avoid giving enemy planes easy targets.

For Molly and for readers, Emily offers multiple lessons. As Molly learns, she is fortunate to live where she does and not to have to face the harsher side of the war. Although Molly has faced rationing and worrying about her father, Emily's war experience included tragedies close to home, such as the death of her dog and regular bombings in her neighborhood. The two girls also learn that their differences don't mean they can't be friends, as long as they offer each other a little understanding. Emily is both a sensitive, kind friend for Molly and a different perspective on World War II for Molly and readers.

> "In England the bombing isn't exciting at all," Emily said. **"It isn't a game.** It's terrible. People and . . . things get hurt. **They get killed. You Americans don't know."**
>
> *HAPPY BIRTHDAY, MOLLY!*

In the 1940s, roller skating was all the rage.

The English Princesses

Molly and Emily slowly begin to bond over the English princesses, Elizabeth and Margaret. Emily tells Molly that the princesses dressed alike when they were young girls, and this gives Molly one of the best ideas she's ever had: She and Emily will pretend to be the princesses! The girls wrap themselves up in the fantasy, dressing alike and walking imaginary dogs on jump-rope leashes.

When Mom asks Molly how she wants to celebrate her birthday, Emily suggests that she can have an English princess tea party. Molly loves the idea so much she wants Emily to share her birthday, to make up for all the birthday parties she's missed during the war.

Enemies?

When the girls start planning the party, Emily has a lot to say about what a proper English tea party is and is not. There are no hot dogs or peanut butter sandwiches or ginger ale. There are meat-paste sandwiches and tea—with milk, if you must. *And there is no birthday cake.* Molly simply can't take it anymore!

Girls in England show their support for Britain's Royal Air Force. By the time Emily comes to live with the McIntires, she has seen hundreds of planes fly overhead and can identify aircraft from several countries.

> "You and your dumb old tea party," Molly said. **"I don't want milky tea and lemon tarts!"**
>
> *HAPPY BIRTHDAY, MOLLY!*

Allies Again

On the day of Molly's birthday, she wakes up feeling awful about what she said to Emily. She tries to think of what Dad would do. He would say that no birthday party is more important than a friend's feelings. Just as Molly begins to apologize to Emily, her bedroom door is flung open. Mom and Brad burst into the room, shouting, "Happy birthday!"

Then Jill and Ricky come in, carrying two surprise presents: puppies! After watching Molly and Emily drag their jump-rope leashes around, they decided the princesses deserve real dogs. As Ricky puts it, "Yeah, so you can stop acting like nuts, talking to dogs that aren't there."

Emily's Pajamas (left) and Bennett (below). There have been various versions of Bennett. This one was released in 2022.

> "I think I'll call my puppy Yank," said Emily, "because it's a good American dog." "I'm going to call my puppy Bennett," said Molly, "after my good English friend."
>
> *HAPPY BIRTHDAY, MOLLY!*

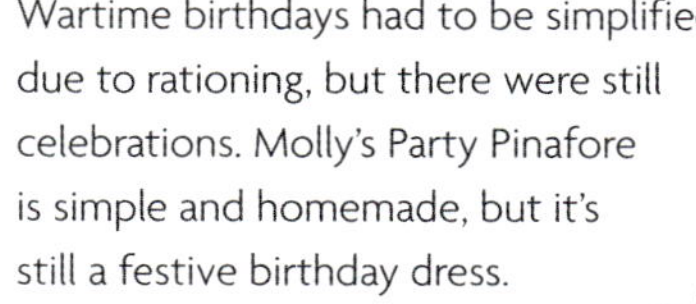

Wartime birthdays had to be simplified due to rationing, but there were still celebrations. Molly's Party Pinafore is simple and homemade, but it's still a festive birthday dress.

This prototype of Molly's Birthday Crown includes notes from the product designers to guide manufacturers on where to punch the holes and apply gold foil.

No birthday tea party would be complete without a tea set—and, as Molly would insist, a birthday cake!

Pleasant's Inspiration

As Pleasant and Valerie developed the first three Molly stories, designers were busy creating Molly's product line of outfits, accessories, clothing for girls, and furniture—much of it inspired by Pleasant's memories of her 1940s childhood. In this photo of Pleasant on her eighth birthday, she wears a dress with rickrack trim, just like Molly!

Pleasant Company staff re-created Pleasant's childhood photo for the company's tenth anniversary.

Molly Saves the Day, written by Valerie Tripp and illustrated by Nick Backes, published in 1988

Molly Saves the Day

Molly loves everything about summer camp from the moment she arrives: the big sky, the sparkling lake, the pine-scented air, and living with her friends in Tent Number Six. Molly especially loves nature hikes and learning the names of plants and trees and birds. There's something for everyone at Camp Gowonagin! The days fly by, just as they did for Pleasant when she was a young camper at Red Pine Camp in northern Wisconsin.

Summer camps were built as places for children to study nature and have fun outdoors. Campers lived in tents, cooked over open fires, and had no electricity. They felt as if they were really living in the wilderness!

An old camp friend of Pleasant's wrote to her through Pleasant Company, and Pleasant happily wrote back.

August 13, 1990

Dear Joan,

The world is indeed very small! I <u>am</u> Pleasant Thiele from Red Pine Camp long, long ago. How nice to hear from you and to know that my life has been linked with yours through your children's education and interest in The American Girls Collection. Pleasant Company sends ten million catalogues a year and I have found it a wonderful way to renew long-lost friendships, as sooner or later the catalogue seems to end up in the mailbox of just about everyone I ever knew.

I have just returned from Minocqua where my family (my married name is ... summer home for many years on a lake about fifteen ... two years ago, my husband, ... I have

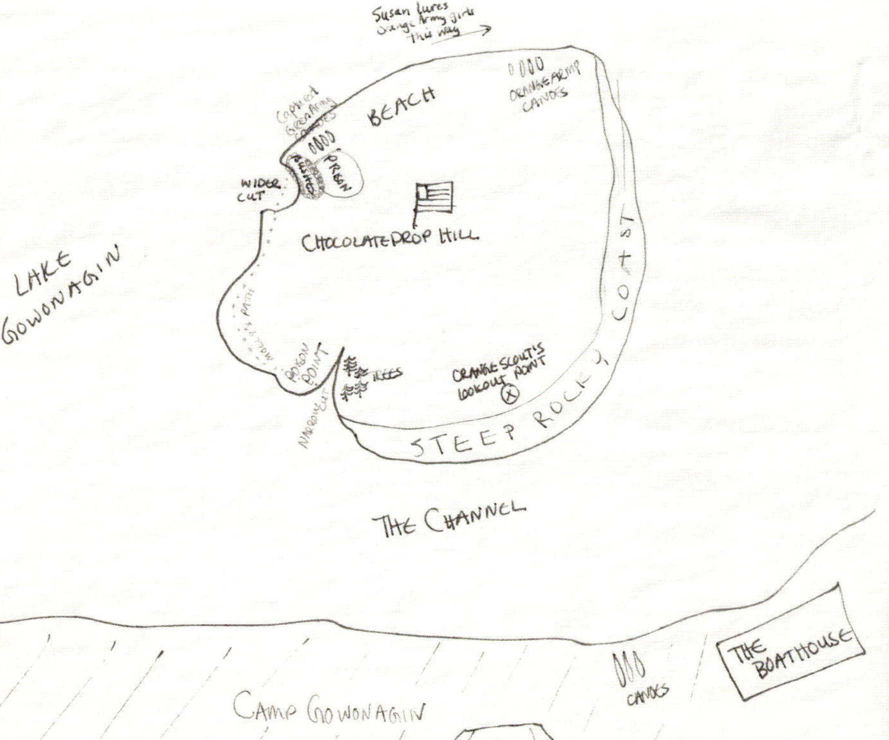

Valerie's hand-drawn map (above) of the Color War locations on Chocolate Drop Island was used as inspiration for the book's artwork (left).

Color War

A goal for this story was to bring World War II into child size by putting Molly in the midst of her own war and giving her a chance to show leadership. When the Color War is announced, Molly pictures herself leading a team to victory, proudly bringing the flag back to camp so everyone can cheer, shout, and sing the camp song. Her dreams of victory are dampened when she finds out that she and Susan are part of the Blue Army, but Linda is part of the Red Army. "Does that mean we're enemies?" asks Susan.

Dorinda Brassy, the leader of the Blue Army, takes the Color War very seriously. She shows the Blue campers an impressive map she has drawn. Molly thinks the plan is too easy. This time, instead of staying silent the way she did about sock knitting in *Molly Learns a Lesson,* Molly stands up and, in a budding moment of leadership, points out to Dorinda that the Red Army will probably have scouts and see them coming across the lake. Dorinda belittles her, playing on one of Molly's greatest fears and biggest failures at camp—swimming underwater:

> "How do **you** think we should cross the lake?" Dorinda asked sharply. **"Should we swim underwater?"**
>
> *MOLLY SAVES THE DAY*

Molly sneaks up on Linda with the can of worms tucked in her shirt.

Molly and Susan show up late to the war, thanks to Susan's less-than-stellar skills with a canoe paddle. All their teammates are in the Red Army's prison, and Linda is the guard.

Molly comes up with a plan that depends on worms. She sneaks to the prison and dumps a can filled with worms and bugs over Linda's head, knowing that bugs are Linda's greatest fear. With that act, Molly frees the Blue Army and steps up as leader, hatching the plan of all plans:

> "**Don't you remember the newsreels we saw of D-Day?"** Molly asked. "The Allies built a long, long dock from the deep water all the way to the shore. Remember? They built it out of barges and boats. They could drive trucks off their big ships and onto their dock, and then all the way to land."
>
> "I don't get it," said Susan. "We don't have any barges or anything. **What can we use to build a dock?"**
>
> **"Canoes,"** said Molly."

MOLLY SAVES THE DAY

The Allied forces took Normandy in an amphibious invasion that inspires Molly's Color War strategy.

Changes for Molly

***Changes for Molly* lives up** to its title with the biggest and best change Molly could hope for: Dad is coming home.

My orders have been changed. I'm coming back to the States to take care of the wounded soldiers there. I'll work at the Veterans' Hospital in Jefferson, so I'll be able to live at home. Of course, no one can tell me for sure exactly when I'll get home. But right now, it looks like I might be there by the eighteenth of March. Maybe in time for lunch!

It will be so wonderful to see all of you! I can tell by the pictures you sent that Ricky is probably a basketball star by now, and Brad isn't a baby anymore. And Jill! You look so grown-up and sophisticated in your prom dress! You've become a beauty just like your mother. And of course, I can't wait to see good old olly Molly and taste Mrs. Gilford's perfect pot roast. I'll be so glad to get home! Hurray for the U.S.A.!

Lots of love,

Dad

Changes for Molly, written by Valerie Tripp and illustrated by Nick Backes, published in 1988

Soldiers received joyous welcomes all across the country, as shown in this Norman Rockwell painting, *Homecoming G.I.* (1945).

Valerie's Hair-Raising Solution

"I wanted Molly to think—wrongly!—that she needed to change her appearance in order to be the lead dancer in the Miss Victory show so that she could impress her dad when he came home from the war."

"Her friend Susan says she'll help Molly by giving her a home permanent. This is why research is so much fun: To find out more about home permanents in 1945, I called the 1-800 number on the side of the Toni Home Permanent box. Very quickly, I was connected to Irving Harris, regarded as 'Mr. Toni' himself, who sounded very perky and very glad to talk.

"When I asked about the permanent, Mr. Toni said, 'Oh, in those early days the setting-lotion chemicals made you smell like a wet dog.' I thought, *Well, if Mr. Toni himself said that, I can say it, too.* So I did."

"I've always been grateful to Mr. Toni for being so honest and **providing me with such a funny line!**"

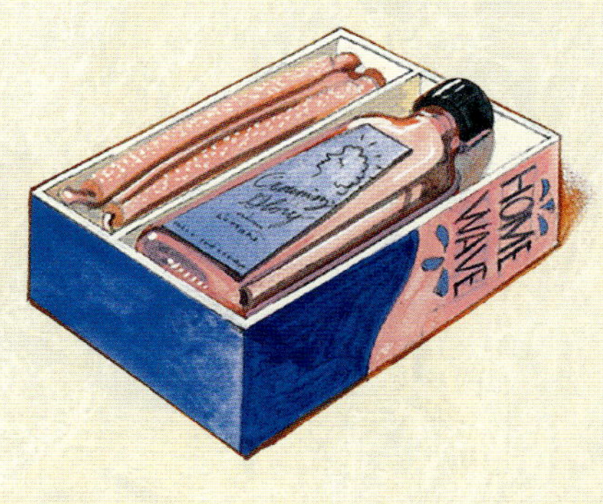

Which Twin has the Toni?

More than 2 million women a month use Toni
. . . the wave that gives that natural look!

The wave that gives that natural look . . . Toni

Molly desperately wants to look glamorous for her big performance, the way a real performer would.

A Close Call

Thankfully, Molly's sister Jill stops the girls from attempting a home permanent—and thus saves Molly from the wet-dog smell. Jill kindly offers to put Molly's hair up in pin curls day after day to make it curly for the show. The only method that keeps the curls in Molly's hair while she dances is the "wet-hair method," which means she has to go out in the freezing cold with her hair still damp and let the pin curls dry gradually before she takes the pins out.

Molly gets to dance in a dress rehearsal the day before the show. Her pin curls are bouncy and perfect, and she takes off her glasses for an extra-glamorous effect. She can't really see the audience, but she hears them clapping and cheering, and she dances her heart out.

Star-spangled shows, like *Yankee Doodle Dandy* (shown at left) and Molly's own hometown show for soldiers at the Veterans' Hospital in Jefferson (shown below), helped keep hopes up on the home front.

Molly's Tap Costume

Home at Last

The dress rehearsal turns out to be the last time Molly will dance the part of Miss Victory. She comes down with a terrible cold and ear infection due to all the pin-curl prep and winds up home alone while the rest of the family still has parts to play. The show must go on! Listlessly, Molly plays with her kaleidoscope and paper dolls and tries not to think about Alison Hargate dancing the role of Miss Victory. It helps that Ricky kindly says that Alison isn't half as good a dancer as Molly is.

Molly thinks her buzzing ears are playing tricks on her when she hears a booming voice call out, "I'm home!" It's Dad! Molly tears out of her room and runs down the stairs and into his arms. They share a long, quiet hug, just the two of them.

"Gosh and golly, olly Molly! You look exactly as I remembered you, just as I've pictured you for two long years. You look perfect!"

> "Perfect!" she said. Then she hugged Dad again. **Absolutely perfect.**"
>
> *CHANGES FOR MOLLY*

Homecoming was a joyous moment for many soldiers and their families, just as it is for Molly and her father.

> "It means so much to Dad to come home and find Molly exactly as she is. **She doesn't need a new hairdo or tap shoes or spotlights. He loves every atom of her exactly as she is.** I loved giving that message to girls."
>
> VALERIE TRIPP

Felicity
Merriman
Lady Dunmore presents her compliments to Mrs Merriman and requests the favour of her Daughter Felicity's Attendance at a Dancing Lesson at the Palace on Saturday January 7 at four o'clock.
Felicity Come! Help! Ben
MEET FELICITY
AN AMERICAN GIRL
~BOOK ONE~
17
74
THE AMERICAN GIRLS COLLECTION®
Lucy 1774

Making Felicity

All of the American Girl characters take the big themes of a historical era and present them in a way that is relatable to girls—perhaps none more so than Felicity. Her stories take place during a time when many colonists wanted independence from the King of England. This theme plays out through Felicity's desire for more independence than a girl in her time would typically have had. Pleasant and Valerie thoughtfully set Felicity's stories in the years before the American Revolution so young readers could witness firsthand, through Felicity's family, friends, and everyday life, how the ideas that formed the foundation of the democracy of the United States were shaped, debated, and tested. They wanted readers to learn, as both Felicity and the colonies do, that with independence comes responsibility for yourself and your world.

> "Just like my readers, Felicity learns to be a responsible member of her family and community, and a good friend."
>
> VALERIE TRIPP

"Finding the girl in history," as Pleasant liked to call the process, was a challenge with Felicity. It was hard to find first-person accounts written by women in the eighteenth century, and next to impossible to find accounts written by or about children. As Valerie dug deeper into her research, she discovered the journal of Philip Vickers Fithian, a tutor who lived in the colony of Virginia around the time Felicity's stories are set. Fithian wrote about his daily experiences teaching—or trying to teach!—colonial children. His journal was an invaluable resource during the development of Felicity's stories.

Pleasant and Valerie worked closely with Colonial Williamsburg as they brought Felicity to life. Dennis O'Toole and Katherine Keena, in the education department at Colonial Williamsburg, shared their knowledge, suggested resources, and read manuscripts. Mary Wiseman, a docent who portrayed Lady Dunmore at the Governor's Palace and trained junior interpreters who acted as historical figures, also lent her expertise and support. Valerie fondly recalls how Patricia Gibbs, a Colonial Williamsburg historian, checked her facts and accuracy as she wrote the Felicity books: "I learned to listen closely—and to love—when Pat would gently say about an element in a story I had written, 'Now that would not have been possible. But what if . . .' Oh, what a great partner in creativity Pat was! Her 'what-ifs' made the Felicity books authentic."

Valerie lived just a couple of hours away from Colonial Williamsburg, and she visited many times with her baby daughter in tow—their first mother-daughter road trips. Valerie would walk around all day, pushing Katherine in her stroller and taking every tour she could find. "We went so often that my daughter learned to walk pushing her stroller in Williamsburg when I was there to do research," Valerie recalls. She could already see that, like Felicity, her daughter was not a "sitting-down kind of girl."

FATHER

MOTHER

Family portraits, such as this painting by Stephen Slaughter, inspired the clothing Felicity and her family wear throughout her book series.

Felicity's home reflects the importance of symmetry and order seen throughout Colonial Williamsburg. This sketch by Valerie Hodgson and the illustration by Randall Berndt were created for Felicity's Scenes & Settings.

Felicity's color palette is expressed in her illustrations, outfits, furniture, and accessories. Portraits at left and on next page by Dan Andreasen

NAN

WILLIAM

GRANDFATHER

ROSE

MARCUS

ISAAC

The Question of Freedom

In the years before and during the American Revolution, calls for independence from the king and the British Parliament echoed throughout Williamsburg's streets, taverns, and public buildings. Yet there were profound contradictions between the Revolution's rhetoric of freedom, liberty, and equality and the reality of the day-to-day lives of most of the colonial town's population.

In Virginia and in all the thirteen colonies, slavery was an entrenched institution, codified in law, that treated people as property and denied them basic rights and freedoms. In New York City, 20 percent of the population was enslaved. In Charleston, South Carolina, 55 percent were enslaved. Slavery had an enormous impact on the social, political, and economic lives of people in Williamsburg, where more than half the population was Black, and most were enslaved. Felicity's stories include Rose and Marcus, who are enslaved and work in the Merrimans' household and store, and Isaac, a young free man who is a drummer in the militia. Even though Isaac is free, as a Black man in Williamsburg he would have faced restrictions, prejudice, and danger. For all the Black residents of Williamsburg, true liberty would have meant freedom from enslavement for themselves and their loved ones.

Despite overwhelming constraints, Black people resisted enslavement and fought for freedom. Matthew Ashby, a free Black man in Williamsburg, earned enough money to secure freedom for his wife and children through a complex and arduous process. Phillis Wheatley, an enslaved poet, became the first Black American to publish a book of poetry. She gained her own freedom and used her work to challenge the nation's moral conscience. Still others, like the more than 5,000 Black people who served with the Continental Army, helped defeat the British. These hard-won achievements reflect the determination and resilience of Black communities who recognized the promise of the Revolution's rhetoric, even if it did not apply to them.

Isaac's drumbeats keep the Patriot soldiers in step as they march across the village green in Williamsburg.

This watercolor shows soldiers who fought in the Revolutionary War, including a Black soldier from the First Rhode Island Regiment.

James Lafayette, a spy for the Patriots, remained enslaved throughout the war and successfully petitioned the government for his freedom after the colonies won their independence.

The colonists' eventual victory in the War of Independence did not bring independence, rights, or freedom to enslaved people. Slavery was a deeply rooted system that persisted in the United States for nearly a century, until the Thirteenth Amendment abolished it nationwide in the 1860s.

During the 1770s, independence was shaped primarily by—and for—white male property owners. For so many people living in the colonies who were excluded from the full rights of citizenship, the Revolution opened some doors but left many firmly closed. Generations of Americans fought to expand liberty's promise to all people, and the fight continues today.

Although enslaved people were not usually educated, Phillis Wheatley learned to read and write at a young age.

Remember the Ladies

Other Williamsburg residents, including women like Felicity's mother, also lived under laws and customs that denied them full independence.

In the 1770s, women faced significant legal restrictions. Under the laws of coverture, a married woman's property, earnings, and even her children belonged to her husband. She could not vote, serve on a jury, or hold public office. Abigail Adams, recognizing the gap between Revolutionary ideals and women's lack of rights, wrote to her husband, John Adams, during the Continental Congress in March 1776:

Portrait of Abigail Adams by Benjamin Blyth in 1766

> **"I desire you would Remember the Ladies, and be more generous and favorable to them than your ancestors.** Do not put such unlimited power into the hands of the Husbands."
>
> ABIGAIL ADAMS

The House and Furniture of the Solisiter General have fallen a prey to their own merciless party. Surely the very Fiends feel a Reverential awe for Virtue & patriotism, whilst they Detest the paricide & traitor —

I feel very differently at the approach of spring to what I did a month ago, We knew not then whether we could plant or sow with Safety, whether when we had toild we could reap the fruits of our own industery, whether we could rest in our own Cottages, or whether we should not be driven from the sea coasts to seek shelter in the wilderness, but now we feel as if we might sit under our own vine and eat the good of the land — I feel a gaieti de Coar to which before I was a stranger, I think the Sun looks brighter the Birds sing more melodiously & Nature puts on a more chearfull countanance we feel a temporary peace, & the poor fugitives are returning to their deserted habitations. Tho we felicitate ourselves, we sympathize with those who are trembling least the Lot of Boston should be theirs — but they cannot be in similar circumstances unless pusilanimity & cowardise should take possession of them — They have time & warning given them to see the Evil & shun it — I long to hear that you have declared an independancy — and by the way in the new Code of Laws which I suppose it will be necessary for you to make I desire you would Remember the Ladies & be more generous & favourable to them than your ancestors Do not put such unlimited power into the hands of the Husbands. Remember all Men would be tyrants if they could. if perticuliar care & attention is not paid to the Laidies we are determined to foment a Rebelion, and will not hold ourselves bound by any Laws in which we have no voice, or Representation — That your Sex are Naturally Tyrannical is a Truth so thoroughly established as to admit of no dispute, but such of you as wish to be happy willingly give up the harsh title of Master for the more tender & endearing one of Friend Why then not put it out of the power of the vicious & the

Coral bead necklaces were a popular good-luck gift for colonial girls. The coin in Felicity's hand is called a bit.

Meet Felicity

Meet Felicity, written by Valerie Tripp and illustrated by Dan Andreasen, published in 1991

***Meet Felicity* wastes no time** in showing us that Felicity is a horse-loving girl of action and intuition. When she hears that Jiggy Nye, the disreputable tanner—who turns animal hides into leather—has a new horse, she hurries off to see it. When she arrives at the tannery and sees Jiggy Nye raise his whip to strike the horse, she stops him by shouting "No!" Felicity can't bear to think of the magnificent creature in the hands of that scoundrel. Early one morning, while it's still dark, Felicity slips out of her bedchamber and runs to Jiggy Nye's pasture. There, she begins a beautiful friendship with the horse she names Penny, which is short for inde*pen*dence.

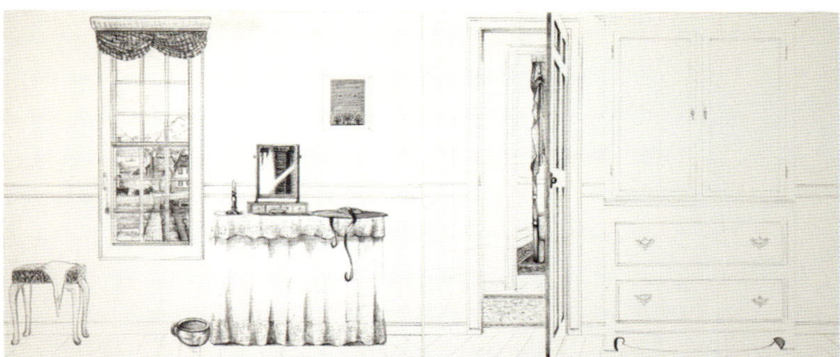

The sketch by Valerie Hodgson and painting by Mike Wimmer of Felicity's bedchamber, created for Felicity's Scenes & Settings

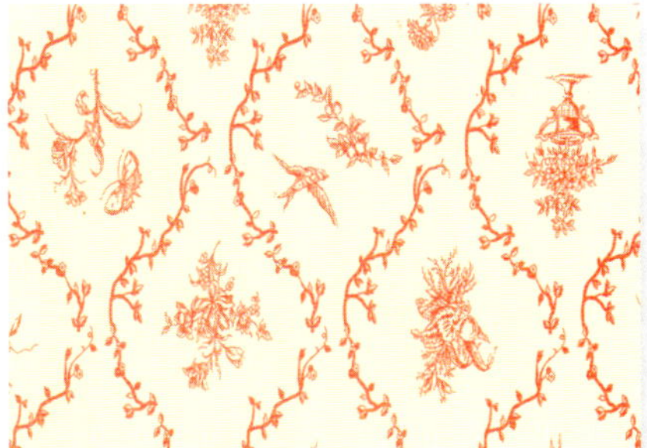

Product designers contrasted the delicate florals and birds on Felicity's red toile counterpane with the bold red-check pattern of her bed hangings.

Holly Easland designed Felicity's clothing. She interpreted the pattern for Felicity's Meet dress from a 1770s print, with pink and plum roses strung on ribbons of cornflower blue.

The palette above shows colors from Felicity's Meet dress.

Felicity's Night Shift is edged with lace around the sleeves and neck, and her matching cap has lappets, or long flaps, that tie under her chin.

Note that "Lucy" was an early name possibility for Felicity. Pleasant came up with the name Felicity, which was atypical in Virginia in colonial times. Pleasant loved the nickname Lissie, which appears on the garters that hold up Felicity's stockings.

Ben's Breeches

"In breeches your legs are free," Felicity tells Ben. "You can straddle horses, jump over fences, run as fast as you wish." Felicity longs for the independence that boys and men enjoy, especially when her petticoats slow her down during her secret visits to see Penny. When Felicity finds a pair of Ben's breeches in the mending basket, she decides Ben won't mind if she borrows them. Ben's breeches make it so much easier to run and visit gentle Penny, and eventually to ride her. When Felicity hears Jiggy Nye say he will kill Penny, Felicity makes a daring plan to set her free. But will she ever see Penny again?

BEN

Women and girls in Felicity's time were expected to ride sidesaddle, as this painting from the 1800s shows. It was more challenging to ride sidesaddle—you can see why Felicity wanted to borrow Ben's breeches so she could ride astride!

Penny is a chestnut mare, a blood horse trained to be a gentleman's mount. The term "blood horse" dates back to the 1600s and is another name for a thoroughbred, or purebred, horse.

Penny

“I pushed strongly for Felicity to be a ‘horse girl,’ because so many girls (including me) love horses. My readers inspired me to write about a girl who loves horses because so many of them love horses and other animals. **I understood.** When I was their age, I wanted a horse so badly that I pretended my bicycle was a horse. I even left tufts of grass by its front tire!”

VALERIE TRIPP

ELIZABETH

Felicity Learns a Lesson, written by Valerie Tripp and illustrated by Dan Andreasen, published in 1991

Felicity Learns a Lesson

In *Felicity Learns a Lesson*, Felicity and her new friend Elizabeth Cole are on opposite sides of a political issue. Elizabeth's Loyalist family supports the king's rule, while Felicity's Patriot family believes the colonies should govern themselves. Through her friendship with Elizabeth, Felicity—and readers—learn that people can disagree with those they love, and love people with whom they disagree. The way Felicity resolves the problems in their friendship shows that there are ways to be respectful while standing firm in your beliefs.

Apple Butter Day

In the opening scene, we find Felicity sitting high on the roof of her house, happily picking apples to make into apple butter. She's relishing the fresh air and sunshine while avoiding the dim, stuffy kitchen house, where she's supposed to be learning the skills of housewifery by stirring endless pots of mush to make apple butter. Felicity complains to her mother that all the dull stirring seems like a great deal of work for a little bit of butter. Her mother laughs and says she used to think that, too, when she was Felicity's age.

She cuts an apple in half across its middle and shows Felicity the "flower" hidden inside. Then Mrs. Merriman gently guides Felicity to the generous view that caring for her family and for other loved ones has value, even in doing chores that are unseen.

Felicity's Work Gown was inspired by the striped dress in this illustration.

The sketch by Valerie Hodgson and illustration by Mike Wimmer of the kitchen house, created for Felicity's Scenes & Settings

Felicity hates when her stays are laced too tight—a metaphor for her chafing at the restrictions imposed on girls in the colonial era.

Felicity's Undergarments give her gowns the shape that was stylish during colonial times. Her stays lace up to ensure good posture. Pocket hoops tie around her waist to give her dress the right fullness. She wears her embroidered pocket under her dress—all of her dresses have slits so she can reach into her pocket.

Lessons with Miss Manderly

A few nights later in the parlor, Father and Mother announce that Felicity will soon begin lessons with Miss Manderly, a gentlewoman who will teach her all the things she will need to know in order to take her place in polite society: fine handwriting, fancy stitchery, and the proper way to serve tea. These are exactly the "sitting-down kinds of things" that Felicity dreads with all her heart. It doesn't help at all when Mother says that two young ladies who have just arrived in the colonies from England will be joining the lessons. They will surely know the proper way to do everything already. Felicity's heart sinks.

To everyone's surprise, during their first tea lesson, Felicity's loose tooth falls into her teacup. Laughing, Miss Manderly tells the girls she doesn't know the polite thing to say in this situation and ensures the tooth's safe return to Felicity.

In colonial times, tea leaves were stored in a wooden tea caddy. Felicity's dark blue teacup and saucer feature an elegant fruit pattern. Queen cakes were a favorite treat in colonial households.

Felicity and Elizabeth have a grand time playing with Elizabeth's mother's wigs. "Oh, my darling Ben!" Felicity teases. "It is I, your beautiful Bananabelle! You have stolen my heart away!" When Annabelle catches them, Felicity is unfazed by her threat to tattle. "I will tell Ben you are sweet on him," she coolly replies.

A Bright Spot

Lessons with Miss Manderly turn out to have a bright spot: Elizabeth Cole, the younger English sister who is just Felicity's age and loves horses as much as Felicity does. Elizabeth's older sister Annabelle, however, looks down on Felicity for being a colonist and a shopkeeper's daughter. She also belittles Elizabeth and calls her Bitsy, a name both Elizabeth and Felicity hate. Annabelle does have a vulnerability, though. She is sweet on Ben. Felicity uses this knowledge to her advantage to stand up to Annabelle both for herself and for Elizabeth. She also gives Annabelle a nickname that will forever rankle her: Bananabelle. Valerie Tripp researched lists of goods imported to Williamsburg to be sure Felicity would know about bananas.

Early sketches and fabric swatches for Felicity's Laced Jacket & Petticoat

"My father is not a traitor!" Felicity shouts.

To Drink Tea, or Not to Drink Tea?

The girls' differences cause trouble when Mr. Merriman decides to stop selling tea in his shop. When Annabelle accuses Felicity's father of being a traitor and Elizabeth doesn't rise to her defense, Felicity storms out of Miss Manderly's tea lesson. Mother counsels her to try again, and it takes all Felicity's courage to go back to Miss Manderly's the next day. She wants to be loyal to her father and doesn't want to drink tea, but she also wants to show good manners at Miss Manderly's tea table. Luckily, she remembers there is a way to do both, with an action that is polite and at the same time subversive and revolutionary. She turns her teacup upside down, places her spoon across it, and says, "Thank you . . . I shall take no tea."

"It is always my hope that my readers will see that a child their age had an opinion about political differences and acted upon her beliefs so that my readers will then decide how they feel, and think about actions they might take. **Their decisions and actions are more important than Felicity's because they will be shaping the real world we all live in.**"

VALERIE TRIPP

Thomas Jefferson wrote the Declaration of Independence while seated in a handsome writing chair like this one.

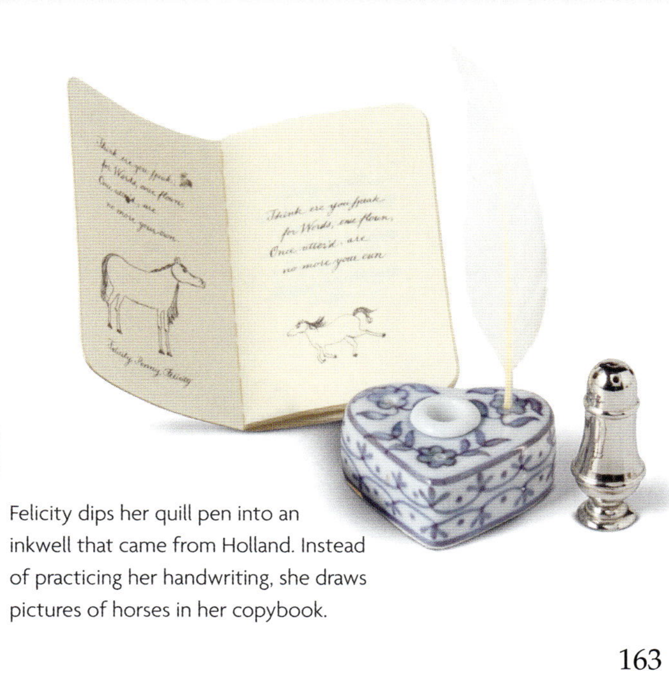

Felicity dips her quill pen into an inkwell that came from Holland. Instead of practicing her handwriting, she draws pictures of horses in her copybook.

Lady Dunmore
preſents her compliments
to Mrs Merriman and
requeſts the favour of her
Daughter Felicity's Attendance
at a Dancing Leſson at
the Palace on Saturday
January 7 at
four o'clock.

Felicity's Surprise

Felicity's Surprise, written by Valerie Tripp and illustrated by Dan Andreasen, published in 1991

***Felicity's Surprise* begins with** an invitation to a dancing lesson at the royal Governor's Palace. Felicity is happy and excited at the thought, until she thinks about the actual dancing. Even her curtsies are wobbly—how will she ever dance gracefully in front of Lord and Lady Dunmore?

A Meaningful Gown

Felicity, who doesn't usually fuss about clothes, plans to wear her old brown "best" dress to the Palace. But as the lesson draws near, she begins to believe that a new gown will give her

confidence and improve her dancing. Then one day, when Felicity and her mother go to the milliner's shop, they see a fashion doll. The doll's dress is exactly what Felicity is dreaming of! Kind Mrs. Merriman promises to make the dress for Felicity, even though she is busy with holiday preparations.

A rough sketch for the scene illustrated at left

There is one person who doesn't think Felicity should go to the dance lesson: her father's apprentice, Ben—a headstrong Patriot. He doesn't believe Felicity should dance before Lord and Lady Dunmore, who have treated the colonists so poorly. Father, however, sees the invitation as a kindness. "If our children can dance together," he says, "then perhaps we adults can settle our differences without fighting."

The fashion doll in her royal blue dress can be seen at far left in Colonial Williamsburg's millinery shop in 1991.

A thumbnail sketch from the art director guided the illustrator in creating the final painting.

"On one of our visits to Williamsburg, Pleasant and I stopped in at the milliner's shop. Pleasant gasped and grabbed my arm when she saw the fashion doll in her royal blue dress. **Without saying a word, we both knew we'd found Felicity's doll, and the dress Felicity would wear to the Governor's Palace.**"

VALERIE TRIPP

Mother fastens a pearl earring to a blue silk cord to make Felicity's choker.

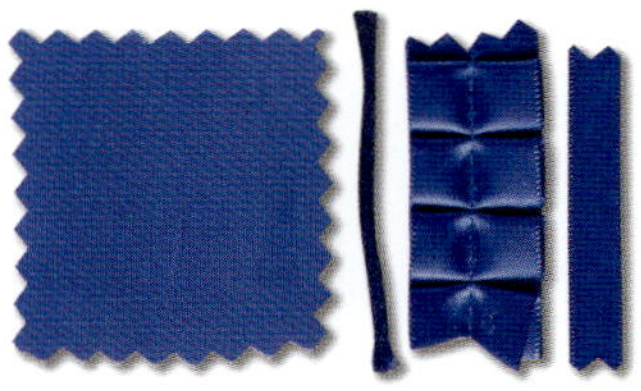

This is the dress Mother promises to make. The brilliant blue taffeta gown is trimmed with blue satin pleating and dainty lace on the sleeves and stomacher. Since colonial girls had few clothes, they often freshened up a dress with a new stomacher. Felicity's stomacher is decorated with pink ribbons and pearl beads.

Fashion dolls showed colonial women what stylish ladies in Europe were wearing, so they could copy them.

Kindness at Christmas

Before she can finish Felicity's dress, Mother becomes very ill. While selflessly taking care of her mother, Felicity realizes what is truly important—the well-being of loved ones. Having a fancy gown, or even going to the dancing lesson at the Governor's Palace, becomes unimportant. Mother's recovery is the only thing that matters.

Felicity spends all her time tending to Mother and playing with Nan and William to distract and comfort them.

Even in the thumbnail sketch, the emotion of this scene comes through.

When Elizabeth finds out that Mother is ill, she secretly works to finish Felicity's gown—an act of friendship and of hope. On the day of the dancing lesson, Mother is feeling better, and Elizabeth surprises Felicity with the beautiful blue gown. But who will escort Felicity to the Palace? Father needs to stay with Mother, and Felicity cannot go unescorted. One final kindness comes from an unexpected place. Ben, the fiery Patriot who has been staunchly against Felicity dancing with Loyalists, steps up to escort her.

When Felicity asks what changed his mind, he replies, "You did. I watched you take care of your mother. I saw how you cheered Nan and William even when all of the things you had hoped for looked impossible. I began to think your father was right. Christmas is the time when our hopes for peace and happiness should come true."

The catalogue introducing Felicity and her Elegant Tea Party in 1991

How to Bring History Alive

A SPECIAL MESSAGE TO PARENTS

When I first heard about Williamsburg I was probably eight years old. I had been poring over the family photo album, lingering long on my parents' wedding pictures, imagining myself, as all little girls do, someday wearing that beautiful gown with its froth of airy veil. Today, many years later, I can still remember the blurry snapshots of Mother and Daddy on their honeymoon in front of a picket fence, a windmill, and a rose-covered arbor. They were in Williamsburg, the caption said, a place forever etched in my childhood memory as a pretty place for happy times.

Years passed, and one day I did wear that same wedding gown, and one day, many years later, I did go to Williamsburg. This time I was a corporate wife accompanying my husband to a business meeting, pleased to be going to that place of the snapshot memories.

Little did I know what awaited me. The picket fences and windmill were still there, but nothing had prepared me for the depth of detail, the breadth of vision that I found in Colonial Williamsburg. It was more than a pretty place for happy times, it was simply the best living classroom of American history I could ever imagine.

Everywhere I looked the past came alive—not in an imaginary fantasy world, for Colonial Williamsburg is not peopled with cartoon look-alikes or landscaped with amusement park attractions. It is a world pulsing with real life stories.

As I strolled through Williamsburg that early, gentle morning, I realized that George Washington, Patrick Henry, and Thomas Jefferson had walked the same street more than 200 years before. They, too, had nodded to the apothecary sweeping his front steps and to the maid hurrying to the smokehouse for breakfast bacon. They, too, had dodged the child skipping along beside his hoop and the horses clip-clopping to the blacksmith. They, too, had spotted the gardener hoeing his beans before the day got too hot in the very same garden I was looking at. It is the juxtaposition of these simple, homely details of everyday colonial life alongside the great dreams of liberty and independence first forged in the grand public buildings of this place, that makes Williamsburg such a stunning experience, such an astonishing brush with history.

The idea for The American Girls Collection was born there as I sat under an arbor to rest and to absorb all I had seen and felt. How could I as a teacher help bring history alive for children in the same way Colonial Williamsburg had just brought it alive for me? How could I help children see that through all the changes wrought in the dailiness of American life over the past two hundred years, the vision of our forefathers has endured?

I created The American Girls Collection to celebrate those changes and to honor that vision, to bring the remarkable story of our nation's past alive for a new generation of American girls. It will be wonderful fun to join them in Williamsburg this August, to watch the stories of Felicity and the magic of that extraordinary place ignite their imaginations as it did mine so long ago.

Pleasant T. Rowland, President

Felicity's Elegant Tea Party

In the summer of 1991, nearly 11,000 girls and their grown-ups came to Williamsburg from forty-eight states to celebrate the introduction of Felicity. After being welcomed by Pleasant Rowland, guests watched a theatrical fashion show depicting clothing commonly worn during Felicity's era.

Author Valerie Tripp then introduced the play *Tea for Felicity.* After the final scene was completed, the character of Miss Manderly instructed her "pupils" in the audience about the fine art of serving tea, along with making polite conversation, just as Felicity was taught so many years ago.

The 450 guests at each of the twenty-four parties were treated to raspberry tea, plus an array of colonial delicacies including Shrewsbury cakes, ginger cake, queen cakes, marzipan, and tiny tarts—all served on historically accurate place settings and silver platters.

A girl-sized souvenir tea set from Felicity's Elegant Tea Party matched the pattern of Felicity's teacup.

Pleasant Company's Special Events team spent eight months preparing for the tea party, which was the largest event ever hosted at Colonial Williamsburg. From August 15 to 25, 1991, it went down in history as the program with the highest number of guests in attendance—surpassing even the Economic Summit held there in 1983!

Each girl received a gift package that included the book *Meet Felicity*, a craft kit, a mob cap like Felicity wears, a bookmark, a poster, and a Felicity bag and button. A wonderful map of Felicity's Williamsburg enabled her fans to walk through the streets of the past while experiencing a typical day in the life of the Merriman family.

Felicity's launch at Colonial Williamsburg was a happy full-circle moment for Pleasant. Felicity's Elegant Tea Party was held in the same place where she first dreamed about teaching history through characters and play.

Girls enjoy the displays of Felicity's books, fashions, and accessories.

> "As I strolled through Williamsburg . . . I realized that George Washington, Patrick Henry, and Thomas Jefferson had walked the same street more than 200 years before. They, too, had nodded to the apothecary sweeping his front steps and to the maid hurrying to the smokehouse for breakfast bacon. . . . **It is the juxtaposition of these simple, homely details of everyday colonial life alongside the great dreams of liberty and independence . . . that makes Williamsburg such a stunning experience.**"
>
> PLEASANT ROWLAND

Happy Birthday, Felicity!

Happy Birthday, Felicity!, written by Valerie Tripp and illustrated by Dan Andreasen, published in 1992

In this story, the conflict that has been simmering in Williamsburg between the colonists and Lord Dunmore boils over. His raid on the colonists' gunpowder divides Patriots and Loyalists even more sharply. This is an especially difficult situation for the Merriman household, since Felicity's grandfather is visiting, and he is a Loyalist.

When the story opens, it's the start of spring, and Felicity is looking forward to two exciting things: It will soon be her tenth birthday, and her beloved grandfather will be with them to celebrate. When Grandfather arrives, he brings two precious gifts: a sweet little lamb and a beautiful guitar that belonged to Felicity's grandmother. He tells Felicity that she must treasure the guitar, and Felicity agrees to keep it in the parlor, safely stored on a high bookcase.

Notes taken for the cover sketch of *Happy Birthday, Felicity!* during a phone conversation with Patricia Gibbs, Colonial Williamsburg historian

Designer Holly Easland illustrated several dresses before one was chosen for Felicity's birthday outfit.

Felicity wears an apron called a pinner with this outfit. In Felicity's day, snaps and safety pins had not yet been invented. Colonial girls and women used straight pins to fasten their aprons to their dresses.

The young girl seated at the table wears a pinner while she practices her penmanship.

Musical instrument makers had to master the use of tiny, delicate saws to carve exquisite rosettes like the one in the middle of Felicity's guitar.

The Guitar

Annabelle brings her own guitar, which she is learning to play, to lessons at Miss Manderly's. With her usual snobbishness, she refuses to allow Felicity to touch the guitar. The day before her birthday, Felicity impulsively brings her grandmother's guitar—without permission—to her lessons so that Miss Manderly can tune it. After the lesson, Felicity and Elizabeth go to the Coles' garden and then, forgetfully, Felicity leaves her guitar behind when she goes home. Alarmed, she runs back to the Coles' garden in the rain to retrieve her guitar.

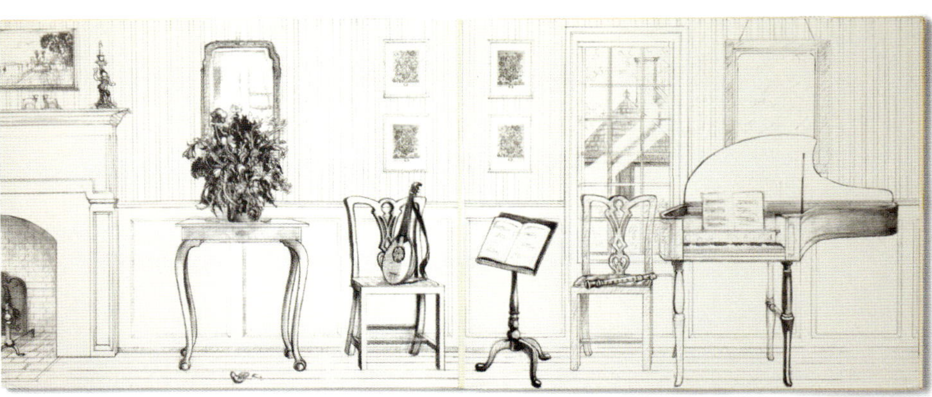

The sketch by Valerie Hodgson and illustration by Mike Wimmer of Miss Manderly's parlor, created for Felicity's Scenes & Settings

Horrible sounds fill the room. When Annabelle plays, the guitar sounds whiny, tinny, and twangy. And her singing is even worse.

Sounding the Alarm

The guitar is right where Felicity left it, but as she starts to leave, she accidentally overhears something that will change life in the colonies forever: Lord Dunmore is planning to steal the colonists' gunpowder that very night. Felicity knows she must tell someone who will believe her.

When Felicity returns home, she disappoints her parents and grandfather in two ways. First, she has nearly ruined a cherished family heirloom. And second, because she has proven herself so untrustworthy, the adults think she's telling falsehoods about Governor Dunmore and the gunpowder.

That night, Felicity wishes she could forget what she overheard, but she cannot. She awakens Ben, and together they ask their friend Isaac for help. When Felicity peeks over the wall of the gunpowder Magazine, she sees British soldiers stealing the gunpowder. Isaac beats his drum, the soldiers flee, and outraged colonists vow that they will never trust the governor again.

A Happy Birthday?

The next morning is Felicity's birthday. When she walks downstairs, she wonders if Father, Mother, and especially Grandfather will ever trust her again. The news of the governor's betrayal has been especially hard for Felicity's grandfather to hear, given his loyalty to the king. Still, Grandfather is an honorable gentleman who admits when he is wrong. When Felicity enters the parlor, he comes forward carrying a vase of flowers. In the center of the arrangement is a stubborn weed from Felicity's garden. "Aye, 'tis your weed," he says. "I decided something that is so determined to grow must be respected. And I think someone as brave as you must be forgiven a mistake."

Grandfather arranged flowers in the five fingers of the porcelain quintal vase. The glass salvers forming the two-tiered centerpiece hold a great cake, marzipan fruits, and tarts. The figurine was inspired by one made in Derby, England.

Felicity Saves the Day, written by Valerie Tripp and illustrated by Dan Andreasen, published in 1992

Felicity Saves the Day

***Felicity Saves the Day* opens with** Felicity happily running and playing. She's spending the whole summer at her grandfather's plantation, as she has done every summer of her life. This visit, however, holds a special surprise: The plotline of Felicity's hope for Penny's return resolves in one of the most memorable and heartfelt scenes in her series.

A Wild Horse

When a friend brings some horses for Grandfather to consider adding to his stable, Grandfather asks Felicity to come with him. He values her eye for horses. As Felicity gazes across the small herd, she spots one horse at the far end of the pasture, kicking up its heels and running wildly.

Felicity gasps and runs to the horse as fast as she can. She makes herself slow to a walk as she comes nearer. She stands still and holds out her hands. "Come to me, Penny," Felicity says. The horse nickers and takes one step, then two, toward Felicity. Then she gently nudges Felicity's shoulder, and Felicity reaches up and puts her arms around Penny, her beloved horse, whom she's found again at last.

Notes taken for the cover sketch of *Felicity Saves the Day* during a phone conversation with Patricia Gibbs, Colonial Williamsburg historian

"I knew we would find each other again someday," Felicity whispers.

This painting, entitled *Miss Juliana Willoughby*, by George Romney, inspired designer Holly Easland as she imagined Felicity's summer outfit.

Felicity stays cool and comfortable on hot, steamy days in this airy summer gown. The sleeves and neck are edged with eyelet, and the luxurious sash features butterflies and garden nosegays. Felicity's lace cap and wide-brimmed straw hat help shade her face from the sun.

Prints like this one inspired Felicity's Summer Gown and her battledore and shuttlecock product.

Slavery on the Plantation

Plantation owners exploited the forced, unpaid labor of enslaved men, women, and children who had no freedom or rights. Enslaved people worked under harsh conditions to plant, tend, and harvest crops. They cooked, cleaned, cared for children, made clothes and furniture, and kept livestock fed, groomed, and healthy.

To perpetuate slavery, laws known as slave codes were enacted to control the lives of enslaved people and prevent them from holding property, traveling without permission, or even learning to read. Complicit in perpetuating slavery were merchants and manufacturers in Northern cities, whose profits depended on the sale of tools, clothes, and shoes made in factories in the North and sold and used in the South. Northern textile manufacturers soon depended on the cotton crop grown by enslaved labor in the South. The entire economy of the colonies depended on slavery.

Enslaved people resisted the slave codes and carefully planned ways to oppose them. They ran away, learned to read in secret, worked slowly on purpose, burned crops, pretended to be sick, tried to earn money to buy their freedom, and petitioned the government for freedom.

In this ca. 1798 painting, enslaved women are forced to hoe land under the watch of an overseer. No matter how hard they worked, the overseer could punish them at any moment.

Enslaved people developed their own art, music, religious beliefs, and stories based on African traditions. Words we still use today—like yam and banjo—come from various West African languages. Spirituals are religious folk songs created by enslaved people, based on African music styles. These songs expressed the singers' suffering and protest, and their hope for freedom.

Even after long days of work, enslaved people made time for joy and community through music and dance, preserving their traditions and strengthening their resilience.

Some drumbeats signaled codes for escape.

The Note in the Bird Bottle

Felicity, Nan, and William bring Grandfather the gift of a bird bottle from their father's store. At William's urging, Felicity checks every day to see if there is a bird's nest in it, but there never is. One day, though, something else is there. It's a scrap of cloth wrapped around Ben's wooden signal whistle. On the cloth is a note written in berry juice.

Tending to Ben

When Felicity finds Ben in the woods, one of his legs is wrapped in bloody rags. He's heard that General Washington is going to start an army of Patriots, and he aims to become a soldier and fight with them.

Newspapers used versions of this cartoon to encourage everyone in the colonies to work together for independence. The parts of the snake are labeled with the first letters of the colonies. "NE" stands for New England.

When Felicity asks Ben if he talked with her father about this, Ben tells her that he already knows Mr. Merriman will not let him break his promise to him.

> "I always thought it was a promise you made to yourself, **to do what you said you would do,**" Felicity replies, **"no matter how hard it was."**
>
> *FELICITY SAVES THE DAY*

Felicity's sense of justice, which begins in *Meet Felicity* when she stands up for a mistreated horse, has developed and matured, just as the colonists' own questioning of British authority intensifies as the war looms nearer. The theme of trust, too, continues to grow and become more personal to Felicity. After bravely exposing the governor's deceit in *Happy Birthday, Felicity!*, she has earned the certainty and confidence to tell Ben some hard truths: "You are a coward, Ben Davidson. It's cowardly to run away, to break promises, and to hurt those who need you and trust you."

Hard to Refuse

Felicity is now a girl who is willing to take risks and advocate passionately for her family and friends. Ben finally listens to her and comes back to face Mr. Merriman and apologize. With respect, Felicity says to her father, "You could let him go be a soldier, Father. The fighting won't last forever. You could trust Ben to come back to you when the fighting is over. I know you could trust him." Father decides to take Felicity's advice, with the provision that Ben has to wait a little more than a year to be a soldier, until he turns eighteen.

Felicity's growing maturity and confidence aren't lost on Grandfather. "Felicity, the world is changing," he says. "'Tis changing too fast for an old man like me to keep up with it." He smiles at Felicity. "But how can I mind growing older, when I can watch you growing up, becoming a fine young lady, full of strength and wisdom and love." Grandfather decides that Penny is too fast for him, too, and asks Felicity if she will take Penny back to Williamsburg with her. Felicity can hardly contain her happiness. Indeed, she will. And she will take good care of Penny, too, she promises with all her heart.

Felicity knows how to help Ben when she gets his desperate message. Grandfather has taught her about healing plants. She collects lavender and witch hazel in her gathering basket and grinds them with a mortar and pestle to make a healing poultice for Ben's leg.

Changes for Felicity

Felicity's series ends just as the Revolutionary War begins. Throughout her stories, we've seen Felicity mature from a headstrong, self-centered, impatient girl to a more thoughtful, courageous, and confident young woman. The coming war will change the colonies and change her in ways we can't predict, but we know one thing for certain: Felicity will face it bravely.

Changes for Felicity, written by Valerie Tripp and illustrated by Dan Andreasen, published in 1992

Unexpected News

When Grandfather tells Felicity and Elizabeth that Penny will soon have a foal, Felicity is so happy that she wants the world to know. She and Elizabeth trudge off, wearing their pattens, through the slushy streets to Father's store so that Felicity can share the good news. Father's store looks a little different these days. Men from all over the colonies are coming to Williamsburg to join the army to fight against the king's soldiers. Many of them wear the dark, fringed hunting shirts that are the uniform of the Virginia army.

After Felicity and Elizabeth tell Father about Penny, they volunteer to make a delivery to Mr. Pelham, the town jailer. While at the jail, they find out that Jiggy Nye, the man who once abused Penny, is there in debtors' prison. He is ill and near to death. Felicity and Elizabeth take pity on Jiggy Nye and decide to meet the next afternoon to bring him supplies.

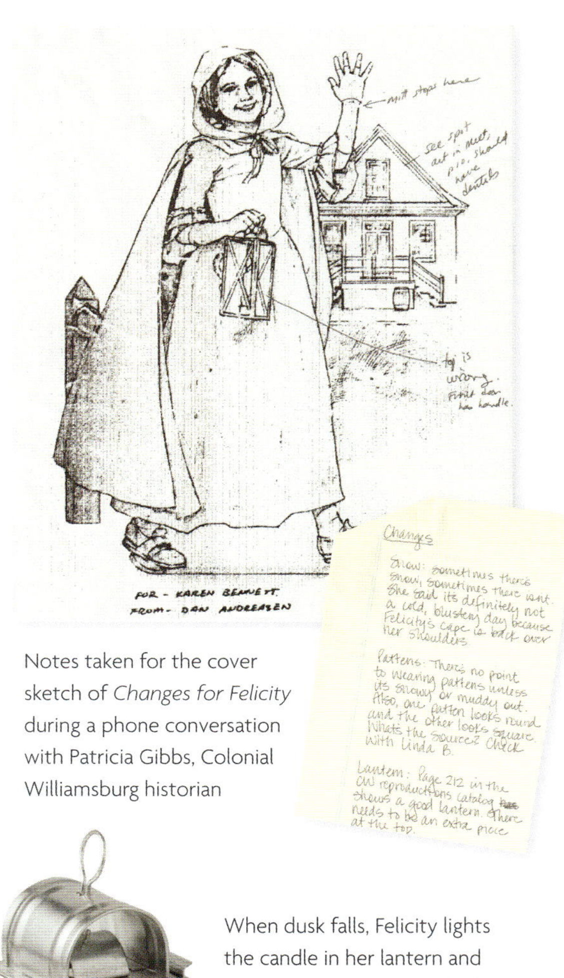

Notes taken for the cover sketch of *Changes for Felicity* during a phone conversation with Patricia Gibbs, Colonial Williamsburg historian

When dusk falls, Felicity lights the candle in her lantern and walks to Father's store, which is always one of her favorite places to go.

If it's muddy and slushy outside, Felicity ties pattens to her shoes to keep her feet above the puddles!

Felicity finds a way to get a message to Elizabeth. The next Sunday at church, she quickly gives Elizabeth her sampler of stitches as Mrs. Cole hurries Elizabeth along. The sampler reads, "Faithful Friends Forever Be."

Friends Divided

When Felicity knocks on the Coles' door the next afternoon, she is turned away with no explanation. Felicity is confused and worried. Is someone sick? Have the Coles gone away? She finds her answer at the jail, after she delivers Jiggy Nye's supplies: Mr. Cole has been arrested and imprisoned for being a Loyalist. *No wonder I wasn't allowed into the Coles' house today,* Felicity thinks. *They know Father is a Patriot. They probably don't trust anyone in the colony today.*

In wintry weather, Felicity uses her embroidered muff of eggshell-white satin and wears her soft leather mitts.

Felicity wraps herself in her cheerful scarlet Cardinal Cloak to brighten even the gloomiest day. It ties closed with a beautiful red satin ribbon to keep out the chilly winter winds.

A Sad Good-Bye

Very soon after learning of the Coles' plight, Felicity's sadness deepens unexpectedly. Valerie Tripp explains, "Felicity's grandfather, who is an Enlightenment figure, dies. He is a Loyalist, so symbolically he had to die to show the defeat of British rule. But I also wanted to show that his Enlightenment ideas of the perfection of the human soul, the rights of all to flourish, did not die, nor does Felicity's love for him."

"As it happened," Valerie continues, "my own father died while I was writing the Felicity stories. I poured out my sorrow in a rush and later used that outpouring in the Felicity book to show Felicity's sorrow about her grandfather's death."

Unbeknownst to everyone, Grandfather had set in motion two profound acts of love for Felicity before he died. First, he helped free Mr. Cole from jail, in hopes that Felicity could be reunited with her best friend. And second, he left money for Jiggy Nye in full payment for Penny, so Felicity would never have to worry about losing her again.

Designer Holly Easland studied portraits of women equestrians from the 1700s when she created Felicity's Riding Habit.

> "It is good to remember happy times with your Grandfather," Mother said. "Indeed, as long as you remember him, **he won't be truly gone from you.**"
>
> *CHANGES FOR FELICITY*

Felicity's handsome Travel Trunk has brass accents and is lined with wallpaper featuring an antique pattern of brick-red and blue cherries.

Felicity's forest-green Riding Habit is a gift from her grandfather. It has a fitted waistcoat jacket elegantly adorned with gold. The matching wool skirt is full and perfect for riding sidesaddle. A fancy tricornered hat edged with gold trim and a handsome plume of feathers finishes the look.

Felicity loves the stable. In it are all the things she needs to care for Penny and her foal: feed bags, hay bales, a bucket and brush, a wheelbarrow, a rake, a shovel, and a mortar and pestle.

To the Rescue

Felicity awakens one night to learn that Penny is having her foal! When Penny begins to struggle during the birth, there is only one person Felicity thinks of for help. Just as we saw in *Meet Felicity*, she runs through the darkened streets of Williamsburg to the edge of town, to a tumble-down shack next to the tannery. She knows the only person who can help Penny is the man who once hurt her: Jiggy Nye. When he answers the door, he tells Felicity he owes her a kindness and agrees to help. Soon, the foal is lying warm and safe next to Penny. But when Felicity turns to thank Jiggy Nye, he is gone.

When Father returns from settling Grandfather's estate, he is surprised to learn that Felicity considers Jiggy Nye a friend. And he surprises Felicity with news of his own: He's decided to become a commissary agent, traveling to collect supplies for the Patriots' army. He'll need to rely on Felicity to help at home and at the store. Felicity assures him she's ready for those challenges, and she has a sacrifice of her own to make: She wants Father to ride Penny on his travels. "I will be happy knowing that you and Penny are together, looking after each other. I will trust each of you to bring the other back to me safely."

> "By the time the Felicity books were completed, Katherine was old enough to have them read aloud to her. **For the first time, I was the mother of an American Girl fan.** I saw the power of Pleasant's comprehensive and brilliant idea all over again."
>
> VALERIE TRIPP

Master Tinsmith Jenny Lynn at work with her childhood Felicity doll. Jenny read her first American Girl books when she was in third grade and soon after visited Colonial Williamsburg, where she took one of Felicity's tours. From that day forward, she knew she wanted to work at the living history museum. Today, Jenny is the first woman to serve as Journeyman Supervisor and Master Tinsmith at Colonial Williamsburg. Her work focuses on demonstrating the craft of making tin items such as cups, coffeepots, and saucepans to visitors. She credits American Girl with inspiring her love for history, saying, "The books and dolls definitely spurred my interest in history. . . . I became that kid who was obsessed with history class and loved reading any kind of historical fiction."

AmericanGi
ember/October 1996
resh!
w Costumes to
ake for Halloween
risp!
ake Sharp,
nappy Photos
Delicious!
uper School
unches to Pack
AmericanGi
$3.95
May/June 1996
Sign Up!
AG Readers' Coolest Clubs
Stand Out!
Being Proud of Being Different
Speed Ahead!
Biking Tips from a Pro
erican girl
$3
The Al
Anima
Issue
American girl
May • June 1993
$3.95
WOW!
It's Double Dutch
WHIZ!
A Super Bike Party
WHEE!
Life Without TV
eri
k-to-
view

AmericanGirl
SINGLE!
One Summer
Away at Camp
DOUBLE!
Two Cowgirls
Rope 'n' Ride
TRIPLE!
Three Story
Contest Winners
AmericanGirl
March/April 1996
P, YIP,
ppee!
abet
n Winners
R-eat!
Surprising
WOW!
anGirl
AmericanGirl
November/December 1996
$3.95
Frosty
Wonderful Wintry
Food and Fun
Fancy
Styling a Skater
Funny
Poems About
Your Family
erican

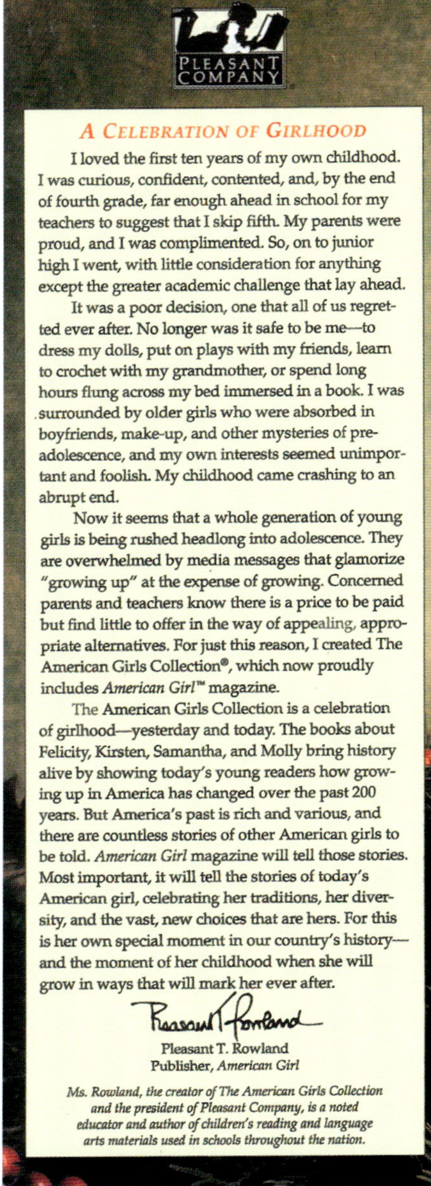

PLEASANT COMPANY

A Celebration of Girlhood

I loved the first ten years of my own childhood. I was curious, confident, contented, and, by the end of fourth grade, far enough ahead in school for my teachers to suggest that I skip fifth. My parents were proud, and I was complimented. So, on to junior high I went, with little consideration for anything except the greater academic challenge that lay ahead.

It was a poor decision, one that all of us regretted ever after. No longer was it safe to be me—to dress my dolls, put on plays with my friends, learn to crochet with my grandmother, or spend long hours flung across my bed immersed in a book. I was surrounded by older girls who were absorbed in boyfriends, make-up, and other mysteries of pre-adolescence, and my own interests seemed unimportant and foolish. My childhood came crashing to an abrupt end.

Now it seems that a whole generation of young girls is being rushed headlong into adolescence. They are overwhelmed by media messages that glamorize "growing up" at the expense of growing. Concerned parents and teachers know there is a price to be paid but find little to offer in the way of appealing, appropriate alternatives. For just this reason, I created The American Girls Collection®, which now proudly includes *American Girl*™ magazine.

The American Girls Collection is a celebration of girlhood—yesterday and today. The books about Felicity, Kirsten, Samantha, and Molly bring history alive by showing today's young readers how growing up in America has changed over the past 200 years. But America's past is rich and various, and there are countless stories of other American girls to be told. *American Girl* magazine will tell those stories. Most important, it will tell the stories of today's American girl, celebrating her traditions, her diversity, and the vast, new choices that are hers. For this is her own special moment in our country's history—and the moment of her childhood when she will grow in ways that will mark her ever after.

Pleasant T. Rowland
Publisher, *American Girl*

Ms. Rowland, the creator of The American Girls Collection and the president of Pleasant Company, is a noted educator and author of children's reading and language arts materials used in schools throughout the nation.

Pleasant's own childhood experiences were at the heart of *American Girl* magazine's mission.

The masthead for *American Girl* magazine included a representation of a 1990s girl full of energy and confidence. Her in-house nickname was "Electric Girl." She became multicolored in 1995.

Making American Girl Magazine

Pleasant also considered the name *Spunky* for the magazine, but ultimately she named it after its audience: *American Girl*.

The idea for a magazine just for girls was an important part of Pleasant's original business plan. In those early days, Pleasant and Valerie were working on a concept called *Sunshine Magazine*, but Pleasant decided to wait and develop it in a later phase of her business, after the historical character books and dolls were realized. When the historical side of the business grew strong enough, it was time to extend The American Girls Collection into present day, to send the message that you—the girl, the reader—are a part of history, too.

The idea for *American Girl* magazine also grew out of Pleasant's own experience entering junior high school a year early. Her teachers recommended she skip fifth grade, since she was so far ahead in school. Although Pleasant was academically ready for junior high, she soon found herself surrounded by older girls whose interests were shifting in more mature directions, such as crushes and fashion, while Pleasant still preferred imaginative play. "No longer was it safe to be me," Pleasant recalls.

Fast-forward to the early 1990s, and Pleasant saw her own junior high experience amplified by relentless media messages that told a whole generation of girls they needed to grow up faster, instead of celebrating the joys of girlhood at their own pace. Pleasant wanted to create a safe space where girls could be girls, with no ads pressuring them to grow up too fast.

American Girl magazine quickly grew to become the largest magazine for girls and one of the ten largest children's magazines in the country—three times as large as its closest competitor, *Girls' Life*.

An Idea Takes Shape

Pleasant knew she wanted to include history and the historical characters in the magazine to build on what her audience already knew and loved: strong, smart, heroic girls. She also wanted a lively mix of contemporary content, including profiles of real girls doing fun and interesting things (rodeo riders, ballet dancers, soccer goalies); short, entertaining news flashes spotlighting girls' ideas and achievements; good fiction by award-winning authors; colorful illustrations and fresh photography; and activities, crafts, jokes, and puzzles. She wanted to create a magazine that delivered the inspiring message: "You're great—just the way you are."

American Girl magazine debuted in the late fall of 1992 with a 65-page Premier issue. Key creatives on the magazine in its early years included Nancy Holyoke, the first editor, as well as Judy Woodburn (editorial director), Michelle Watkins (senior editor), and Kym Abrams (art director).

American girl

PREMIER ISSUE 1992

FIND-ITS! Just for fun, be a detective! Look for the 7 questions hidden throughout the magazine, and see if you can uncover the answers in this issue of *American Girl.*

All answers to games and puzzles are on page 48.

Meet our cover girl, Mary. Mary loves dancing to her boom box and playing with her all-black cat, Night Train.

Dear Girls,

Welcome to *American Girl,* the magazine all about you, the American girl of today. ★ Filled with your sparkle and spirit, it celebrates your moment in history, linking you to the long, proud tradition American girls have shared for generations. ★ *American Girl* will have stories about these four fictional American girls whom you will come to know very well, along with articles about the times they lived in. ★ There will also be stories about girls who lived in other times, including girls of today like you—because you're a part of history, too! ★ I hope this and every issue of *American Girl* gives you hours of fun and oodles of new ideas.

Pleasant T. Rowland
Publisher, *American Girl*

Letters from You

The Premier issue encouraged girls to write in, and they did—by the thousands. Girls' voices were the heartbeat of the magazine, and their words not only contributed to the content but also helped shape its direction. Staffers read and cherished every letter. They sent each girl a postcard to let her know her letter had been received and was very much appreciated.

2-26-98

Dear American Girl,
I have written to you before about your lack of Jewish content, for example Hanukkah. I just wanted to thank you for including Liana Katz paper doll. It was very nice to see.

Dear A.G.
In your Jan/Feb. issue you had a small article on Locks of Love. Ever since your article I wanted to help. At first I wasn't sure because I was scared, but then my mom and I went shopping and there was a little girl who was bald. Ever since then I dedicated my hair to Locks of Love. In fact, I'm in girl scouts and my silver project is Locks of Love. I've convinced so many people to donate their hair and when my hair is long enough I'm going to donate. Thanks for changing my life.

April 22, 1997

Dear Americah Girl,
I would like to comment on the story in the May/June issue of Americian Girl. I really appreciated the story, "A doll house for Dana". I also have a stepfather, and I miss not having to share my mom. The story made me realize that my stepdad can be so much fun! Thank you for including such a lovely story.

Dear American Girl,
I sent in a letter about 3 months ago about braces. I was mad because all of your cover girls have "braces-free" teeth! It's as if you are saying that only girls with "perfect smiles and teeth" are good enough to be a cover girl. When I opened up my May-June issue I was very happy that you put in an article for us "brace faces" out here! Please have the next girl with braces!!!
Carolyn
Age 12

P.S. How do you choose your letters for Letters from you?

Dear American Girl,
I'm 12 years old and I'm growing alot! In your March/April issue you had a couple pages on our bodies growing. I'm glad you put that in, because my body had been feeling strange! Even more so, because I'm in gymnastics and it demands alot out of my body. I'm always sore after my 3½ hour workout. But your articles taught me more about my body! Thankyou so much!
Sincerly,
Sarah

Dear American Girl, In your March\April 1998 Issue for Paper-Toppers The Early Boaterstyle picture of the girl in the hat looks just like me! Do you know who she is? I'd like to know if we are related. Hats off to your article! I liked it!

Lauren
age 9

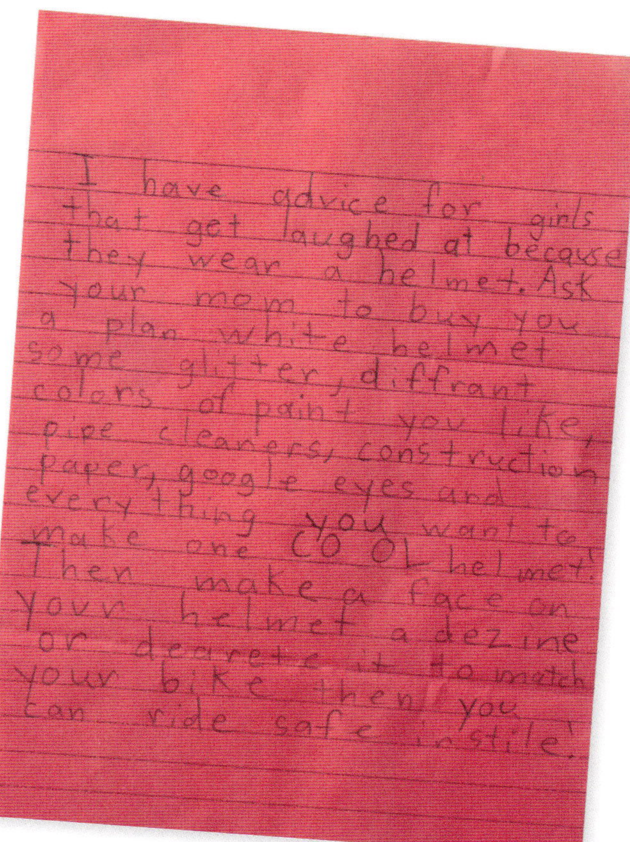

I have advice for girls that get laughed at because they wear a helmet. Ask your mom to buy you a plan white helmet some glitter, diffrant colors of paint you like, pipe cleaners, construction paper, google eyes and everything you want to make one COOL helmet! Then make a face on your helmet a dezine or decrete it to match your bike then you can ride safe in stile!

Dear American Girl.
Thank you for showing ways of helping others not just ourselves in the July/August 99 issue. If everyone did this it would make the world a better place.

American Girl!

Dear American Girl,
My name is Rachel and I love reading and writing stories! In your July/August issue the winning stories were published. I enjoyed them so much I wished there was more. So I think you should print in you November/December issue the other un-published stories. Thank you, though, I appriceate, you ecnolweged them on the bottom of the end of the winning story Nanna's Beach House. But the wining stories were so good I wanted to read more, more, MORE! I'm sure the other girls worked hard, too, so, their stories, I belive should be published, also. I'm positive theother american Girls nation wide who enjoyed the winning stories who enjoy the others!

Respectfuly, american girl,
Rachel

P.S. The July/august issue was my favorite!

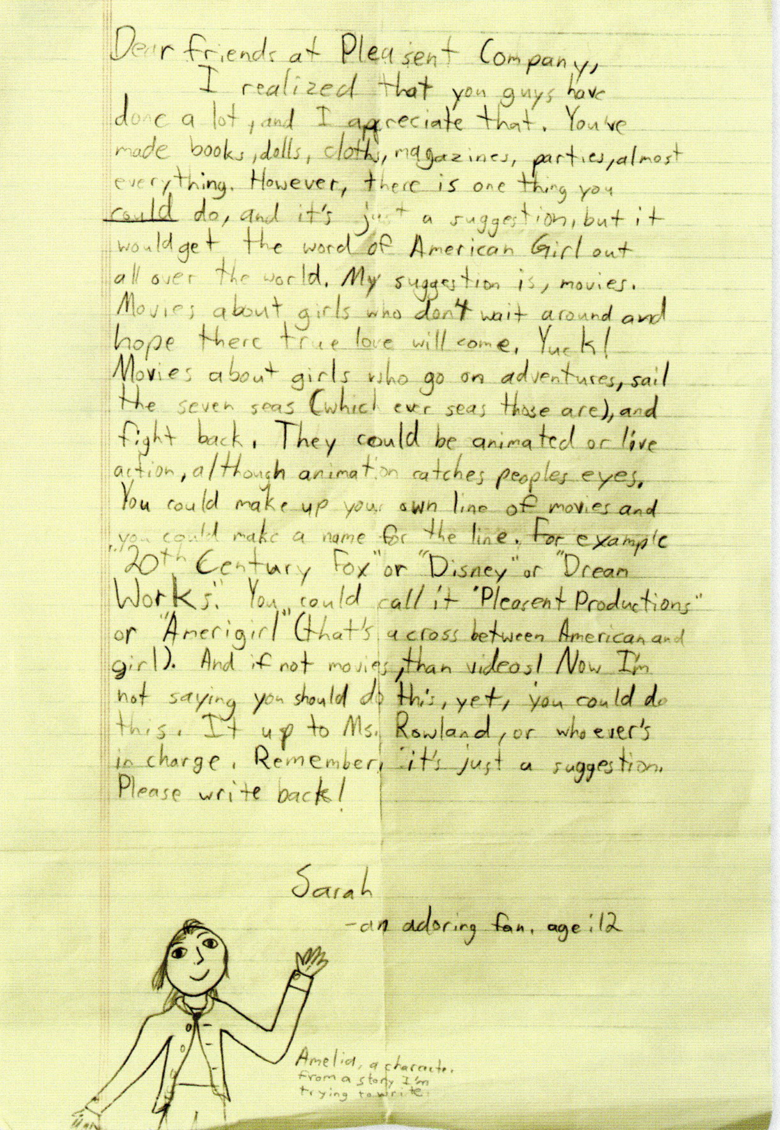

Dear friends at Pleasent Company,
I realized that you guys have done a lot, and I apreciate that. You've made books, dolls, cloths, magazines, parties, almost everything. However, there is one thing you could do, and it's just a suggestion, but it would get the word of American Girl out all over the world. My suggestion is, movies. Movies about girls who don't wait around and hope there true love will come. Yuck! Movies about girls who go on adventures, sail the seven seas (which ever seas those are), and fight back. They could be animated or live action, although animation catches peoples eyes. You could make up your own line of movies and you could make a name for the line. For example "20th Century Fox" or "Disney" or "Dream Works". You could call it "Pleasent Productions" or "Amerigirl" (that's a cross between American and girl). And if not movies, than videos! Now I'm not saying you should do this, yet, you could do this. It up to Ms. Rowland, or who ever's in charge. Remember, it's just a suggestion. Please write back!

Sarah
-an adoring fan, age: 12

Girls Like You

The magazine's pages were filled with girls' faces and voices. Their letters shaped features such as Talk It Out, which gave girls the chance to share their opinions about topics that were important to them: *Have you ever been told you can't do something because you're a girl? Have other kids pressured you into doing something you didn't want to do?* Girls loved learning from one another and seeing their photos and words of advice in the magazine.

Talk It Out

Peer Pressure

We asked readers: Have other kids ever pressured you into doing something you didn't want to do?

Once, some kids wanted me to tell a friend that all the people at our lunch table didn't like her. That was untrue, because I liked her. I absolutely did *not* go along with them. I made the right decision, because if I hadn't backed out of the situation, my friend would've felt really bad.

Jordan
Age 13

One of my friends was pressured to fight with someone. She walked away because fighting doesn't solve anything. You don't have to do it. You can say, "That's not a great idea," or walk away.

Teria
Age 11

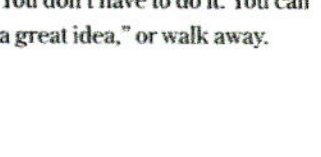

Sometimes kids pressure you to …

The fact that "everyone else is doing it" is not a good reason to do something, although I've used those words so many times I think they're imprinted on my brain. It's important to know right from wrong and let *that* be your reason to do something.

Lisa
Age 12

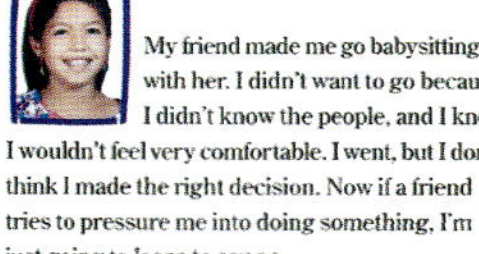

My friend made me go babysitting with her. I didn't want to go because I didn't know the people, and I knew I wouldn't feel very comfortable. I went, but I don't think I made the right decision. Now if a friend tries to pressure me into doing something, I'm just going to learn to say no.

Danielle
Age 11

One friend of mine always wants to play games I don't want to play. If I don't do what others are doing I feel weird. But when I think back on it later, I feel stupid that I thought I should do what everybody else did.

Katie
Age 10

The next time kids pressure me to do something I don't want to do I'm going to tell them, "I have my own mind, and with it I decided the answer is *no!*"

Kirstin
Age 11

It's your choice and your life. You should think through the consequences. Ask yourself, "If I do this, how will I feel inside? Will I get in trouble? Will my parents be mad?" Think it through!

Jennifer
Age 12

You know right from wrong. You should make your own decision—one that you can live with.

… my advice to other girls. If … n't want to do something, the … r is simple—*don't!*

What to Do If It Happens to You

If what the crowd wants to do doesn't seem like a good thing to you:

It probably isn't. Ask yourself, "Would I do this if my friends weren't pressuring me?" If the answer's "No," then don't do it now. Tell the others you're not interested or you have something else to do. If that little voice inside your head says "Don't," listen!

2 If a friend gets mad because you won't go along with the group:

Try letting it blow over. Your friend may be mad for a day or so, but a real friend won't hold it against you. In fact, she may respect you for standing up for what you believe is right. If she stays mad, tell her you're sorry she's upset. But you don't have to apologize for not joining in.

Let's Talk Some More

Talk It Out has changed! Instead of going to schools, *American Girl* now invites readers to send in answers. Some will be printed in a future issue.

Next subject: Divorce. What advice would you give to girls whose parents are getting divorced? If your parents are divorced, tell us what has helped you adjust.

Send your answers and a school picture to: *American Girl*, 8400 Fairway Place, Middleton, WI 53562. Deadline: October 1, 1994. Be sure to include your name and age.

SEPTEMBER/OCTOBER 1994 9

Talk It Out

Divorce

We asked: What advice can you give girls whose parents are getting divorced?

After my parents got divorced, it took me a long time to get used to our new lifestyle. It felt strange not having both parents in the house. I was sad and wished they would get back together, but I realized it was better this way. They weren't fighting all the time.

Sheena
Age 10

If you feel you can't talk about divorce with your parents, keep a secret journal with all your emotions in it. It really helps.

Chelsea
Age 10

My parents have been divorced since I was six years old. My advice for other girls is this: Always remember that a divorce is not your fault. Often mothers and fathers are happier and better parents when they're apart.

Ashlen
Age 11

One thing I did when my parents got a divorce was go to a counselor. With a counselor, you can let out your feelings. You can tell them anything, and they won't tell anyone else.

Never forget the parent you don't live with. You can keep a framed picture of him or her, make a scrapbook, or make a collage out of pictures. Whenever you feel sad, look at the pictures.

Laura
Age 10

If you miss the parent who doesn't live with you, call that parent at a special time every night so you can hear his or her voice.

Athalee
Age 11

What to Do If It Happens to You

1 If it seems as if your world has turned upside down:

When your parents divorce, you may feel angry, cry a lot, or even have trouble in school. When you feel upset, try to figure out exactly what's bothering you. Are you worried you won't get enough time with your mom? Are you afraid you'll miss your dad? Write down the problem. Then think of two ways to solve it. Share your ideas with both parents.

2 If your parents want you to choose sides:

Divorce scares parents, too. Your father might be afraid you'll care more for your mother than for him, and vice versa. Parents may do things to test your love. If you feel pressured to choose … you feel. You don't …

8 AMERICAN GIRL

Talk It Out

"No Girls Allowed"

This month we asked readers: Have you ever been told you can't do something because you're a girl?

When I wanted to sign up for karate, the office told me only boys could do it. They thought girls would hurt themselves or wouldn't like the suit. I thought the suit was cool! If this happened again, I'd gather together some friends and parents who felt the same way and make a complaint.

Heather
Age 9

In my art class, a group of girls were working on a papier-mâché cow. The teacher told us to get a piece of wood for the cow's head. But he gave the saw to the boys to cut the wood, instead of letting the girls cut it. It made me feel helpless.

Molly
Age 11

I was told that I could not shoot a BB gun because I was a girl. How did this make me feel? I hated it as much as I hate liver.

Sara
Age 9

My cousin told me girls weren't supposed to play football because it's a rough game. I gave him a piece of my mind and began playing, just as I had intended to. If someone ever says something like that again, I will say "Oh, poppycop!" and do it anyway!

God-is
Age 9

We're allowed to do anything boys do if we're good enough at it. But I don't think girls should compete with boys in sports. A girl isn't as strong. Her body isn't made to work at the same level as a boy's.

Elizabeth
Age 11

I think everybody's equal. Although we all have different abilities, they aren't based on whether you're a boy or a girl. If I can or can't do something, it's not because I'm a girl but because I'm an individual, and that's what I personally can or can't do.

Amanda
Age 12

I am a girl who plays hockey. I think girls and boys are equal in most things, even those that have been traditionally for one sex only.

Maia
Age 10

I don't think there's anything a girl can't do that a boy can. And I think boys can play dolls like girls can play cars and trucks.

Melanie
Age 10

If people ever tell me I can't do something because I'm a girl, I'll tell them they're wrong. I can do whatever I want. It doesn't matter if I'm a girl or a boy.

Stephanie
Age 12

Don't listen to people who say you can't do things. Just ignore them and walk away. They can't put down your self-confidence.

LaTonya
Age 11

You should always look at a disappointment as a constant fight to keep going. Try and try until you make it. Never give up!

Lisa
Age 9

What to Do If It Happens to You

1 If other kids say, "Girls can't do this": Don't accept it. Say, "Come on, you know that's wrong!" If you can, just join in. If they still won't let you participate, talk to individual kids from the group afterward. There may be only one or two who want to keep you out. If you can win a few people over, they may stick up for you the next day, when you go back to try again.

2 If someone assumes you don't want to do something, but you really do: Tell the person how you feel. If a teacher asks a boy to saw a piece of wood or carry a big stack of books for you, say, "I'd really like to do the sawing myself." If you don't know how, ask the teacher to show you. That's why he or she is there!

Let's Talk Some More

Talk It Out is changing! Instead of visiting different schools, *American Girl* now invites readers to send in answers. Some will be printed in a future issue.

Next subject: Is it ever O.K. to tell a secret someone has shared with you? Give examples from real life that support what you say. Why do you feel the way you do?

Send your answers and a school picture to: *American Girl*, 8400 Fairway Place, Middleton, WI 53562. Deadline: August 1, 1994. Be sure to include your name and age.

8 AMERICAN GIRL

JULY/AUGUST 1994 9

Girls Express

Buzzword

American girls everywhere are using this buzzword this season:

tantalizing

Say it: "TAN-tuhl-eye-zing"

What it means: desirable or teasingly out of reach

Where it comes from: Tantalus is a character in an ancient Greek *myth*, or story. He told a secret and was forced to stand chin-deep in water as punishment. Looking at the water around him, he became thirsty. But each time he tried to drink, the water receded so he couldn't reach it.

One way to use it: "The bright blue mountain bike grew more tantalizing each time Erin passed the bike shop."

The buzzword is tucked somewhere into this issue of *American Girl*. Can you find it?

Fifteen Truly Lovable Things

With Valentine's Day around the corner, this is the perfect time to think about things you love. But don't think things have to be perfect to be lovable. Here's a list of wonderful, fabulous, imperfect things we ♥:

unpopped popcorn from the bottom of the bowl
the runt of the litter
overly toasted marshmallows
the old family car
the Liberty Bell
photo-booth pictures
lumpy pillows
our families
blankets with frayed trim
worn-out sneakers
Mom's bad jokes
Dad's attempts to be cool
a friend's crooked smile
jeans with holes
crazy dogs and snooty cats

It's perfectly clear: What's not perfect about something is often what makes it lovable!

Girls Express

Girls Express featured girls' letters, stories, poems, artwork, and achievements. Polls encouraged girls to share their thoughts about what they wanted to be when they grew up, which ice cream flavor they thought was the best, and how much homework they had each night. Girls could see the results of each poll in a future issue, along with a new question for readers to weigh in on. Each issue also introduced a Buzzword, a fun new vocabulary word that girls were encouraged to search for within the pages of the magazine and use in their everyday lives.

Girls Express illustrations by Paul Meisel

Art from You

The magazine staff showcased girls' artwork throughout the magazine: in themed galleries within the Girls Express feature (seasonal, animals, self-portraits), and in contests such as "Create Your Own Invention," "Design a Beach Towel," "Make a Rainbow Creation," and "Create a Cookie." Girls often decorated their envelopes, too!

A Magazine Fan

In the late 1990s, a young girl wrote a letter to *American Girl* demonstrating her art skills and asking to illustrate for the magazine. That girl, Kimberly Shrack, has gone from aspiring artist to professional illustrator and is now anticipating the release of her debut picture book, *Spooky Scouts* (McElderry Books, Fall 2026). She believes the inspiration of *American Girl* played a role in her journey.

> **“*American Girl* really helped me believe I could do anything.** Not in a ‘girls can do anything boys can do’ kind of way, but in a ‘why not me?’ kind of way. That mentality has been paramount to my career as an illustrator. Someone is creating the art for these products and magazines and books . . . **so why not me?”**

Kim hopes that this inspiration can be passed along to the next generation of American girls—her two daughters (ages 8 and 5): “Being a parent to girls has given me a new perspective on just how special *American Girl* magazine and books were, especially for that age. They made me feel like girls—myself included—were capable of a whole lot more than most people thought. I want my girls to feel that way, too, and have the same confidence I had when I wrote to the magazine.”

The doodles Kim sent in to *American Girl* magazine

For Kim, the magazine was a particular influence: “The thing about *American Girl* that made it different from other magazines aimed at kids was that it took girls seriously during an age where it can often feel like the whole world is rolling their eyes at you. The things we like are too silly. Our problems are unimportant. We’re too emotional, too sensitive, just *too much.* But when I read *American Girl*, I didn’t feel that way. I felt like my interests were cool. My problems were important. That feeling a lot wasn’t a bad thing. I felt like I mattered, not just as a kid, but as a person. That’s why I reached out to *American Girl* about illustrating. It made me feel like I could do anything.”

Kim’s artwork today

More Character Stories!

The worlds of the American Girl historical characters expanded with new short stories in the magazine. Girls loved reading about Molly meeting a movie star thanks to housekeeper Mrs. Gilford, Felicity taking a dare that led to disaster, Addy's little sister helping her find a way to make her dreams soar, and more. Each story was accompanied by an engaging "Looking Back" essay that provided historical context, just as in the characters' stand-alone books.

MOLLY and the MOVIE STAR

FICTION 1944

BY VALERIE TRIPP

Molly McIntire burst into the kitchen running so fast her brown braids stuck straight out behind her. "Guess what!" she exclaimed.

"What?" asked Mom. She and Mrs. Gilford, the housekeeper, were peeling potatoes at the sink.

"My class is collecting money to buy a War Bond at the big rally a week from Saturday, and *I'm* going to give the money to Melody Moore!" Molly was so excited her voice squeaked. "Can you believe it?"

"My goodness!" said Mom.

"Who's Melody Moore?" asked Mrs. Gilford.

Molly gasped. "You mean you don't know?" she said. "Melody Moore is a *very* famous movie star. She's coming to *our* town. Everybody will come to the rally to see her, and she'll sing and dance and make everybody feel patriotic and happy so they'll buy War Bonds."

"Well," Mrs. Gilford began, "War Bonds are a good thing, but—"

"Oh, I know!" interrupted Molly proudly. "That's how I was chosen to give our money to Melody Moore. I explained War Bonds the best of anyone in my class. I

ILLUSTRATED BY NICK BACKES

8 9

Molly pushed the mop across the floor. "I'm doing it," she said.

"See that you do," said Mrs. Gilford as she turned to go.

The trouble with Mrs. Gilford is that she has no imagination. She only cares about boring things like scrubbing floors, Molly thought. *Mrs. Gilford could never be like a heroine in a movie. She could never do anything brave or dramatic. Never.*

On Friday morning, Mom asked, "How did Molly do with the chores, Mrs. Gilford?"

Molly stood still. She was not sure what Mrs. Gilford would say.

"Well," said Mrs. Gilford, "she hasn't sorted the laundry yet."

Mom turned to Molly. "You'll sort the laundry

be very late. After dinner, I want you to sort the laundry. Put everything that needs to be mended in the basket. Your mother can drop the mending off at my house tomorrow morning on the way to the rally. She has to go early. I have no wish to go to that circus of a rally myself." Mrs. Gilford tied her scarf

was a great idea!

Quickly, Molly ran upstairs with one of Ricky's socks that didn't have a hole. She took the envelope with the money out of her book bag, folded it, and put it in the toe of the sock. It was perfect! It was just like in the movie! Molly

"No," said Ricky.

"Cross your heart?" Molly asked desperately.

"Cross my heart and hope to die and spit on it," said Ricky. "What's—"

But Molly was already gone. She flew down the stairs to the kitchen. Jill was sitting at the table, calmly drinking juice. "Jill!" gasped Molly. "Did you take one of Ricky's socks out of my room last night?"

"No," said Jill.

"Where could it be?" wailed Molly. "I hid the money for my class's War Bond in the sock, and now it's gone. The money I'm supposed to hand to Melody Moore today is gone!"

"What?" exclaimed Jill. "Why did you put the money in a sock?"

"I wanted it to be like in Melody Moore's

12 13

Felicity Takes a Dare

By Valerie Tripp

Illustrated by Dan Andreasen

It's spring! The fair is in town. Felicity knows that today will be a day she'll never forget. And she's right!

"Look at me!" cried Felicity Merriman. "I'm a high-wire dancer, just like at the fair!"

Felicity climbed onto the fence as her sister Nan and brother William watched. The old fence was unsteady, but Felicity held her arms out from her sides, found her balance, and walked heel-toe, heel-toe along the top of it. Then she stood on one foot and gracefully pointed the toe of the other foot in front of her.

"You *do* look like the high-wire dancers, Lissie," said Nan. "Oh, I can't wait to see them at the fair today!"

"I want to see everything," said Felicity. "Especially the racehorses."

All through the winter, everyone in Williamsburg looked forward to the spring fair. People came to town from near and far to enjoy the

41

mud on them all.

Nan wailed in dismay. William, who liked mud, shrieked with delight, "Again! Again!"

All the noise brought Mrs. Merriman rushing from the house. "Children!" she

to the fair, her stitching became faster and faster and crookeder and crookeder. When at last the girls finished their hems, they showed them to Mother.

"Your hem is fine, Nan," said Mother. "Yours is not perfection, Felicity. But it will

wide-eyed as they balanced on a wire strung between two poles.

"The wire is much narrower than our fence," Nan said.

"Aye, and much higher, too," answered Felicity. "I'd love to try to walk on it."

"Gracious!" exclaimed Mother. "Just looking at it makes me dizzy. Come along to the fiddlers' tent. Let's listen to the music."

Mother, Felicity, and Nan clapped their hands and tapped their feet to the fiddle music, but William covered his ears. "Too squeaky!" he said.

Felicity was happy when they finally came to the pens for the prizewinning farm animals. She knew the racehorses must be nearby. She and Nan and William mooed at the friendly cows and gasped at the size of the huge oxen. The children admired the prize pig, who was fat and pink and peaceful, and laughed aloud at the way the prize chickens fluttered and fussed.

Together We Sail

BY CONNIE PORTER

ILLUSTRATED BY JOHN THOMPSON

All Addy's hopes seem shattered. Then she discovers just what it takes to make kites fly and dreams soar.

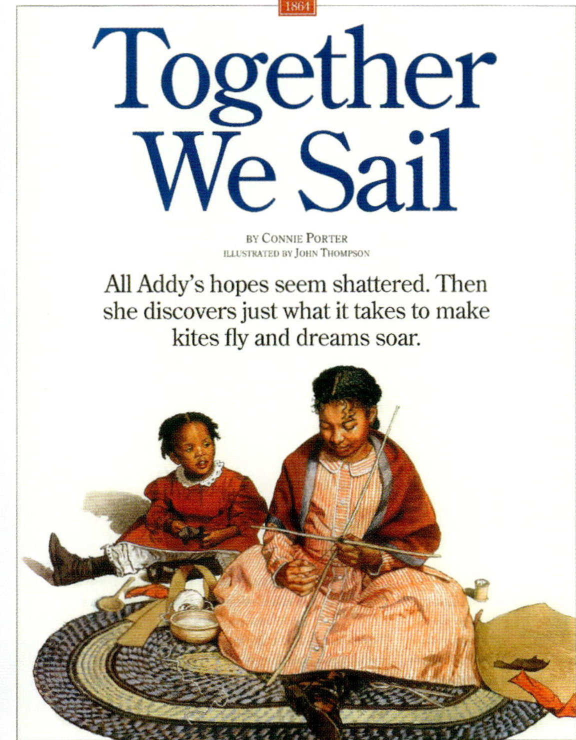

Addy sat on the floor, cutting paper for a kite she was making. It was Sunday afternoon, and her whole family—Momma, Poppa, Sam, and Esther—was together in their room in the boarding house. A strong spring breeze blew through the window and made the paper flutter.

"Ain't it something," said Addy, smoothing it down.

"Ain't what something?" asked Momma. She was sitting at the table with Poppa, cutting scraps of cloth for the kite's tail. Poppa was paring down strips of wood for the frame.

"All that go into making a kite—paper, glue, wood, string, cloth, this spool Sam bought me," Addy said. "Can't none of them fly, but all together they make something that can. It's like they all need each other to do it."

"It's kind of like a riddle," said Sam, who was down on the floor playing with Esther. "One by one they fail, but together they sail."

"I like that riddle," said Poppa. "Lots of things in life is like that."

"My kite is gonna sail the highest and longest at the kite festival next week," said Addy, beaming.

"I'm sure it'll do fine," said Poppa. "But it ain't going nowhere without a frame. You ready for the wood about now?"

"I'm ready," said Addy.

"I'm ready," Esther repeated, climbing over Sam and plopping down next to Addy.

"No, you can't help me, Esther," insisted Addy. She tried to pick Esther up and move her away.

"No!" screamed Esther. "I want to help."

"Now, you be nice to your sister, Addy," Momma said.

Addy let go. "I'm being nice to her," Addy said. "But she already knotted up some of my string and glued her fingers together."

"Addy, give me a piece of paper. I'll draw with her," Sam said. "Come here," he said, coaxing Esther back to him.

Poppa handed Addy the wood. She had to slide her paper under the table to make room.

"I can't wait until we move into our new place at the end of the month," Momma said. "We gonna have much more space."

Earlier in the week, the family had looked at the new apartment. Addy could hardly believe it. Two whole rooms! The apartment had a stove, so Momma could make their meals. There were four long windows that let in plenty of sunlight. The rent would cost an extra three dollars a month. With Poppa, Momma, and Sam working, they could afford it, but there wouldn't be any extra money. Addy loved the new apartment, but worried about leaving her boarding-house friends.

"I'm gonna miss M'Dear and the Goldens," Addy said now.

"We only moving a few blocks away," said Momma. "You can come back and visit whenever you want."

"It won't be the same," sighed Addy. She made a cross of the two pieces of wood and began binding them together with string.

"Wait," Poppa said. "Your frame ain't square." He got down on the floor next to Addy. "It's a little crooked." Poppa shifted the wood and held it while Addy tied the frame together.

10 AMERICAN GIRL — MARCH/APRIL 1996 11

"You ain't. You a baby," said Addy.

"She *is* a baby, so you got to be patient with

clapped her hands together sharply.

"Addy," Miss Dunn said. "I need to see you after school."

12 AMERICAN GIRL

desk. She had a stern look on her face.

"I want you girls to know, I didn't keep you after school for talking, though I could have," Miss Dunn said. Then she smiled. "You girls

have had a wonderful year of studies. That's why I've recommended you both for the Institute for Colored Youth for the fall!"

Addy and Harriet squealed in delight.

"Miss Dunn, you serious?" asked Addy.

"I most certainly am," replied Miss Dunn. She handed each girl a letter. "I want each of you to take this home," Miss Dunn said. "Give it to your parents. It explains more about the school. Congratulations."

Addy walked away from Miss Dunn's desk shaky with excitement. Ever since she had heard about the Institute for Colored Youth, the I.C.Y., she'd dreamt of going there. The I.C.Y. trained black students to be teachers. She would be a *teacher*, just like Miss Dunn!

With the letter grasped tightly in her hand, Addy grabbed her school sack. She couldn't

MARCH/APRIL 1996 13

Paper Doll

A paper doll based on a real, present-day American girl and her ancestors was at the heart of one of the most unique features of the magazine. The paper doll celebrated the history and traditions of the women in a girl's family, going back as many generations as they could remember. Girls could pop out the doll, cut out clothing, and dress her up in outfits that her mother, grandmother, and even great-great-grandmother wore when they were girls.

The illustrated outfits shown here represent a variety of girls' backgrounds from several different issues of the magazine. Paper doll illustrations by Susan McAliley.

The paper doll feature was written and edited by Harriet Brown and researched by Rebecca Sample Bernstein.

A Lasting Community

***American Girl* magazine quickly became** a community space where girls felt celebrated, respected, and comfortable being themselves. They trusted the magazine to answer their deepest and most personal questions about friendships, siblings, parents, school, bullies, puberty, hygiene, crushes, feelings, pets, growing up, money, and more. Various experts shared their advice to ensure that *American Girl* consistently delivered trustworthy guidance. The Help! column received so many questions that several volumes of Help! books were published to print answers to even more questions than the magazine's pages could hold. Advice books in the Care and Keeping of You and Smart Girl's Guide series also got their start from readers' Help! letters.

HELP!

Dear *American Girl*,
My mother is always making me clean my room. It's my room, and my things, so why shouldn't I have it as clean or as messy as I want?
Annoyed and Confused

Sure, it's your room, but what you do—or don't do—with it can affect others. So you and your mom need to agree on some ground rules. Together, make a list of what absolutely must be done, and how often. Should the dirty clothes be in the hamper once a week so Mom can wash them? Should your games be off the floor every Saturday so Dad can vacuum? Stay on top of the important things, and your mom may be willing to live with some creative clutter.

★

Dear *American Girl*,
Some of my friends treat me like a spare tire that you stick into a trunk until you need it to fix a flat. They treat me badly, and when they are bored, they want to play with me. What do I do?
Spare Tire

By playing with these kids, you are giving them the message that their unkind behavior is O.K. So get busy playing with your other friends or doing fun things by yourself. Make up your mind that you won't drop everything to hang out with these friends when they decide to call. If they see you're not just waiting around for them, they may begin to treat you with more respect.

★

Dear *American Girl*,
I'm nine years old, and I love babies and little kids. But I can't babysit. I know I'm responsible, but my parents won't let me!
Impatient to get older

Even though it may be too soon for you to babysit, you don't have to sit on the sidelines! Ask if you can be a parents' helper instead, watching and playing with young kids when their moms or dads are at home. It's a great way to learn about babysitting—and earn money, too.

★

Dear *American Girl*,
My mother and father are divorced, and they still fight! My mom says my dad doesn't care about anyone but himself. When I go to my dad's, he says, "She's just saying that so you won't like me." Who should I believe?
Which one?

A divorce ends a marriage, but it doesn't always put an end to the angry feelings parents have. And now that they're living apart, your parents are carrying on their fight through you. Luckily, it's not your job to sort out who's right and who's wrong. When your parents criticize each other, tell them it hurts your feelings. Tell them you want to stay out of the argument. If they keep putting you in the middle, just keep reminding yourself that parents aren't like sports teams: you don't have to choose a side.

MARCH/APRIL 1996 47

Dear *American Girl*,
I can't fall asleep. I read every night and listen to music, but nothing works. I even tried going to bed at all different times. Sometimes I'm awake after my parents have fallen asleep. What should I do?
Sleepyhead

Help! illustrations by Scott Nash

I talk Too Much!

Dear *American Girl*,
I talk TOO much! I talk my family's ears off! My sister and brother call me "Jibber Jabber."
Jibber Jabber

I hate piano!

Dear *American Girl*,
I hate piano! I've been playing it for about four years, and I don't like to practice. I'm getting to the hardest part in the piano books, and it makes me want to quit. I've told my parents I hate it, but they tell me to keep going.
Piano Hater

Dear *American Girl*,
The girl who sits next to me in class always cheats off my paper! Our teacher told her to stop, but the girl said she doesn't cheat. I can't move, so what can I do?
Not Fair

Dear *American Girl*,
I'm taking swimming lessons, and I'm not very good. I'm the oldest in my class! Worst of all, someone I used to babysit is in the class. It is so embarrassing.
Humiliated

A Legacy of Girlhood

At the height of the magazine's popularity in the late 1990s and early 2000s, *American Girl* reached 750,000 subscribers and could receive over 70,000 pieces of mail in just one year. The magazine was honored with numerous awards from the Parents' Choice Foundation, National Parenting Publications, and the Eddie Awards from *Folio* magazine, and it was twice-nominated for a National Magazine Award. Through the years, some things inevitably changed: Features and columns came and went as girls' tastes and interests evolved, the magazine was redesigned several times, and innovative features were introduced, such as a short story contest that published winners' stories in the magazine. Through twenty-seven years of publication, one thing remained constant: The staff always listened closely to their readers, learned from them, created a safe space for girls to be themselves, and dreamed up new ways to delight the *American Girl* audience.

Story Contest!

It's time for *American Girl*'s second annual story-writing contest. Here are the rules:

1. This year we want you to write a story about wishes. Your story could be about a wish coming true for someone—or about one that *didn't* come true. It could be about someone who is granted a wish that doesn't work out as she thinks it will! Sorry, no stories about characters in The American Girls Collection are allowed.
2. Your story should be no longer than eight handwritten, single-spaced pages. If your story is typed, it should be no more than three pages.
3. Include: your name, address, phone number, and AGE. A parent must sign your story and state that you wrote it yourself.
4. Send your story to Story Contest, AmericanGirl 8400 Fairway Place, Middleton, Wisconsin 53562. DEADLINE: Mail your story no later than February 7, 1995.

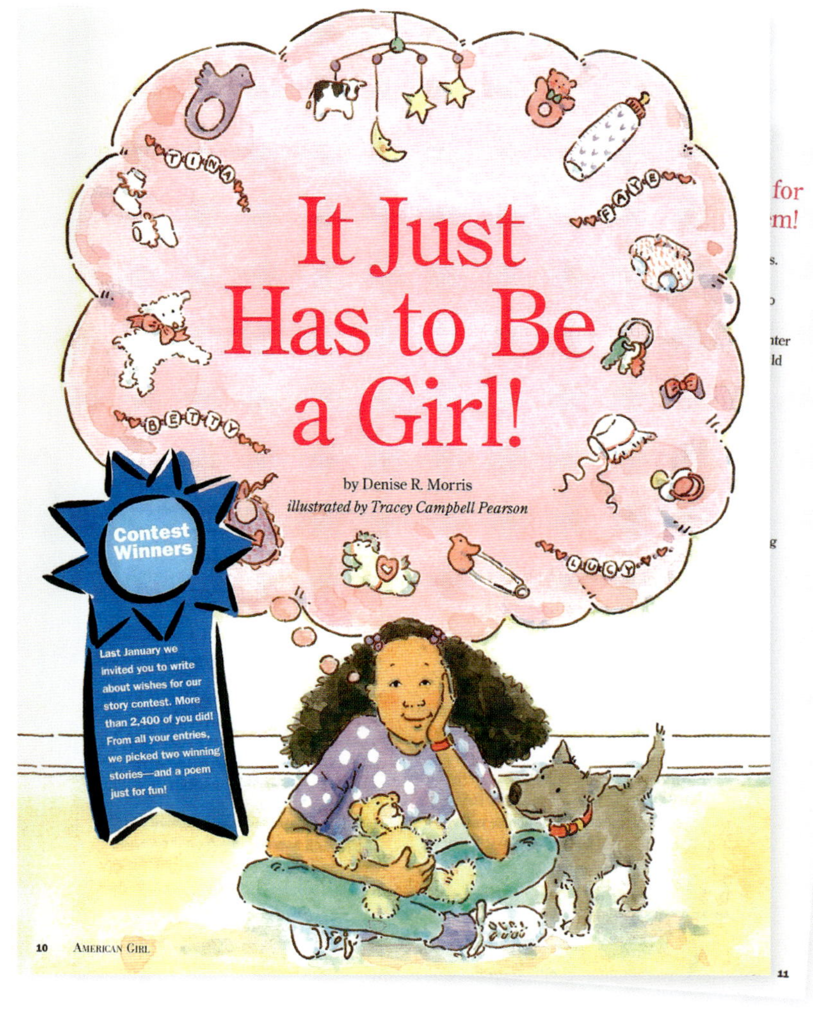

It Just Has to Be a Girl!

by Denise R. Morris

illustrated by Tracey Campbell Pearson

Contest Winners

Last January we invited you to write about wishes for our story contest. More than 2,400 of you did! From all your entries, we picked two winning stories—and a poem just for fun!

10 American Girl

11

The award-winning Mini Mag was a feature for girls to cut out, fold together, and read with their dolls.

Best Things EVER About Working on AG Magazine:

1. Above Pleasant T. Rowland's name on the masthead was a little picture of a Big Cheese.
2. Planning themed birthday parties and sleepovers.
3. Poring over girls' letters, which made us laugh and cry on a daily basis.
4. Girls trusted us so deeply! What a privilege to be a part of their growing up.
5. Testing recipes, games, and crafts (glitter everywhere!).
6. Reading thousands of short story contest entries.
7. Making sure every story delivered a strong ending—a "ping." In the magazine, that was indicated by a ★ at the end of the article.
8. Telling knock-knock jokes on the regular.
9. Receiving thank-you letters from parents, including a single dad who said, "Thank you for helping raise my daughter."
10. Working with people who cared as deeply about girls as you did. ★(ping!)

Contributed by magazine alumnae: Julie Finlay, Therese Kauchak Maring, Michelle Watkins, Laurie Herr, Jinger Peissig Schroeder, Jessica Hastreiter Nordskog, Aubre Andrus, and Barbara Stretchberry

Addy
Walker
MEET ADDY
MEET ADDY
AN AMERICAN GIRL
~BOOK ONE~
18
64
THE AMERICAN GIRLS COLLECTION®
SANDERS' UNION SERIES
SANDERS' UNION READER
NUMBER ONE
FOR PRIMARY SCHOOLS AND FAMILIES
FORD'S DRES
June 9, 1865
Dear Friends,
Can you help us find our family? Please Solomon and Lula Morgan. They caring for our dear baby Esther Walker. We last seen them last summer on the plantation belonging to Master Stevens. The plantation is some twenty miles north of Raleigh. We need information about Samuel Walker also. He about 17 years old. He was sold from the Stevens plantation last summer. We dont know where he was sold to. If you can help us, write to Ben Walker on South Street in Philadelphia, Penn. We want to find them very much because we love them all.
Ben Walker

BRUSHES BASKETS BROOMS
HALF DIME
Happy Birthday, Addy
From your friend
M'dear
April 9, 1865

The development team identified Yoruba culture for Addy's heritage. Yoruba culture has long incorporated beads into the designs of ceremonial attire, with early designs using locally made glass, stone, and shell beads. These ceremonial slippers (bata ileke) from the late nineteenth to early twentieth centuries reflect traditional Yoruba design, crafted with colorful European glass beads.

Making Addy

Pleasant's original concept in 1984 included a Civil War–era Black character as part of The American Girls Collection. To tell that story and tell it well, Pleasant knew she needed to find just the right experts. After Pleasant Company achieved initial success, development work began on the character who became known as Addy Walker.

Pleasant's first priority, even before selecting an author or illustrator, was forming an advisory board of Black historians, educators, and museum curators to guide Addy's development. Although Pleasant originally thought of setting Addy's stories during the Civil War, she asked the advisory board to consider the full breadth of Black history in the United States, including the Harlem Renaissance and civil rights era, when exploring potential stories for the company's first Black historical character. It was an important decision: Addy would be Pleasant Company's first character of color, representing only one of the many possible stories about Black life in America to be told.

After much discussion, the board unanimously agreed that it was crucial to understand the history of slavery in order to fully grasp later chapters of Black life in the United States. Just as the country was divided by the Civil War, Addy's family would be separated by slavery. Addy's story starts in slavery, and by the end of the first book, she begins her escape to freedom in the North. The series would reflect both the harsh realities of enslaved people and the challenges and possibilities of a life in freedom.

Once Addy's time period had been decided, story editor Bobbie Johnson read a wide range of children's books by Black authors. She recommended author Connie Porter, whose debut novel, *All-Bright Court*, was named one of the American Library Association's Best Books of 1991 and a *New York Times* Notable Book. Although the novel wasn't written for children, the young character Mikey, a boy who struggles to stay hopeful, resonated with Pleasant and the advisory board, who felt it was important for Addy's story to express hope despite challenging circumstances.

Meet Addy cover illustration by Melodye Rosales

Published in 1991 by Houghton Mifflin Company

Addy's Advisory Board

Although Pleasant Company had a full-time historical researcher and had consulted outside experts for the development of previous characters, the following esteemed panel formed the company's first formal advisory board:

- **Lonnie Bunch,** founding director of the Smithsonian's National Museum of African American History and Culture
- **Cheryl Chisholm,** film producer and former director of the Atlanta Third World Film Festival
- **Spencer Crew,** Robinson Professor of American, African American, and Public History at George Mason University
- **Violet Harris,** researcher and expert on multicultural literature and Black American children's literature
- **Wilma King,** historian and expert on American slavery
- **June Powell,** former expert with the National Afro-American Museum and Cultural Center in Ohio
- **Janet Sims-Wood,** former librarian and scholar at Howard University who specialized in the stories of Black women

This seven-member board evaluated plot outlines, book manuscripts, story illustrations, and drafts of the "Looking Back" essays at the end of each book. They reviewed prototypes of the Addy doll and guided the design of Addy's clothing, furniture, and accessories.

> "Before I wrote one word, I read about the issues and facts of slavery for months. **I relied heavily on the scholarship of the advisory board,** who brought their expertise to guide and support the accuracy of what I included in the text."
>
> CONNIE PORTER

Photo from 1993, when the advisory board met in Washington, D.C. Left to right: Pleasant Rowland, Connie Porter, Sally DeBroux (product designer), Bobbie Johnson (in front), June Powell, Janet Sims-Wood, Wilma King, Violet Harris, Polly Athan (historical researcher, in back), Cheryl Chisholm

Addy adviser Spencer Crew, left, went on to become the director of the Smithsonian's National Museum of American History (NMAH). Lonnie Bunch, who also advised on Addy's development, now serves as the Secretary of the Smithsonian Institution and is the first African American to hold this position.

Connie holding an early prototype of the Addy doll

Connie Porter

CONNIE PORTER, AUTHOR

When Connie traveled to Middleton in 1992 to meet with Pleasant for the first time, she felt a bit like Dorothy as she journeyed through Oz—not sure she wanted to embark on such an uncertain path. Connie recalls that one of the most memorable things Pleasant shared with her was the idea of legacy: To help bring Addy's story to life would be a chance to do more than write books; it would be a chance to introduce a character who would have an impact on readers for decades to come. Connie had never truly contemplated the legacy of a character before. The more she thought about that, the more she wanted to help bring Addy to life, to give her a voice:

> "**The biggest takeaway should be the humanity of Addy and her family.** She is a little girl, a sister, a daughter, a friend, a person full of hopes and dreams. She represents the millions of ancestors that most Black families will never know. **Addy's stories are a chance for the ancestors to speak, to express how they felt in their time, in their own voices.**"
>
> CONNIE PORTER

"What I discovered on my journey with Addy is that I had everything I needed within me to make the journey. More than anything else, I have been inspired by Addy's courage, and it has bolstered mine. Wherever it is we call home, no matter how far the wind may take us, may we all find the confidence to release the courage we need as we journey."

Enduring Storyline

Connie wrote these words when the Addy doll was reintroduced in 2024:

"As I write this letter from North Carolina, I feel like I am at a full-circle moment in my life. Last summer, my daughter came to visit, and as I was driving, showing her the sights, I saw them off in the distance—tobacco fields. Beyond were pine-filled stands of trees. I could not help but think of Addy. How she and her family were enslaved in North Carolina. Under this sun. Smothering summer heat and humidity. Freezing winter days and nights, and winds that peck at your bones.

"Addy's story is one that must be heard in the telling of the story of America. There are some truths that are hard to face. When I was writing the books, I felt what Addy was feeling, hurt when she was hurting.

"There were times when I cried, but I also want you to know that there were times when I felt her joy! **It was a light in the darkness. A lightness in my spirit.**"

"I feel honored to have been chosen by Pleasant Rowland to help bring Addy's story to life. It was a chance for ancestors I never knew to speak through Addy, to show the strength and courage it took to walk the path to freedom."

In 2024, American Girl began rereleasing Addy's stories with updates that reflect recent scholarship about slavery, race, identity, and representation. Addy's stories now include resources to learn more about her time and reader questions to deepen understanding. Online conversation guides also provide more ideas for in-depth discussion between girls and their grown-ups about slavery. As scholarship evolves, American Girl is and always will be committed to reflecting that evolution in the stories we tell and the language we use.

MOMMA

POPPA

SAM

ESTHER

AUNTIE LULA

UNCLE SOLOMON

MASTER STEVENS

MISS CAROLINE

Dialect in Addy's Stories

When Connie first discussed dialect in Addy's stories with Pleasant and the advisory board, she told them she wanted an authentic voice for Addy—one that reflected the time and place Addy lived in and the way her Southern family spoke. Connie said her great-grandmother could have been Addy.

> "This is a girl who was denied education and didn't know grammar. **The way she speaks should reflect her honest circumstances.** There's no shame in that, only in assuming that because someone speaks a certain way that they are not intelligent."
>
> CONNIE PORTER

Connie, Pleasant, editor Bobbie Johnson, and the board worked very closely with linguists, children's literature specialists, teachers, and children to give authenticity to the speech but not so much as to impede young readers' understanding. Over the course of the series, Addy's dialect evolves alongside her changing environment and experiences. As she moves from the hardships of the plantation to the freedom of the classroom, her speech, reading, and writing also shift—reflecting not only her changing world but also the different, yet connected, lives she has lived.

Character portraits for Addy's stories by Melodye Rosales

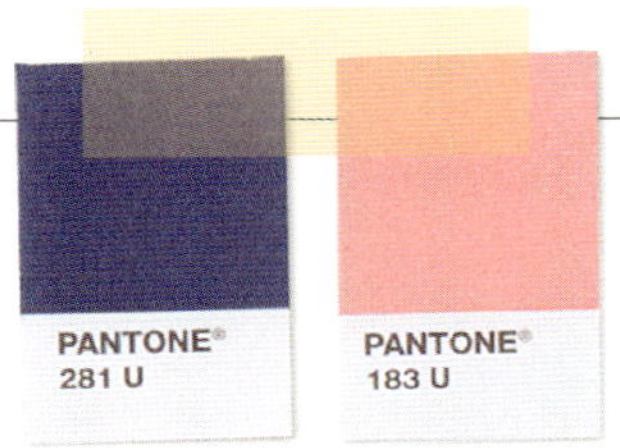

Color samples considered for Addy's Meet outfit

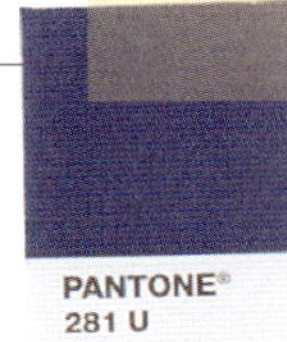

PANTONE®
183 U

Early Designs

This image of a nineteenth-century schoolgirl served as inspiration during Addy's development.

A Dress with a Story

Pleasant, Connie, and the advisory board all felt strongly that girls should meet Addy in the first dress she wore as a free person. They wanted to present her with pride and dignity, both in the doll box and on the cover of *Meet Addy*. Connie had to come up with a way for Momma and Addy to acquire fashionable dresses. This wasn't easy to do, as they spent most of the story in plain shifts on the plantation or disguised as a man and a boy during their escape.

Connie invented the character of Miss Caroline, an abolitionist who helps Addy and Momma reach Philadelphia. When they knock on Miss Caroline's door in the middle of the night, she wastes no time preparing a warm meal for them and finding something to fit them from the donated clothes she saves for runaways. When Addy fastens the shiny white buttons on her cinnamon-pink dress with wiggly white stripes and ties the calico ribbon of her straw bonnet under her chin, she stands straight and tall.

In a 2025 interview with Jaha Nailah Avery for *Essence* magazine, Connie shared: "The dress is symbolic of what had to happen in America in order for slavery to end. Black people stood up, of course, but white people had to stand up, too. Whether part of the abolitionist movement, or those conscripted into the army in the North, many people, Black and white, had to say, 'This is the country we want, and this is the price that we have to pay to get it.' Just like with the situation we're in now as a country, where we will also have to make those decisions."

A color rendering of Addy's Meet dress accompanied by fabric swatches and sample trims

Holly Easland designed all of Addy's dresses. Addy had several placeholder names throughout her story and product development, including "Annie" and "Darcy."

Meaningful Meet Accessories

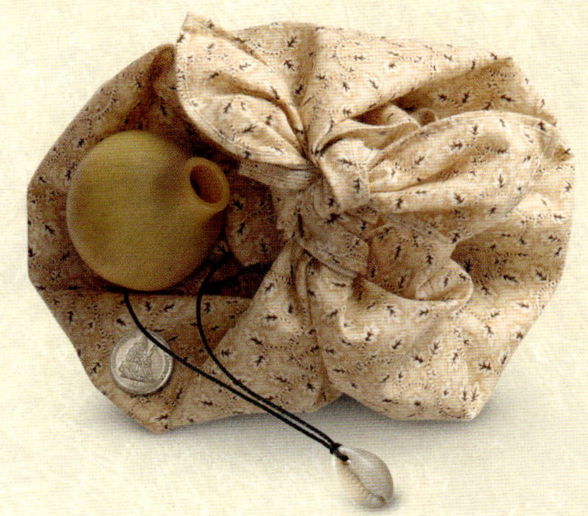

On the night Addy and Momma escape, Addy ties the half dime from Uncle Solomon into the corner of the kerchief she uses as a carrying bundle. She also carries a dried gourd filled with fresh water. The drinking gourd is critical for survival during the escape, and it holds symbolic meaning. In Addy's time, the Big Dipper was also known as "the Drinking Gourd." Its handle points north and helped guide many enslaved people to freedom.

Addy's cowrie shell necklace is a powerful symbol of her unending connection to the people in her past. During their escape, Momma gives Addy this shell, strung on an old shoelace that once belonged to Sam. She tells Addy the shell belonged to her great-grandmother, who was stolen from West Africa when she was a girl. Her name was Aduke, which means "much loved" in Yoruba, a language spoken by the Yoruba people living in modern-day Nigeria, Benin, and Togo.

"I saved her name for you, Addy," Momma said. "Her journey ended in slavery. Yours, girl, is taking you to freedom."

MEET ADDY

Meet Addy, written by Connie Porter and illustrated by Melodye Rosales, published in 1993

Meet Addy

Connie recalls, "I wanted children to see Black people as part of strong, loving families." Even slavery cannot dim the love and light Addy carries for her family in her heart. When slavery tears them apart—just as the nation was divided by the Civil War, North against South—Addy perseveres and never loses hope that they will be together again one day. Addy's determination to reunite her family in freedom is the driving force across all six of her stories. That journey begins in the opening scene of *Meet Addy*, when Addy overhears her parents whispering late at night about plans for the whole family to escape the plantation and live in freedom in Philadelphia.

Original sketch and final illustration by Melodye Rosales

A New Plan

Before Addy's parents can put their plan into action, Poppa and Addy's older brother, Sam, are sold against their will and enslaved on different plantations. Soon afterward, Momma tells Addy that they are still going to escape—even without Poppa and Sam, who know to come to Philadelphia as soon as they can. When Addy asks about her baby sister, Esther, Momma shares the wrenching decision she has made: "Esther might cry any time. Her crying would give us away. . . . I love Esther as much as I love you and Sam, but we can't take her."

Addy and Momma place baby Esther in the care of Auntie Lula and Uncle Solomon, two elderly enslaved people who are like family to Addy. On the night of the escape, Uncle Solomon gives Addy a half dime and tells her,

> "You hold on to that half dime. You gonna need it where you going. Freedom cost, you hear me? Freedom's got its cost."
>
> *Meet Addy*

Paintings from the 1860s helped the development team envision Addy's escape. The man on horseback wears clothing similar to Addy's and Momma's disguises, and the bundles below show how people carried their belongings.

August 1864

Meet Addy Calendar 10/1/92

Sunday	Monday	Tuesday	Wednesday	Thursday	Friday	Saturday
	1	2	new moon 3	4	5	6
7	8	9	1st quarter 10	11	Chapter 1: overhearing parents 12	Chapter 2: selling of Poppa & Sam 13
14	15	16	17	full moon 18	Chapter 3: Addy forced to eat worms; plan to leave 19	Chapter 4: they leave 20
day in cave 21	drowning day in hollow 22	Chapter 5: safe house leave before sunup for east 23	24	3rd qt. 25	26	27
28	General George McClellan nominated for President at Democratic national convention. 29	30	31			

Since many of the scenes in *Meet Addy* take place outside at night, the editor and the historical researcher worked out a calendar to show the phases of the moon at different points in the story.

A Dangerous Escape

Addy and Momma nearly lose their lives while crossing a wide, rushing river at night. Sam taught Addy how to swim, but Momma doesn't know how to swim at all. As they wade deeper, the current grows stronger. It pulls Momma's hand from Addy's, and she disappears beneath the water. Addy dives again and again until she finds her momma trapped in the branches of a fallen tree. With a mighty push, Addy brings them both to the surface, and they make it safely across the rest of the river.

Addy Learns a Lesson

In the second book in Addy's series, Addy and Momma learn lessons on two levels. First, they must learn about their bewildering new life in freedom. And second—equally, if not more important—they begin to manifest Addy's deeply held desire to learn to read.

The story opens with Addy and Momma newly arrived in Philadelphia, standing on a busy pier and wondering if this big, strange city can ever be home to them. Is there room for even two more people in this crowded place? Poppa said this is where freedom is—but Addy feels scared and vulnerable.

Addy
Learns
a Lesson
A School Story
~ Book Two ~
1864
The American Girls Collection

Addy Learns a Lesson, written by Connie Porter and illustrated by Melodye Rosales, published in 1993

The progression from thumbnail sketch to refined sketch to final illustration

Addy tells Sarah how much she wants to learn to read, and Sarah promises to help. On the first day of school, Sarah proudly introduces Addy to their teacher, Miss Dunn.

A First Friend

Then two friendly faces appear from the crowd: Mabel Moore and her daughter, Sarah, from the Freedom Society of Trinity A.M.E. Church. As Mrs. Moore leads the way to the church, Sarah holds Addy's hand while they walk through the busy streets. When Sarah starts to read the street signs out loud, Addy joyfully realizes her dream of learning to read in freedom is within her grasp.

Addy's slate and *Union Reader*

On the first day of school, Sarah and Addy share a double desk. When Miss Dunn announces that the class will copy from the board, Sarah shows Addy how to hold her slate pencil and form the letters of the alphabet. When Addy writes her name for the first time, Sarah gives her a warm smile and tells her she can read her letters plain as day. In Sarah, Addy has found her first friend.

Design rendering for Addy's Double Desk

In Addy's time, 10 percent of the Black population could read and write. That number doubled in the next five years as people gained the education that they had been denied. Education meant true freedom, and literacy opened the door to better jobs and better lives.

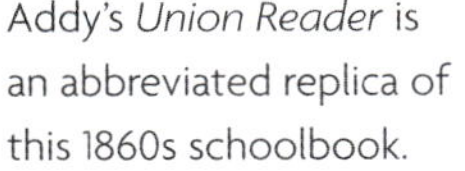

Addy's *Union Reader* is an abbreviated replica of this 1860s schoolbook.

Addy shown in early catalogue photography

This dress, made by an unidentified enslaved woman or women, is the type of garment Momma might sew for herself. Although it's simpler than the fancy dresses she makes in Mrs. Ford's shop, it still requires masterful hand-stitching techniques: gathered sleeves and waist, a "fussy cut" neckline and waistband that showcase the printed design, and delicate piping at the armholes and along the bottom of the waistband.

The Student Becomes the Teacher

Addy's momma works as a seamstress at Mrs. Ford's dress shop. Part of her job is delivering dresses to customers on Society Hill. There's only one problem: Momma can't read. And to keep her job, she has to learn.

Even though Addy is just starting to learn herself, she eagerly offers to help. Using scraps left over from making bread or meat pies for supper, Addy teaches Momma to spell words by forming the letters out of dough. They love making the names *Sam, Esther,* and *Poppa.* "Seeing their names make me feel closer to them," Momma says.

Dressing Smart

The importance of learning to read in the Black community in the 1860s is also shown in this story through Momma's painstaking efforts to make Addy her second outfit in freedom: a new blue skirt and jacket trimmed in black braid, and a crisp white shirt to wear during her spelling match. Connie's choice to make Momma a seamstress gives Momma access to fabrics unavailable to many Black families in Philadelphia at the time. It also ensured that Addy's outfits have close ties to her stories.

School 1864

The Spelling Match

The spelling match is a vindication of Addy's hard-won knowledge. It soon takes on another important dimension: standing strong for a true friend. When Sarah misspells a word, Addy plans to misspell it as well to make Sarah feel better. Then a haughty, manipulative girl named Harriet—whom Sarah had warned her about, though Addy hadn't listened—whispers to Addy that Sarah is dumb. With a flash of anger, Addy thinks, *I'll show Harriet!* and spells the word correctly. By the fifth round, it's down to Addy and Harriet, and the word is *principle.*

> "We all live our lives by principles," Miss Dunn said. Harriet spelled quickly, "P-R-I-N-S-I-P-L-E." "I'm sorry," Miss Dunn said. "That is not correct."
>
> *ADDY LEARNS A LESSON*

Slowly and deliberately, Addy spells *principle* correctly. Beaming, Miss Dunn pins a gold medal on Addy's jacket as the class applauds. Addy is proud that she won, but more than anything, she wants to make things right with Sarah. At lunch, she reads the cookies Momma has put in her lunch pail—and knows just what to do: share them with her true friend.

MISS DUNN

A Role Model for Addy

Addy is happy to learn that her teacher, Miss Dunn, is from North Carolina just like she is. Miss Dunn immediately calms Addy's first-day-of-school jitters by telling her, "I never went to school until my family came north. When I started, some things seemed a little strange. You might feel a bit confused this first week, but you'll soon learn your way."

Miss Dunn's family had been enslaved as well. After they moved north, she attended Philadelphia's Institute for Colored Youth. Because of Miss Dunn, Addy begins to see a path for her future she had never thought possible.

Miss Dunn is an homage to Connie's maternal great-grandmother, Hannah Dunn, born in Alabama in March 1850. Like Addy, she did not know her exact date of birth.

Illustration by Bradford Brown

Addy's Surprise, written by Connie Porter and illustrated by Melodye Rosales, published in 1993

Addy's Surprise

As Christmas draws near, Addy and Momma miss Poppa, Sam, and Esther more than ever. The family has been separated for months, and Addy and Momma have had no word about them. Still, they plan to continue their Christmas tradition of sweet-potato pudding, a dish that Auntie Lula taught Momma to make and that is Poppa's favorite.

"**Last night I dreamed we was all together.** Sam, Poppa, Esther—all of us here in Philadelphia," said Addy. ..."It ain't gonna be just a dream, Momma. It's really gonna happen someday, ain't it?"

ADDY'S SURPRISE

A Source of Strength

Nowhere do Addy's themes of love and determination to reunite her family come through more strongly than at Trinity A.M.E. Church, a fictional church based on Philadelphia's Mother Bethel African Methodist Episcopal Church. The church and its congregation are Addy's first home and family in freedom. Every Sunday, Addy and Momma listen to the pastor's words of hope and comfort. They help with church efforts to raise money to bring people to the North and help feed, clothe, and house them once they arrive.

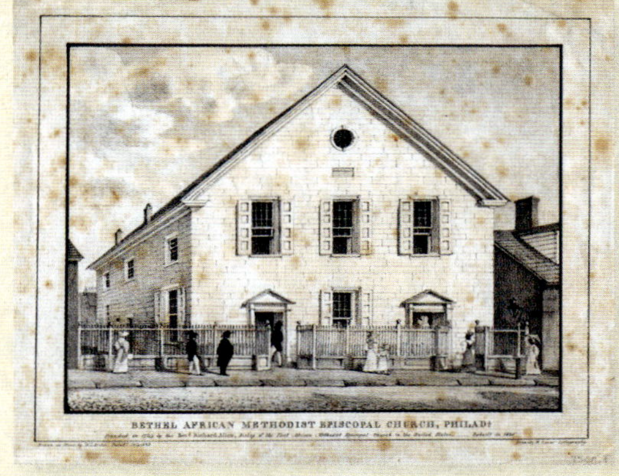

At Christmastime, the church is a place of peace for Addy, Momma, and all the families separated from loved ones. After the Christmas service, the whole congregation gathers in the church basement for a big Christmas dinner. Everyone brings a dish to pass, and they all sit down together like one great big family.

Freedom's Got a Cost

Addy goes to help church members welcome newly freed people at the Philadelphia docks, just as she and Momma were welcomed not long ago. Addy helps carry a baby who reminds her of Esther. Would her sister be as lucky as this baby, finally reaching freedom? *Who's gonna give money for Esther to come to freedom?* she thinks. Later at church, Addy stands in front of the donation box, feeling the coins she holds inside her mitten.

> "Slowly, Addy took off her mitten. One by one, she dropped her coins into the box. The last coin was the half dime Uncle Solomon had given her. She remembered the words he said to her, **"Freedom's got a cost."**
>
> Then she thought of Esther, Sam, and Poppa, still waiting to take their freedom, and **she let the half dime clink into the box with the rest of her money.**"
>
> *Addy's Surprise*

Light and Shadow

From the very beginning of Addy's development, the theme of hope symbolized by the interplay of "light in the darkness" was part of Pleasant's vision for Addy's character and stories. In *Meet Addy*, the reader first sees Addy lying on her pallet in the glow of firelight, feeling safe within Poppa's shadow as he checks to see whether she's awake. During her escape with Momma, the darkness protects them as they run, while the moon and stars shine light to guide their path.

In *Addy's Surprise*, we once again see Poppa's shadow—this time as a shape Addy recognizes during the Christmas shadow play at church, a shape that brings her the greatest Christmas joy she's ever known.

"The children turned to see who had opened the door. It was a tall man. **Though Addy could not see his face, his shadow was a shape she recognized.** . . . Addy knew who was standing in the door, standing there right now, not in a dream, not someday, but right now.

"Poppa," she burst out. **"Poppa, is that you?"**

"Is that my Addy?" came the answer.

ADDY'S SURPRISE

Dresses from the 1860s, like the one shown above, inspired Holly Easland's design for Addy's Tartan Plaid Dress.

Christmas 1864

The Best Gift

When Momma and Addy take Poppa home to their garret, they find a gift from Mrs. Ford: a kerosene lamp shining brightly. Addy reads aloud the note beside it: "May the hope of the Christmas season shine in your lives always."

The words and the gift are lovely and moving, but that's not why Poppa begins to cry.

> "I'm crying because I'm so happy," Poppa said. **"I'm so proud you can read."**
>
> *ADDY'S SURPRISE*

Addy's Quilt

West Africans brought rich textile traditions to America. Enslaved people blended these with new techniques to create beautiful quilts from scraps, taking pride in their craft despite having few possessions. The inspiration for Addy's quilt was an antique quilt called *Album Quilt,* made in 1854 by Sarah Ann Wilson. Although there is no record of the names of the people portrayed in the design, they were likely members of the maker's family. Images of home, the beauty of the natural world, and biblical references were also incorporated into the design. The lion may have symbolized both a biblical figure and a story from Africa passed down through generations.

Early color exploration for Addy's quilt, interpreted from the original by designers Valerie Hodgson and Sally de Broux

The quilt is inscribed "Sarah Ann Wilson Aug 1854" on the bottom row. Though little is known about Wilson, she may have been a free Black woman living in New York.

Addy's Launch

In 1993, Addy Walker became the fifth character in The American Girls Collection. In a memo to all employees dated June 28, 1993, Pleasant wrote,

> "Serious racial issues divide America today, and each of us, within our own sphere of influence, must do what we can to help heal these wounds. Pleasant Company's sphere of influence is enormous. The honest and compassionate presentation of Addy's experience that The American Girls Collection portrays will impact the attitudes, feelings, and behavior of a whole generation of young Americans. I firmly believe that Addy will make a difference—an important and lasting one that all of us can be extremely proud of."
>
> PLEASANT ROWLAND

In 1993, *Meet Addy* was the tenth bestselling new children's book of the year, according to *Publishers Weekly*. Booksellers voted the Addy series "Best Children's Series of 1993."

Connie Porter signing books at Black Books Plus in Manhattan during her author tour

The Addy doll, her first three books, and the accompanying products launched in September, when over 30,000 people met Addy at the National Council of Negro Women's annual Black Family Reunion Celebration in Washington, D.C. Connie Porter traveled across the country on a four-city author tour that drew over 15,000 people to events at bookstores, schools, libraries, and museums.

Even with this overwhelmingly positive welcome, Addy—a Black doll whose story begins in slavery—was regarded as a polarizing character. For some, her story did not feel right to tell in a children's book accompanied by a doll; for others, she provided language to confront racism and to humanize slavery—an institution defined by its attempt to strip humanity away. Parents admired Addy's courage and perseverance, seeing her as an inspiring example for all children. They saw Addy as a positive role model for their daughters, regardless of race. Over the years, girls from a variety of racial and cultural backgrounds and lived experiences proudly carried their Addy dolls to book signings, events, and lunch at American Girl Place. Still, many parents wished their daughters had more Black dolls and stories to choose from in Pleasant Company's catalogue. Today, the historical line also includes Claudie, a girl living in 1922 during the Harlem Renaissance, and Melody, a girl growing up in 1964 during the civil rights movement and the rise of Motown.

Addy made her debut on *The Oprah Winfrey Show* during the 1993 holiday season. Oprah thought Addy's Sweet Potato Pudding accessory was so adorable that she highlighted it on the show. Right after the segment aired, Pleasant Company's phone lines went down due to the unexpected call volume!

According to Connie, "Children are curious and truly excited about history. Those visits remind me of the wonderful part about writing for children—the world is still new to them, and they're still exploring it."

Pleasant Company was one of the initial contributors to the building project of the Smithsonian's National Museum of African American History and Culture (display of Rosa Parks pictured at left). Below, from left to right: Robert McCormick Adams Jr., Secretary of the Smithsonian Institution (1984–1994); Claudine K. Brown, Director of the National African American Museum Project; Julia Prohaska, PR Director, Pleasant Company

In 1994, to honor Black History Month, Pleasant Company donated over $78,000—5 percent of all January and February sales of Addy books, dolls, and accessories.

> "Over the years, Pleasant Company partnered with groups as diverse as the Deltas to companies like Scholastic **to bring free and low-cost books to readers, and has done much more to give back to local communities and encourage and promote conversations about race and history.**"
>
> CONNIE PORTER

Inspiring a New Generation

When she was eleven, Brit played the role of Addy in a production held at her public library.

Brit Bennett was an avid reader and fan of Addy's books as a young girl. She grew up to become the *New York Times* bestselling author of *The Mothers* and *The Vanishing Half*. Brit had always wanted to create an American Girl character, and she got her chance with Claudie Wells, a girl who grows up in Harlem during the 1920s.

In her foreword to *Meet Claudie*, a passage reads: "When I began to write, I knew that I wanted to honor the work of Connie Porter, the trailblazing author of the Addy series. She took on the challenge of writing a story about a girl, around my same age then, who had survived the horrors of slavery. She taught generations of children about the brutality of slavery, as well as the strength and bravery of a family determined to make itself whole again. She made me want to tell stories, too.

"A while ago, when I first considered writing this book, I had a chance to talk with Connie Porter on the phone. It was thrilling to speak to a writer who wrote books that I loved so much when I was little. Did she know, I wanted to ask, how important her books were to generations of girls? But before we hung up, Ms. Porter said, 'Maybe one day, thirty years from now, a girl who read your book will call to tell you she's a writer now.'"

> "And you know what? **I hope to hear from you then.**"
>
> BRIT BENNETT

Brit and Connie at the launch event for Claudie

Claudie illustrations by Laura Freeman

Happy Birthday, Addy!, written by Connie Porter and illustrated by Bradford Brown, published in 1994

Happy Birthday, Addy!

Like many people who had been enslaved, Addy doesn't know when her real birthday is. *Happy Birthday, Addy!* tells the story of how she chooses just the right day for her birthday. The story is set in springtime, full of hope and new beginnings. Poppa has been back with Momma and Addy for three months, and the addition of his wages from driving an ice wagon has made it possible for the family to move out of the garret above Mrs. Ford's shop and into a boardinghouse.

Freedom?

Life is better for the Walker family once Poppa arrives in Philadelphia—but he, too, quickly recognizes the irony of freedom in the North. When Addy rides along on his delivery route, she sees a group of white girls enjoying ice cream inside Natkin's Confectionery Shop. Without thinking, Addy blurts out how much she'd like a dish of it, even though she knows the shop doesn't serve Black people.

> "I'm telling you, Addy, this is some kinda freedom," Poppa said. **"I can deliver ice to make ice cream, but I can't even buy my own daughter a dish of it."**
>
> *HAPPY BIRTHDAY, ADDY!*

When Poppa finds a busted-up ice cream freezer left for trash, he determines to fix it up so they can make their own ice cream at home.

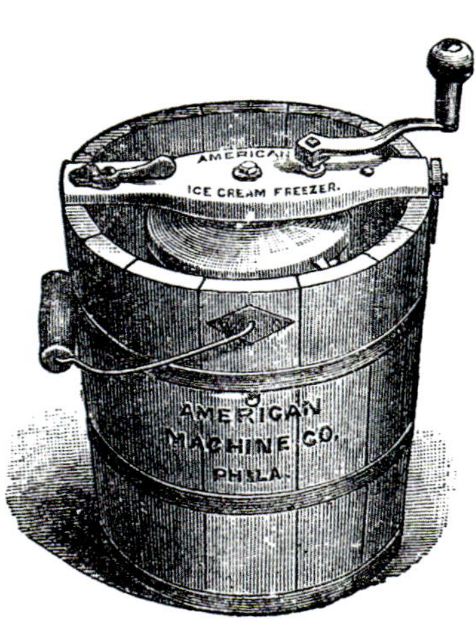

Historical references like the pen-and-ink drawing above inspired Addy's Ice Cream Freezer.

The inclusion of Sunny is an homage to the theme of freedom versus confinement found in Maya Angelou's famous memoir, *I Know Why the Caged Bird Sings*.

The Seer

A new character is introduced in *Happy Birthday, Addy!*: M'dear, the mother of Mr. Golden, who owns the boardinghouse where Addy and her family now live. She represents the archetype of the Seer, a wise character who can perceive hidden things and helps guide the protagonist and the story.

Addy first meets her right after M'dear moves into the boardinghouse. Addy follows the sound of birdsong down the hallway and sees a bright yellow canary singing in his cage. When M'dear introduces herself and her bird, Sunny, Addy notices that M'dear's eyes are cloudy. M'dear intuits Addy's unspoken question:

> "Didn't know I was blind, did you?" Mrs. Golden asked.
>
> Addy answered quickly, "No, ma'am. If you blind, how did you know I was standing outside your door?"
>
> "I got plenty of ways of seeing," answered Mrs. Golden.
>
> *HAPPY BIRTHDAY, ADDY!*

It's M'dear who tells Addy that slavery has taken away so much from Black people, but that there's one thing Addy can take for herself: her birthday. She assures Addy that when the right day comes along, she'll know.

The Inspiration for M'dear and Sunny

> "The beautiful, statuesque woman on the right in this picture is my dear Aunt Ruth, my father's sister. **Her likeness was used for M'dear. Her children called her by that nickname, and in the latter years of her life, like M'dear, she was blind.**"
>
> CONNIE PORTER

Pleasant had a friend with a bird named Sunny, which turned out to be the perfect name for M'dear's canary. Sunny symbolizes Addy's longing for a freedom that eludes her, even though she's living where freedom is supposed to be. When Addy asks if Sunny is sad and lonesome in his cage, M'dear tells Addy that sometimes he does sound that way. However, she adds, "That cage can't contain Sunny's spirit. It soars right out from behind those bars. That's what's important for all of us. To let our souls sing out."

Ironstone plates such as this one inspired Addy's tableware. Notice the tea-leaf motif rendered in copper luster with a crackle finish.

An Almost Perfect Day

On April 9, 1865, Addy and her family wake in the middle of the night to the booming of cannon fire. At first, they think the war has come to Philadelphia—until they hear joyous cheering, whistles blowing, and church bells ringing. General Lee has surrendered. The war is over at last.

> **This was the day she had been waiting for.** It was not perfect. If it were, her brother and sister would be right there with her, but this was the best day she could imagine without them.
>
> She turned to Momma and Poppa. **"I want today to be my birthday,"** Addy said.

HAPPY BIRTHDAY, ADDY!

Early design ideas for Addy's birthday dress

The off-the-shoulder apron style was popular in the 1860s.

Addy Saves the Day, written by Connie Porter and illustrated by Bradford Brown, published in 1994

Addy Saves the Day

In *Addy Saves the Day*, hope takes the form of a garden that Addy, Momma, and Poppa plant to grow vegetables. The money they raise selling the harvest will help them fund their search for baby Esther and Addy's older brother, Sam. In the two months since the war ended, Addy and her family have worked tirelessly to find their loved ones.

Heartless Harriet

"Well, well, well, if it isn't the little plantation girl," a sharp voice says while Addy is watering the garden. Addy looks up and sees Harriet. When Addy tells her that Poppa is going to find Esther and Sam, all Harriet has to say is "Oh yes. You told me about your lost brother. He's the one you think *might* have been a soldier." Harriet smiles a superior smile. "My uncle served with distinction in the Third Infantry. He'll be home any day now. My mother says she expects he is a hero and will have the medals to prove it."

> "If only Addy knew as much about her brother Sam as Harriet knew about her uncle!"
>
> ADDY SAVES THE DAY

Photographs like this one and firsthand accounts of the Civil War inspired events in Addy's stories and served as references for characters, like her brother Sam. Notice that this soldier poses with a book, perhaps to show that he could read.

At harvest time, Addy heaps her basket high, imagining that each ripe vegetable will bring her family one step closer to being together again.

Harriet personifies the cruelty and ignorance Addy's momma and poppa teach her that she must rise above. Poppa says, "You got to know, Addy, anger and bitterness can be like weeds. If you let them grow, pretty soon they take over and there ain't room for nothing else." By the end of the story, Addy has an opportunity to do just that. She finds Harriet hiding in a closet at church, crying. The uncle whom Harriet once bragged about has died in the war. Addy, the voice of hope, the light in darkness, has this to say to the girl who treated her so callously:

> "I'm so sorry. I truly am. **I know you loved your uncle. I know you were proud of him.**"

ADDY SAVES THE DAY

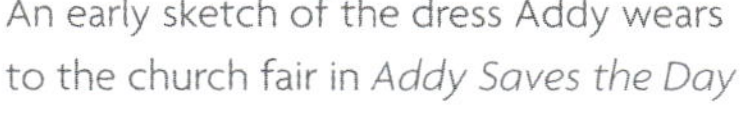

An early sketch of the dress Addy wears to the church fair in *Addy Saves the Day*

Riddle Me This

Addy's church is putting on a fair to raise money for the hospitals crowded with men wounded in the war. Addy has the idea to make puppets and put on a show. She makes her soldier puppet say a riddle Sam once told her:

"Riddle me this," Addy makes the soldier ask the dog. "What's smaller than you, but can put a bear on the run?"

Suddenly Addy hears a young man say, "That's an easy riddle. Even my little sister know that one. It's a skunk." Addy's heart fills with hope. There's only one person who would know that riddle and speak those words. Sam has come home.

Poppa makes slide whistles to sell at the church fair.

> "Addy ran out from behind the booth **and threw her arms around Sam.**"

ADDY SAVES THE DAY

Changes for Addy

Changes for Addy, written by Connie Porter and illustrated by Bradford Brown, published in 1994

The final book of Addy's series reunites her family in freedom at last, but there is sorrow amidst the joy. Addy and her family receive a letter from a volunteer at the Quaker Aid Society in Raleigh, North Carolina. She has seen Lula, Solomon, and Esther at a freedmen's camp. They said they were headed to Philadelphia! Every day, Addy bundles up and trudges through the icy cold streets until it gets too dark to see, tirelessly visiting aid societies, churches, and hospitals.

One evening, when she should be heading home for supper, Addy decides to make one more stop at the First Baptist Church. In the twilight, she sees the shadowy shape of a woman helping a child down the steps. Esther and Auntie Lula have come to freedom at last.

Images of children's fashions in *Godey's Lady's Book* helped designer Holly Easland create Addy's Winter Coat.

The Importance of Education

While Addy is focused on her whole family being reunited, she discovers that Sarah's family is struggling financially. As a result, Sarah has to quit school to work so she can contribute to the family's income. Connie shares, "Writing about Sarah having to leave school was emotional for me. Having grown up poor, one of nine children, I very much knew that in order to escape poverty, I needed to be educated. My parents, who grew up in the segregated South during the Great Depression, knew this and encouraged me and my siblings to pursue education."

Addy wears this wool coat as she searches the Philadelphia streets for Uncle Solomon, Auntie Lula, and Esther.

The girls in this family photo are wearing coats similar to Addy's.

Addy's voice is loud and clear as she reads the Emancipation Proclamation.

The rosette on Addy's sash features a portrait of President Abraham Lincoln.

Addy's Patriotic Party Dress came with a passage from the Emancipation Proclamation on a scroll.

The Emancipation Proclamation

...I do order and declare that all persons held as slaves within said designated States and parts of States are, and henceforward shall be, free....

Done at the city of Washington, the first day of January, in the year of our Lord one thousand eight hundred and sixty-three....

By the President:
Abraham Lincoln

Pass It On

Two days before Christmas, Auntie Lula dies. Addy is supposed to read the Emancipation Proclamation at church, but she doesn't think she can. Her dream of having her whole family together in freedom will never come true. Momma comforts her, reminding Addy why she gave her the cowrie shell necklace: "This shell was to remind you that we are linked to the people in our past forever. They live in our hearts. Their lives, and their strength and courage, are part of us even though they gone."

Momma's words give Addy strength. That night, she stands before the congregation and reads the powerful words that changed her family's life forever. When she finishes at midnight, the church bells ring out and the congregation explodes with joy.

Addy stands on tiptoe, trying to find her family. She feels a small hand slip into hers: Esther's.

> **"Where we going, Esther?"** Addy asked. Esther smiled back. "Home," she said. "That's right", Addy said. **"We going home together."**

CHANGES FOR ADDY

Josefina
Montoya
Meet Josefina
An American Girl
~ Book One ~
18
24
The American Girls Collection®
Ya viene amaneciendo, ya la luz del día nos dio. Levántate de mañana, mira que ya amaneció.
María Francisca Montoya
María Josefina Montoya

Making Josefina

Although Josefina didn't debut until 1997, the idea of a character from the American Southwest was part of Pleasant's vision from the very beginning. After Addy's launch, discussions began to make this vision a reality. Pleasant encouraged the staff to research possible locations from California to Texas. Story editor Peg Ross had done her graduate study in anthropology in New Mexico and wanted to highlight the deep history of the state. Santa Fe was founded even before the Pilgrims landed in Massachusetts! Pleasant and Valerie Tripp were both enchanted by the region's rich blend of cultures and languages, and soon New Mexico became a natural choice for Josefina's setting. "The buildings are earth-covered adobe, smooth, plain, austere from the outside," Valerie recalls. "You have to go inside to see the bright colors, hear music and laughter, smell delicious cooking aromas. So, too, Josefina is reserved, shy, and quiet until you get to know her and see that on the inside she is full of music and mischief and life."

Valerie spent so much time in the Santa Fe Public Library that there was a seat in the Southwest Reading Room she began to think of as her own. She read books by New Mexican writers such as *We Fed Them Cactus* by Fabiola Cabeza de Baca, and she relied on works by Marc Simmons, Tey Diana Rebolledo, and Orlando Romero, who later became advisers on the Josefina series. She especially loved reading the original typewritten onion-skin manuscripts of the WPA project interviews from the 1930s. The WPA interviewers collected just the sort of information Valerie was after: home remedies, lullabies, gossip, recipes, folktales, life stories, prayers, and sayings.

Valerie loved learning by doing, too. She took cooking lessons in Santa Fe, and she visited museums such as El Rancho de Las Golondrinas, La Hacienda de los Martinez, the Palace of the Governors, and the Wheelwright Museum. She went to several pueblos for festivals and dances, and visited weavers, dyers, sheepherders, and farmers. She immersed herself in the material culture and music of the time.

> "The music alone was immensely important and organic to the story because **I used lots of musical imagery as a metaphor in Josefina's stories:** Josefina and her sisters struggle to live in harmony after the death of their mother."
>
> VALERIE TRIPP

A sketch and the final painting by Jean-Paul Tibbles capture the joy that Josefina feels when she hears music.

The sketch by Valerie Hodgson and illustration by Mike Wimmer for Josefina's home, part of Josefina's Scenes & Settings

Josefina's Advisory Board

An esteemed panel of historians, scholars, curators, and experts guided the creative development of every aspect of Josefina's stories, illustrations, and products:

- **Rosalinda B. Barrera**, Professor of Curriculum and Instruction, New Mexico State University, Las Cruces
- **Juan R. García**, Professor of History and Associate Dean, College of Social and Behavioral Sciences, University of Arizona, Tucson
- **Sandra Jaramillo**, Director, Archives and Historical Services, New Mexico State Records Center and Archives, Santa Fe
- **Skip Keith Miller**, Co-Director/Curator, Kit Carson Historic Museums, Taos, New Mexico
- **Felipe Mirabal**, former Curator of Collections, El Rancho de Las Golondrinas, Santa Fe, New Mexico
- **Tey Diana Rebolledo**, Professor of Spanish, University of New Mexico, Albuquerque
- **Orlando Romero**, Senior Research Librarian, Palace of the Governors, Santa Fe, New Mexico
- **Marc Simmons**, Historian, Cerrillos, New Mexico

"Time and time again, they gently steered me, kept my course true, and educated me. The advisers instructed me on the large cultural and historical issues and on the subtleties, too, such as comportment, forms of address, tone, status of children, attitude, and etiquette. All those things contributed essential details about life in Josefina's time."—Valerie Tripp

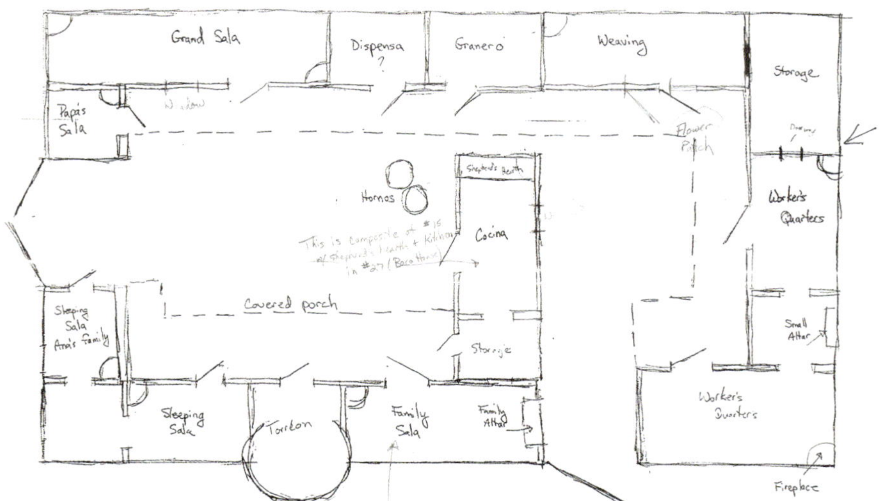

Historical researcher Kathy Borkowski made this drawing of the interior of Josefina's house to guide the planning for the illustrations and to keep them consistent.

The advisers for Josefina met regularly to review manuscripts and product prototypes. Above, Tey Diana Rebolledo examines a petticoat for Josefina's school outfit.

The team relied heavily on Marc Simmons, a prominent historian of New Mexico and leading expert on the Spanish colonial period. He also lived in a hand-built adobe home without running water or electricity, much like Josefina's world.

Advisory board members Felipe Mirabal and Juan García review Josefina's Christmas Dress. Felipe helped guide the portrayal of religion and celebrations in the stories, often emphasizing the quiet, steady faith characteristic of Josefina's family and culture.

Abuelas

Valerie relied on another essential group of people as she developed Josefina's stories. She spent many hours talking with elderly Hispanic women whose families had lived in New Mexico for generations. "When I visited, the women would tell me family stories. They'd show me how their mothers and grandmothers had taught them to fold laundry, and they'd talk about cooking, sewing, and teaching children prayers. Every time, after a while, the women would show me an album or a room full of family pictures, and they'd talk about the family members with love and frankness.

"I drank it all in—the stories, the lessons, and the expressions. I quoted some directly in Josefina's stories. For example, one expression was 'Don't make your thread too long or the devil will catch on to the end of it.' Almost every time, in addition to what they were telling me, the women showed me what was important. Invariably, while we were talking, a teenager would amble in, say, 'Hi, Abuelita,' and poke around the refrigerator."

> "I was seeing **the importance of family and the easy flow of generations,** unchanged since Josefina's time."
>
> VALERIE TRIPP

Illustration above and family illustrations on opposite page by Jean-Paul Tibbles

A young girl learns how to wash wool at El Rancho de Las Golondrinas.

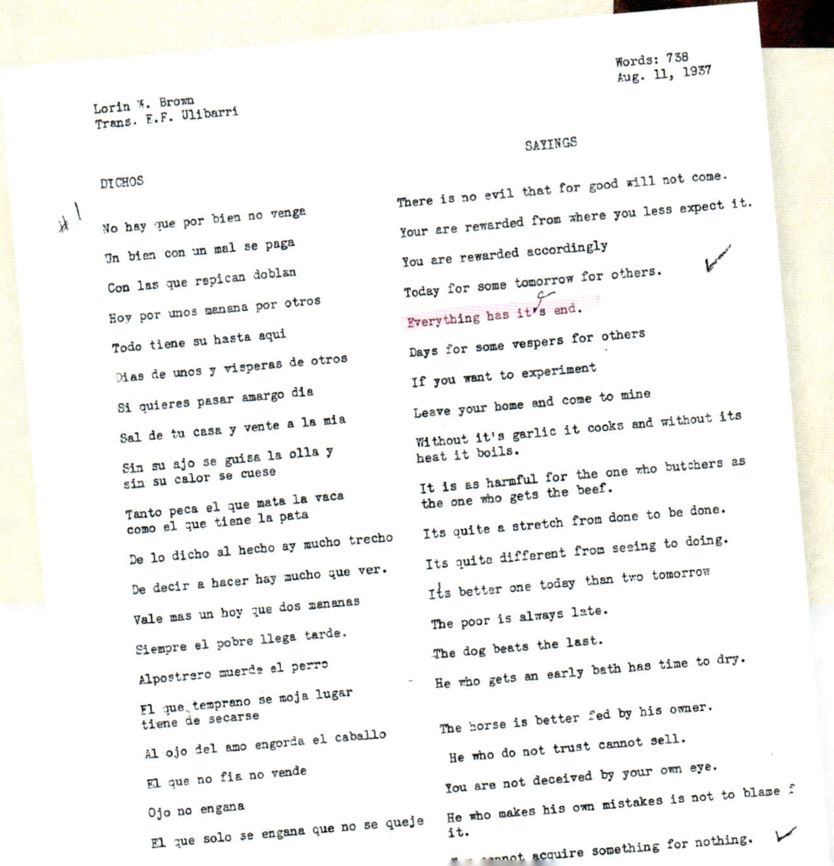

Lorin W. Brown
Trans. E.F. Ulibarri

Words: 738
Aug. 11, 1937

DICHOS	SAYINGS
No hay que por bien no venge	There is no evil that for good will not come.
Un bien con un mal se paga	Your are rewarded from where you less expect it.
Con las que repican doblan	You are rewarded accordingly
Hoy por unos menana por otros	Today for some tomorrow for others.
Todo tiene su hasta aqui	Everything has it's end.
Dias de unos y visperas de otros	Days for some vespers for others
Si quieres pasar amargo dia	If you want to experiment
Sal de tu casa y vente a la mia	Leave your home and come to mine
Sin su ajo se guisa la olla y sin su calor se cuese	Without it's garlic it cooks and without its heat it boils.
Tanto peca el que mata la vaca como el que tiene la pata	It is as harmful for the one who butchers as the one who gets the beef.
De lo dicho al hecho ay mucho trecho	Its quite a stretch from done to be done.
De decir a hacer hay mucho que ver.	Its quite different from seeing to doing.
Vale mas un hoy que dos mananas	Its better one today than two tomorrow
Siempre el pobre llega tarde.	The poor is always late.
Alpostrero muerde el perro	The dog beats the last.
El que temprano se moja lugar tiene de secarse	He who gets an early bath has time to dry.
Al ojo del amo engorda el caballo	The horse is better fed by his owner.
El que no fia no vende	He who do not trust cannot sell.
Ojo no engana	You are not deceived by your own eye.
El que solo se engana que no se queje	He who makes his own mistakes is not to blame for it.
	... cannot acquire something for nothing.

A dicho is a little saying that brings universal truths down to a simple, memorable, bite-sized phrase.

ABUELITO

ABUELITA

PAPÁ

TÍA DOLORES

CLARA

FRANCISCA

ANA

TÍA MAGDALENA

Family and Faith

Hispanic families like the Montoyas relied on their strong faith in God to help them endure the hardships of their lives. The Catholic saints were very important to them; they asked saints for help with daily struggles, large and small, and they thanked the saints for their blessings. Every church and almost every room in the house had images of saints, called santos. The Montoya family prays at an altar in their sala, or parlor, at the beginning of each day and before they bid one another good night.

"In writing Josefina's stories, I was very supported by having been raised as a Catholic," Valerie recalls. "The rites of passage, the ceremonies, the words of the Mass, the songs, the traditions, the sacraments, the holy days of obligation, the stories of the saints—all shaped me, all were organic parts of my own childhood."

Above, a traditional carved figure of a saint, called a bulto, by artist Ernie Lujan. At right, a painted retablo from the late 1800s. Both artworks depict San José, or Saint Joseph.

The Colors of Josefina's World

Santa Fe is in northern New Mexico—known as "the Land of Enchantment." From the brilliant turquoise sky to sun-baked orange-red adobe, from the golden-ocher sunsets to foothills covered in dark green pines, the colors of Josefina's world are unforgettable.

The natural pigments shown at right guided all the colors in Josefina's world.

This color palette, created by New Mexican artist Charles Carrillo for Josefina's project, shows natural pigments and finishes available in the early 1800s.

The colors of the sisters' clothing were informed by the palette of natural colors at left. In the drawing below, notice that Josefina had the placeholder name "Maria" at this time.

Meet Josefina, written by Valerie Tripp and illustrated by Jean-Paul Tibbles, published in 1997

Meet Josefina

As *Meet Josefina* opens, we learn that Josefina and her family are grieving the recent loss of Mamá. Josefina cherishes a carved wooden box that had belonged to Mamá. She calls it her "memory box" because inside she keeps things that remind her of Mamá. Whenever Josefina opens it, the scent of Mamá's lavender soap and the sight of the primroses Mamá had loved give her comfort.

Although not overtly stated in the stories, Mamá's death symbolizes Mexico's recent independence from its historical and cultural parent, Spain. Josefina's quest for healing—for herself and her family—drives her character arc, storylines, and themes.

An early draft of *Meet Josefina* shows the shift from the placeholder name "María Luisa" to "María Josefina." In Mexican culture, it was traditional for girls to have "María" before their given names in reverence to the Virgin Mary.

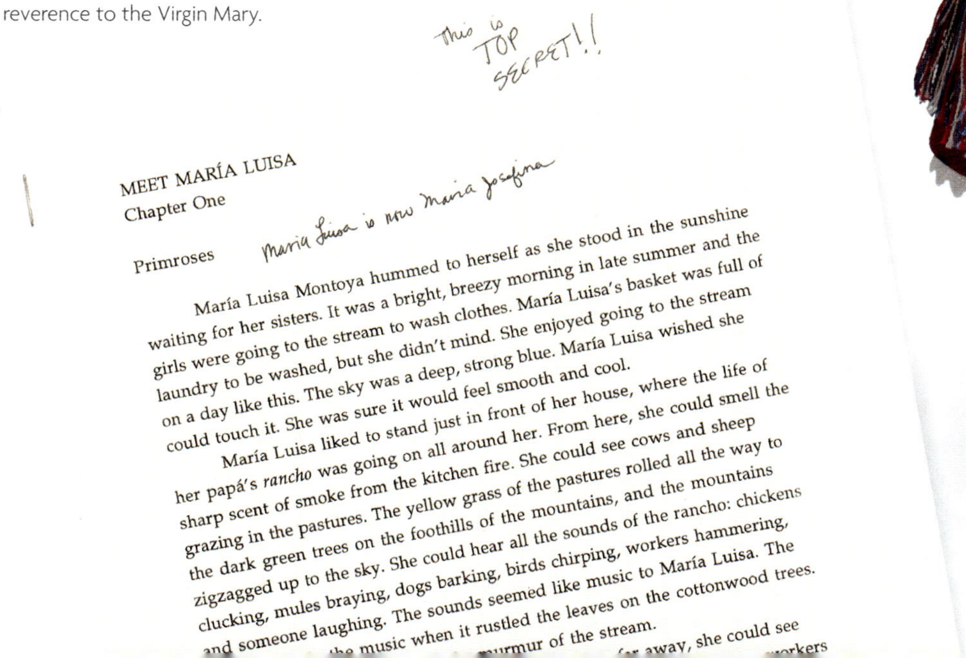

This is TOP SECRET!!

MEET MARÍA LUISA
Chapter One

Primroses   María Luisa is now María Josefina

María Luisa Montoya hummed to herself as she stood in the sunshine waiting for her sisters. It was a bright, breezy morning in late summer and the girls were going to the stream to wash clothes. María Luisa's basket was full of laundry to be washed, but she didn't mind. She enjoyed going to the stream on a day like this. The sky was a deep, strong blue. María Luisa wished she could touch it. She was sure it would feel smooth and cool.

María Luisa liked to stand just in front of her house, where the life of her papá's *rancho* was going on all around her. From here, she could smell the sharp scent of smoke from the kitchen fire. She could see cows and sheep grazing in the pastures. The yellow grass of the pastures rolled all the way to the dark green trees on the foothills of the mountains, and the mountains zigzagged up to the sky. She could hear all the sounds of the rancho: chickens clucking, mules braying, dogs barking, birds chirping, workers hammering, and someone laughing. The sounds seemed like music to María Luisa. The ... music when it rustled the leaves on the cottonwood trees. ... murmur of the stream. ... away, she could see ... workers

Color outfit illustration at left by Judy Smith; cover sketch below by Jean-Paul Tibbles

Fabric options considered for Josefina's outfit

Josefina's Accessories consist of a long, fringed rebozo; a garnet pendant from Mexico City; and a tooled leather pouch that holds her embroidered hankie and jola coin.

Paintings, such as the one above, gave designer Holly Easland inspiration for Josefina's fashions.

Sketches above by Holly Easland

Healing and Harmony

Josefina's stories are set in 1824—when New Mexico was part of the country of Mexico, which had just won its independence from Spain. Although Josefina is actually a Mexican citizen, the advisory board felt comfortable calling her an "American girl" because the cultures of both Josefina's Hispanic family and her Native neighbors are an integral part of America today. This timing for Josefina's stories also includes the arrival of the first americanos, or "Yankee" traders, who traveled west from Missouri along the Santa Fe Trail. The changes underway in Josefina's era left deep imprints not only on New Mexico but on the Southwest and the United States as a whole.

> "In 1824 in New Mexico, the government was in chaos and disharmony. So I made Josefina's family be in disharmony also, because her mother has died. **Josefina's quest in the books is for healing and harmony, just as New Mexico was trying to find political healing and harmony.**"
>
> VALERIE TRIPP

When Josefina's grandfather arrives from Mexico City with his trading caravan, he brings a surprise that will soon change all their lives: their mother's sister, Tía Dolores, who introduces new ideas and fresh ways of doing things.

Art director Jane Varda suggested that Jean-Paul use himself as the model for Patrick O'Toole, the scout for an American wagon train whom Josefina meets in *Josefina Saves the Day.*

Jean-Paul Tibbles

Illustrator Jean-Paul Tibbles caught the attention of Josefina's art director, Jane Varda, when she saw his illustration for the cover of *Becoming Little Women*. She contacted him, and he painted a stunning sample piece for Josefina that showed meticulous attention to historical detail. When Pleasant saw his work, she quickly agreed he was the right choice. Jean-Paul worked from his studio in Great Britain but spent weeks in Santa Fe and traveled throughout New Mexico, studying the people, the architecture, the landscape, and—most importantly—the light.

Jean-Paul has had four paintings shown at the National Portrait Gallery in London. "I'm still working on portrait commissions today," he shares, "which, over the years, has taken me around the United States, Europe, and the UK." He regularly has work accepted by the Royal Society of Portrait Painters, and his paintings have been accepted seven times into the Portrait Society of America's International Portrait Competition.

Marie-Louise is a portrait of Jean-Paul's daughter, Lou. She often served as a body model for Josefina and is wearing Josefina's camisa in this painting.

Tía Dolores insisted on bringing her piano all the way from Mexico City. And no wonder—it's a beauty, with inlaid trim and fancy metal ornamentation. Just like pianos in Josefina's day, girls could lift the lid of the English Square Piano and actually play the keys.

Florecita

One of the most memorable villains in the American Girl canon is . . . a goat. Florecita is the meanest, bossiest goat in the herd—and Josefina's nemesis. She pokes Josefina with her horns, knocks her down, and—in the scene below—eats the primroses she has gathered. Later, Florecita gobbles up a beautiful bouquet Josefina made for Tía Dolores. When the goat eats the flowers in Mamá's precious garden, Josefina's anger is greater than her fear, and she stands up to Florecita for the first time. By the end of the series, Josefina is a girl no goat—or person—can intimidate.

Tía Dolores brings a very grown-up gift to Josefina from Mexico City.

Josefina Learns a Lesson, written by Valerie Tripp and illustrated by Jean-Paul Tibbles, published in 1997

Josefina Learns a Lesson

Tía Dolores

Just as Josefina and her sisters hoped, Tía Dolores comes to live on the Montoya rancho to teach and guide them. With a sigh of relief, the girls are grateful that life can now return to the sure and steady rhythm it had when Mamá was alive. But as the agent of change throughout Josefina's stories, Tía Dolores gently nudges the girls out of their old, familiar ways, which is especially difficult for Josefina and Francisca, the two sisters most opposite in temperament. While Francisca chafes against all the extra work Tía Dolores assigns, Josefina has a hard time mustering the courage to be as brave as Tía Dolores believes she can be.

Josefina's sash is the color of a natural dye called cochineal, made from insects that live on the prickly pear cactus.

Cover sketch below by Jean-Paul Tibbles; color outfit illustration at right by Judy Smith

A color sketch for the weaving shown in the illustration below

Blankets for Sheep

The sisters aren't sure what to make of the bold business idea Tía Dolores presents to Papá: weaving blankets to trade for new sheep to replace those lost in a flood. Papá had never discussed business with Mamá, or with any woman, before. Francisca huffs about waking earlier to fit in this additional task. Josefina doesn't know how to weave and isn't sure that she can, but she's eager to try. "Well," Papá says to Tía Dolores, "if all your weavers are as eager as my little Josefina, you'll turn the wool into blankets and the blankets into sheep in no time!"

Churro sheep, some of which have four horns, were brought to what is now New Mexico from Spain in the 1500s.

Josefina learns to weave on a small Navajo loom.

Josefina goes on an expedition to gather wildflowers, herbs, roots, barks, berries, and leaves to make dyes to color wool for weaving. She brings a pottery canteen filled with water, along with tortillas, squash, onions, fresh goat cheese, and a ripe plum for lunch.

A Troubling Question

When Papá agrees with Tía Dolores's idea of teaching the girls to read and write—something Mamá did not know how to do—it's the last straw for Francisca. In the middle of the night, Josefina hears a small noise in the courtyard, and she finds Francisca crying. Francisca refuses to learn to read and write—not because the lessons are more work, but because she believes all of Tía Dolores's changes are making them forget Mamá. Josefina doesn't want to believe this is true, and yet a deep fear starts to grow within her as she wonders if Francisca is right. Is learning to read and write disloyal to Mamá?

> "Many times I received letters from readers who had a new stepmother, asking me was it okay to love her, too? **Those letters inspired Josefina's situation of being torn between loyalty to Mamá and affection for Tía Dolores.**"
>
> VALERIE TRIPP

Color outfit illustration by Judy Smith

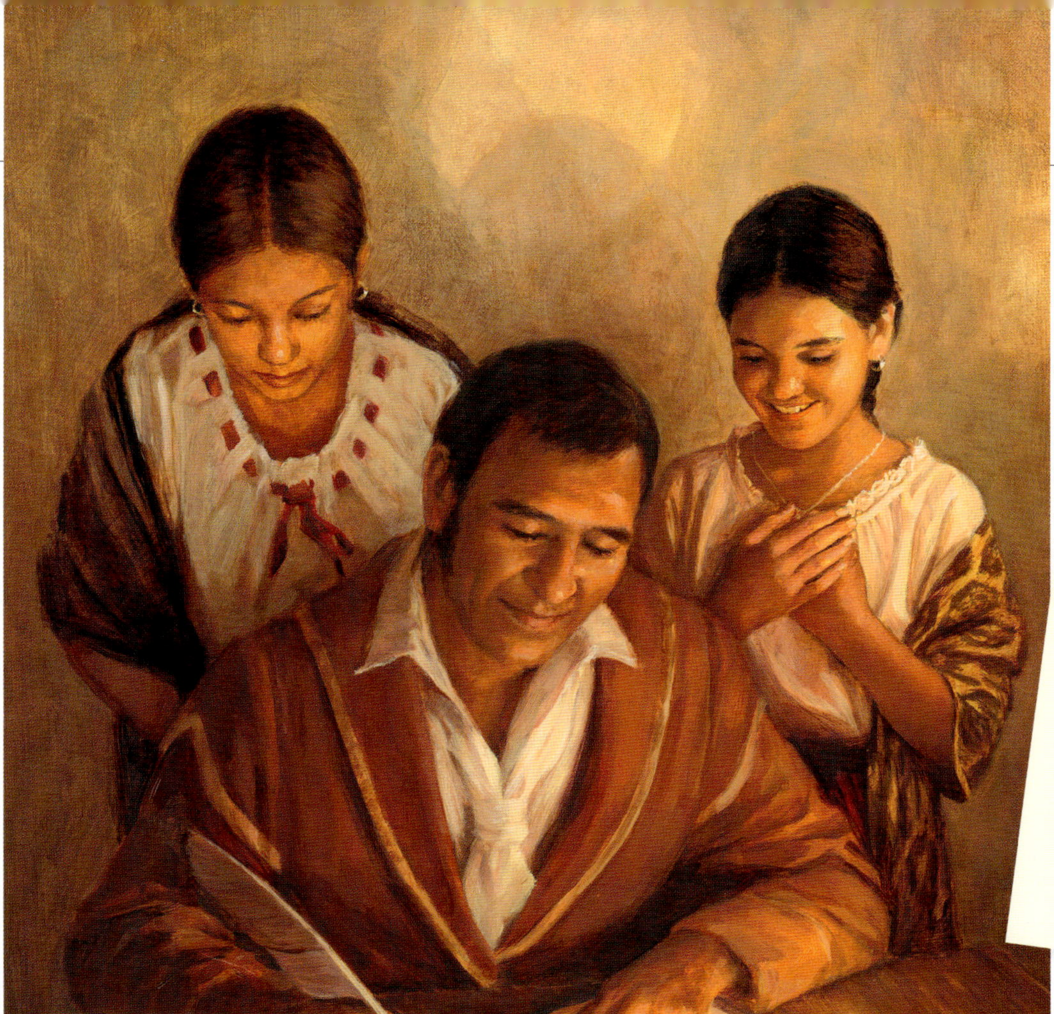

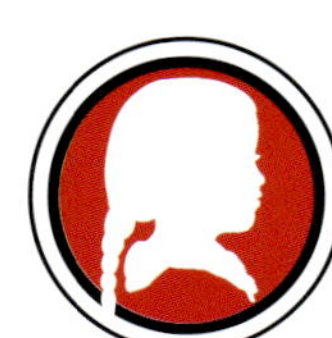

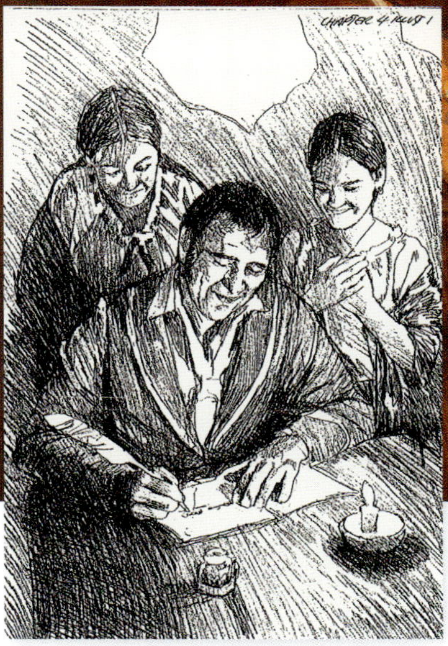

Papá shows Josefina and Clara his fancy signature.

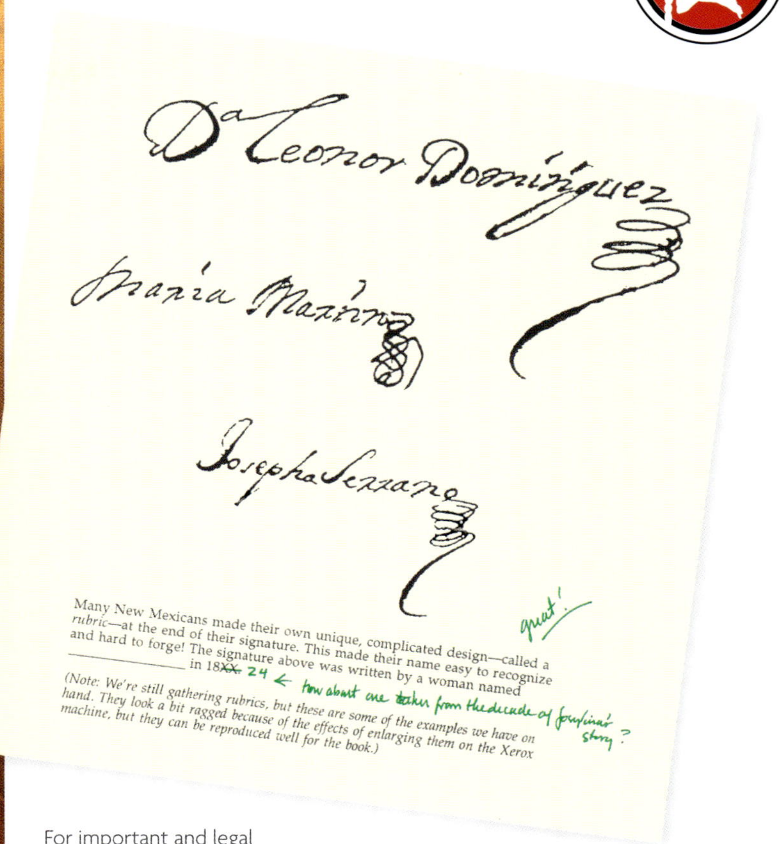
Dª Leonor Domínguez

María Marín

Josepha Serrano

Many New Mexicans made their own unique, complicated design—called a *rubric*—at the end of their signature. This made their name easy to recognize and hard to forge! The signature above was written by a woman named ______________ in 18~~XX.~~ 24 ← how about one taken from the decade of Josefina's story?

great!

(Note: We're still gathering rubrics, but these are some of the examples we have on hand. They look a bit ragged because of the effects of enlarging them on the Xerox machine, but they can be reproduced well for the book.)

For important and legal documents, people in Josefina's time signed their names with a rúbrica, or flourish, that made their signatures difficult to copy.

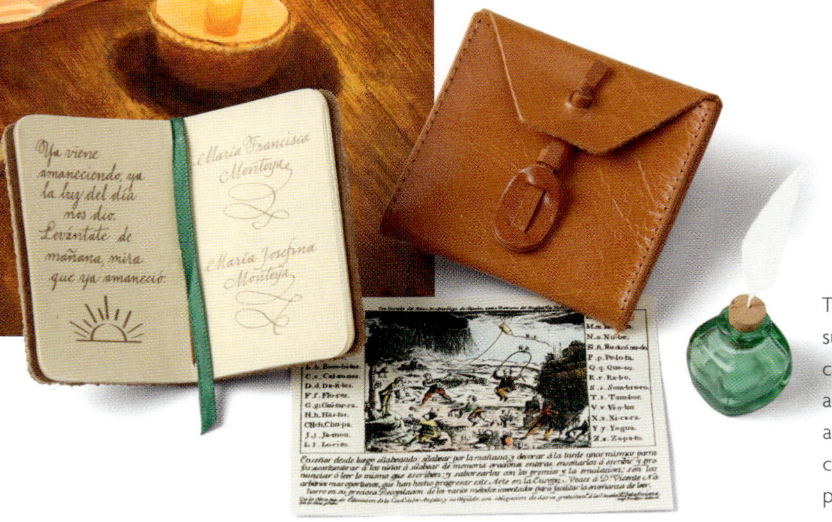

Tía Dolores brings books and writing supplies from Mexico City—a speller called a silabario, a ledger, a quill pen, and a glass inkwell—and gives Josefina and her sisters lessons. The leather cuaderno, or notebook, is filled with poems, proverbs, songs, and sayings.

"Pleasant did my heart proud by saying that her favorite American Girl book is *Josefina Learns a Lesson*, because in it there is a passage that articulates something she had not realized, but loves. In that passage, Josefina expresses to Tía Dolores some reluctance and concern about learning to read. In reply, to encourage Josefina, Tía Dolores says to her, **'Reading is a way to hold on to the past, to travel to places you have never been, and to learn about worlds beyond your own time or experience.'**"

VALERIE TRIPP

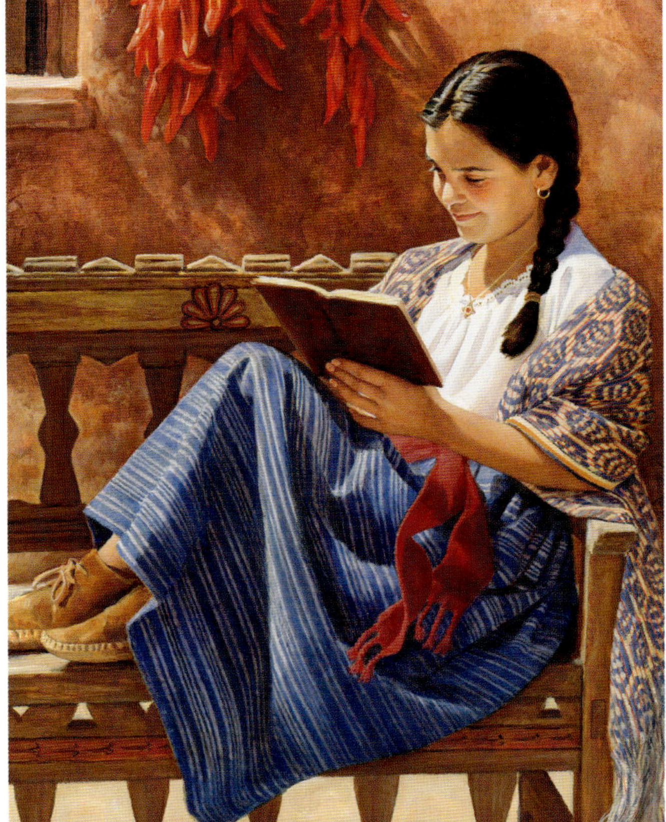

Mamá's Words

Bit by bit, Josefina realizes she is forgetting Mamá's poems, songs, and prayers, which she once knew by heart. Tía Dolores soothes Josefina's heartache with a treasure she keeps hidden in a secret compartment of her writing desk: a little book, bound in soft brown leather. As Josefina turns the pages, she stops at a drawing of four white doves. Tía Dolores reads the words that Josefina feared she had forgotten:

> "Behold four little white doves perched on a rosemary bush. They were saying to each other, **"There's no love like the first love."**"
>
> *Josefina Learns a Lesson*

Tía Dolores's writing desk came up El Camino Real all the way from Mexico City. Designed by Valerie Hodgson, it looks like a plain box on the outside but opens to reveal stunning artwork inside.

An eighteenth-century Mexican writing desk open to show its beauty (above) and closed for travel (below). It has eight drawers you can see, and eight hidden drawers, too!

Artwork for the interior of Josefina's Writing Desk

Josefina's Surprise, written by Valerie Tripp and illustrated by Jean-Paul Tibbles, published in 1997

Josefina's Surprise

Josefina's second Christmas without Mamá marks the beginning of her ability to let go of sharp sadness and feel her grief start to soften. Still, Josefina senses Mamá's presence everywhere: in the chiles she delivers to neighbors, just as Mamá once did; in the voices of Mamá's friends as they praise her love of flowers and her skill with colcha embroidery; and, most achingly, in the beauty of the music at Christmastime.

When Tía Dolores asks Josefina if she would like to play the part of María in Las Posadas, the traditional reenactment of Mary and Joseph's search for an inn on the first Christmas night, Josefina wants to with all her heart. But she's just not ready. Josefina's older sister Clara is struggling, too. When Josefina asks her about the doll named Niña that Mamá had made, a doll passed down to each sister when she turns eight years old, Clara claims she cannot find it. It was Josefina's turn for the doll last year, but without Mamá, it wasn't passed down. This Christmas, Josefina is determined to find Niña so the tradition will continue and the doll can be hers. Josefina looks in every room, in every trunk and cupboard, under every bed, but she cannot find Niña.

Art director Jane Varda tried out different items for Josefina to hold on the cover of *Josefina's Surprise*.

Designers considered this pattern as a bedcover for Josefina, but ultimately chose a hand-loomed Rio Grande blanket.

Josefina delivers ristras, or strings of red chiles, to Señora Sánchez to flavor her famous stew. In return, Señora Sánchez gives Josefina a plump chicken in a bentwood cage.

Josefina's bed is a New Mexican interpretation of a European sleigh bed.

Josefina's Chest has detailed carving, rustic hardware, and mortise-and-tenon joints fashioned just as they would have been in 1824.

Mending

Tía Dolores sees that the sisters are struggling, and in her ever-gentle but persistent way, she guides the girls as Mamá would have. After a tragic flood, the family finds that the altar cloth Mamá had embroidered for the church has been nearly ruined. Tía Dolores slowly and patiently leads the girls through the steps to repair what they think is unmendable: gently washing the cloth, carefully drying and ironing it, and finally working together to make the cloth—and themselves—whole once again. On Christmas Eve, as Josefina goes to the bedroom to get ready for church, she finds the surprise she's been longing for: Niña! Clara admits she hid Niña because the doll was her last gift from Mamá. Josefina kindly says, "We'll share Niña. She'll sleep between us from now on."

Clara makes a beautiful new dress for Niña that matches Josefina's own Christmas dress, designed by Holly Easland.

A fine example of New Mexican colcha from Josefina's time

Color outfit illustration by Judy Smith

Tía Dolores shares a sewing diary that shows all the latest styles from Mexico City. Each sister chooses a pattern and sews her own dress from material that Tía Dolores has given them.

On the last night of Las Posadas, Josefina finds the courage to play María.

Happy Birthday, Josefina!, written by Valerie Tripp and illustrated by Jean-Paul Tibbles, published in 1998

Happy Birthday, Josefina!

An alternate idea for the cover showing Sombrita on Josefina's lap

Josefina's birthday story marks a turning point in her character growth. At the start of the series, Josefina is timid. She's afraid of mean goats, thunderstorms, and singing in front of a crowd. "But just as my readers are growing and changing every day," says Valerie, "Josefina grows in bravery, strength, and self-confidence, while never losing her gentle thoughtfulness." Nowhere does Josefina's strong sense of empathy come through more clearly than in the scene where Florecita, the mean goat who bullied her through the first three books, is giving birth. The goat is in trouble. As Josefina looks down on her enemy, watching her breathing grow slower and weaker, she feels sorry for Florecita and is filled with compassion. When Florecita dies, the fear Josefina has felt for so many years passes away, too.

But with every ending comes a new beginning, and this story brings the sweet arrival of Sombrita, Florecita's orphaned baby goat. Josefina wants to care for Sombrita, but Papá worries that the tiny goat may not survive, and that Josefina's heart will break. Josefina is sure in her answer: "When any of God's creatures is sick or weak we have to try to make it better, don't we?" As she holds out her arms for the little goat, Josefina's journey toward becoming a curandera—a healer—begins.

Blending knowledge of natural remedies, health, and faith, curanderas have been part of New Mexican culture for centuries.

Fun with Mud

In this scene, Josefina and her sisters go to the village to replaster the church, a yearly springtime chore. She is small enough to climb onto the church roof to help spread a new layer of mud plaster. As her sisters call to her to tuck her skirt up so it doesn't get muddy, Josefina realizes that they envy her. *Almost ten is a wonderful age to be*, she thinks, while exuberantly sloshing through the mud and cheerfully ignoring their advice.

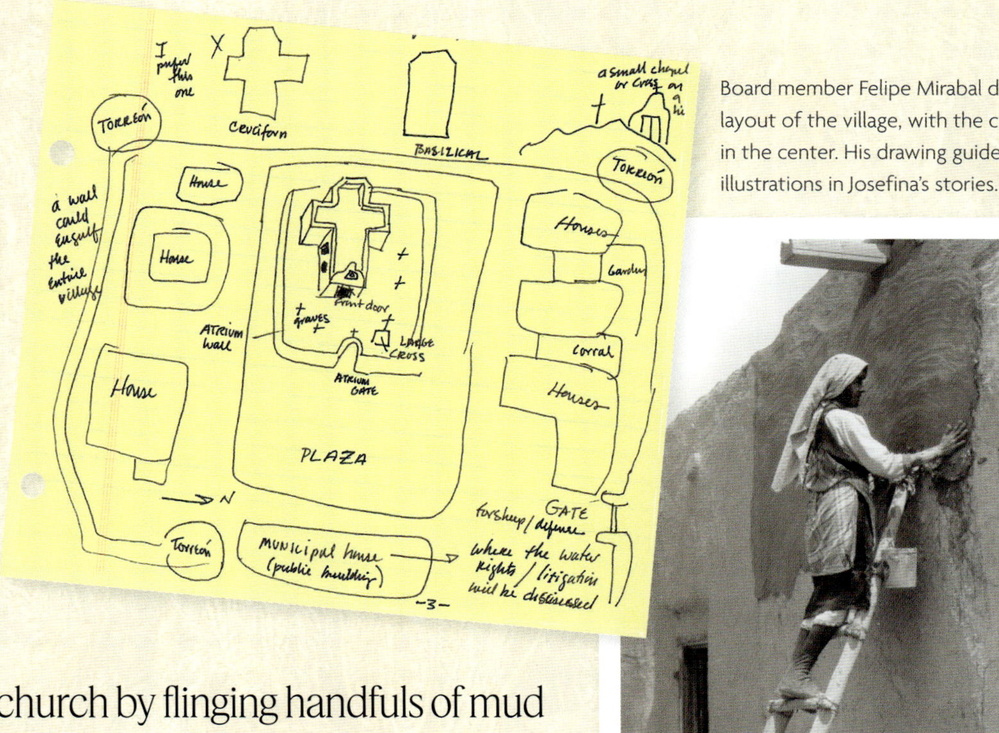

Board member Felipe Mirabal drew the layout of the village, with the church in the center. His drawing guided the illustrations in Josefina's stories.

> “One day, I helped replaster an adobe church by flinging handfuls of mud on the wall and then smoothing them flat. **That was research, too, because replastering is a chore that Josefina and her sisters would have done.**”
>
> VALERIE TRIPP

Hispanic and Pueblo villages both used adobe construction. This Pueblo woman is replastering a wall in the early 1900s.

Historical researcher Kathy Borkowski's goat research guided the development of Florecita and Sombrita.

San Clemente Island goats

Goats

Terms: Female, doe, or nanny goat. Male, buck, or billy goat. Not sure of usage in Spanish Colonial period. Most books refrain from using the nicknames, billy goat or nanny goat.

Usage: Goats used for milk, hides (for rugs), and cheese (soft, white cheese). Also favorite meal was *cabrito* or roast kid.

Horns: any goat can have horns, male or female. Unlike deer, are not hormone related--that is, male deer grow them each season and lose them each season.

Hooves: all goats have split, or cloven hooves, for better climbing.

Grazing: goats prefer a large amount of variety in their diet. Eat many different weeds, also like paper.

Mating: Goats generally mate from late summer to late winter. Doe gives 2-3 kids about 5 months later. When left alone, a doe will nurse for 6-

Josefina names the baby goat Sombrita, "little shadow," because she usually follows Josefina everywhere. Sombrita wears a little silver bell so Josefina can find her if she wanders off.

Courage

Josefina's talent for healing comes into sharp focus when she has to face one of the greatest dangers in New Mexico's dry landscape: a rattlesnake! Josefina is visiting the nearby pueblo, accompanying her father while he visits his longtime trading partner, Esteban, who has a granddaughter named Mariana. She and Josefina have been friends since they were little. While the grown-ups discuss their trade, the girls take their dolls to the stream and make boats for them. Sombrita tags along but is soon nowhere to be found. The girls eventually find her—practically nose to nose with an angry snake!

As Josefina inches slowly toward Sombrita, Mariana stands by with a rock. When Josefina picks up Sombrita, Mariana throws the rock. The snake lunges—and bites her. Luckily, Josefina has learned about healing roots and herbs from her godmother, Tía Magdalena, and she knows that globe mallow root will draw out the venom. She crushes the root and applies it again and again to Mariana's wound until slowly the color comes back to Mariana's face and her breathing becomes steady and even once again.

These Pueblo girls are wearing woven dresses called mantas that are fastened over the right shoulder and tied with a colorful braided sash, similar to Mariana's dress.

The Pueblo People

The multiple terraces of the houses at Zuni Pueblo in 1903

The research for Josefina's stories took the development team to several Pueblo communities outside of Santa Fe to better understand what life might have been like for a Pueblo girl living in Josefina's time. The many Pueblo nations have lived in what is now New Mexico for thousands of years. In the seventeenth century, the Spanish enslaved many Pueblo people and used their labor to build churches and ranchos. Eventually, the Pueblo people rose up against this treatment. By Josefina's time, Pueblo and Spanish families had coexisted peacefully for many years.

Pueblo people are not a single group, but rather distinct communities that share a similar way of life. In Josefina's time, they lived in complex, multistory adobe buildings, created beautiful pottery and weavings, and farmed the land and raised livestock, including sheep and horses. Each village had its own language, government, and customs. Josefina's family might have visited the Cochiti, Kewa, or Tesuque Pueblos, all within a day's ride from the rancho. While they were neighbors and often traded goods, these communities still lived separately and had different traditions and ways of life. Today, Pueblo people live primarily in New Mexico and still value their traditional ways while living in modern homes both on and off their Pueblo reservations.

For protection, pueblos had no exterior doors on the ground floor. If there were intruders, the ladders would be pulled up so no one could enter. Illustration by Susan Moore

Heather Northrop designed Josefina's embroidered gold mantón, or shawl. Both the mantón and delicate black fan are treasures from Mamá.

Saint's Day Celebration

In Hispanic families like Josefina's, children celebrate their saint's day instead of their birthday. In the Catholic Church, each saint is honored on a specific day of the year. Josefina was born on March 19, the feast day of San José. On the morning of Josefina's saint's day, her family awakens her with a lovely morning song:

> **"On the day you were born**
> **All the beautiful flowers were born,**
> The sun and moon were born,
> And all the stars."

HAPPY BIRTHDAY, JOSEFINA!

Early designs and Josefina's birthday dress by Heather Northrop

Josefina's eldest sister, Ana, makes cookies called bizcochitos to eat before breakfast; Francisca decorates the statue of San José on the family altar with flowers; and even practical Clara has a surprise for Josefina: a dainty pair of turquoise-blue slippers to hand down to her. Papá's gift is the best of all: rattles from a rattlesnake, a memento from his own run-in with a rattlesnake as a boy. At Josefina's fiesta, he proudly tells the story of Josefina's own quick thinking and courage, so everyone will know and remember her bravery—and the moment she became a healer—for generations to come.

The redware pottery jar holds an apricot branch—a sure sign of spring.

This flat rendering shows the decorative details of Josefina's pitcher.

For this special saint's day celebration, Tía Dolores bakes a fancy loaf of bread, and Josefina's friend Mariana brings a juicy melon that had been buried in sand all winter to keep it fresh.

Josefina's pitcher was inspired by the beautifully painted Mexican majolica that was prized in 1824. It features a poppy design.

Josefina Saves the Day, written by Valerie Tripp and illustrated by Jean-Paul Tibbles, published in 1998

Josefina Saves the Day

In the Santa Fe plaza, Josefina sees the U.S. flag for the first time. Its stars and stripes are so different from the Mexican flag she is used to.

Josefina's summer story broadens Josefina's contact with the world beyond New Mexico to include American traders who arrive on the newly created Santa Fe Trail from Franklin, Missouri. Josefina and her community are living through the first contact of two worlds—which will soon change both worlds profoundly. Josefina unexpectedly meets her first americano, a scout named Patrick O'Toole, on a hilltop near Abuelito's rancho. This time when Josefina encounters something unfamiliar, she's ready to face it. Instead of the shy girl from *Meet Josefina* who might have hidden or run away from someone new, here we see Josefina greet Patrick politely and confidently lead him to Abuelito's house. Once inside, Josefina takes the role of cultural guide for this young man out of his element. When Patrick tries to talk business with Abuelito right away, for instance, Josefina frowns and shakes her head to let Patrick know that's not polite. After Abuelito and Papá deem Patrick trustworthy, they arrange for him to trade Papá's mules to the americanos on Papá's behalf.

An alternate cover sketch

As Josefina plays her clay flute one sunny day, she meets an American scout named Patrick!

The Violin

Later, Patrick comes for dinner, and Abuelito regales him with tales from his travels on El Camino Real. After dinner, Patrick takes out his violin and soon has everyone clapping along to his lively tunes. When he offers his violin to Papá, the room grows quiet. Papá has not played the violin since Mamá died. He gently picks up the instrument and begins playing a song so full of longing and hope that Josefina gets chills. More than anything, she wants Patrick's violin for Papá. And so, with a boldness reminiscent of Tía Dolores, she strikes a trading deal with Patrick.

The violin, or fiddle, was a popular instrument among travelers because it was lightweight and portable.

Designer Heather Northrop tooled Josefina's vest with a floral and scroll design. The short, cropped length pairs well with an empire-waist dress, which was a fashionable style in the early 1800s.

Josefina knows that Papá's song tells a story full of longing and hope.

When Josefina and Francisca sneak out in the night to find the violin Patrick has promised them, they narrowly avoid trouble.

American Traders Arrive

Historical paintings like the one below helped the development team bring the American traders' arrival in Santa Fe to life. The Santa Fe plaza was always lively, but when traders arrived, it grew even busier, filled with new sights, sounds, and people. Many languages—Spanish, English, French, Comanche, Navajo, Apache, Ute, and several Pueblo languages, including Tewa, Keres, and Zuni—swirled through the plaza as the traders bartered.

Traders stopped just outside of Santa Fe to comb their hair and change into clean shirts before pulling into the plaza.

Josefina is enthralled by all the new sights and sounds of the plaza.

The trading route from Missouri to Santa Fe was called the Santa Fe Trail.

The americanos' covered wagons were painted red, white, and blue. The wheels are taller than Josefina.

Josefina falls in love with this fascinating American toy she sees in the Santa Fe plaza. The buildings look so different from the flat-roofed adobe ranchos of New Mexico! Patrick leaves it as a gift for Josefina, along with the violin for Papá.

Changes for Josefina, written by Valerie Tripp and illustrated by Jean-Paul Tibbles, published in 1998

Changes for Josefina

A reference sketch for Tía Dolores's fashion book from Mexico

By her final book, Josefina is no longer the same quiet, unsure girl we met at the beginning of Josefina's series. The heroine of this book has helped start a blanket-weaving business to save her family's rancho and has boldly traded with an americano. She's braved floods, storms, a deadly snake, and one particularly ornery goat. She knows how to please a crowd with her beautiful singing and delightful piano playing. And last, but far from least, she knows how to read and write. All this growth has happened in less than a year and a half, largely due to the encouragement of Tía Dolores.

This story opens with Josefina and her sisters competently and confidently preparing for a fiesta to celebrate the Feast of the Three Kings, the last day of the Christmas season. Josefina proudly shows Tía Dolores that she knows how to bake a perfect loaf of bread in the horno, and the sisters are happily making spicy stew, meat pies, bizcochitos, and tamales, all with hardly any guidance needed from Tía Dolores. That evening, the fiesta in the rancho's gran sala is one of the best they've ever had. Josefina plays a beautiful waltz on the piano, and Papá asks Tía Dolores to dance. The colorful swirl of dancers seems to fade away, and Josefina cannot take her eyes off Papá and Tía Dolores. With her whole heart, she is sure they belong together.

To create Josefina's Party Dress, designer Heather Northrop studied the fashions of women who visited Santa Fe from Mexico City wearing the latest European styles.

Baking was done in an outdoor horno to keep the heat out of the kitchen.

A sketch by Valerie Hodgson of Josefina's kitchen from Scenes & Settings

Josefina's Cocina Supplies include (clockwise from top): a stick that holds dried corn, squash, and garlic; a copper pot on a trivet; a water jar, gourd dipper, and braided ring; a mano and metate to grind corn; and chiles in a coiled basket.

Josefina and her sisters make dough in the kitchen, then take it outside to bake in an horno.

Josefina's Sarape is made of thick wool to keep her warm on wintry days. Its distinctive design is similar to the highly valued Saltillo sarapes of her time.

Fabric swatches for Josefina's Sarape

Will There Be a Wedding?

Papá is so reserved and polite that Tía Dolores believes he does not have feelings for her, and she wants to get out of the way so he can make a match. She announces that she is leaving the rancho to live with Abuelito and Abuelita in Santa Fe. Josefina cannot bear the thought of losing Tía Dolores, who has become another mother to her. She begs Papá to propose, but he believes Tía Dolores wants to start life anew and loves her too much to stop her. All seems lost, until Josefina helps deliver a letter from Papá to Tía Dolores. When a little heart-shaped milagro falls out, Josefina knows her heart's desire may come true after all.

Josefina hangs a leather pouch called a guadameco around her neck to carry Papá's letter.

Growing Up

"My 'alums,' which is what I call my now-grown-up readers, tell me that when they read Josefina's stories for the first time as a child, they loved the adventure and Josefina's beautiful clothes and learning about life on a rancho. Then when they reread Josefina's stories as an adult or read them aloud to their children, they realized that, gently and honestly, I was writing about trust, love, sacrifice, death, and immortality. **My words expressed feelings they had had when they suffered a loss, and my words comforted them.** Josefina's stories had not changed, but they had."

VALERIE TRIPP

Josefina and Clara look in on a festive fandango, the bright colors of the dancers' dresses whirling by. One day, they'll be old enough to know what it's like to be part of the dancing, like Francisca!

American Girl Place
Theater
SUPER SPORTS GEAR

American Girl Place

Pleasant devoted the first decade of the company to establishing the brand's expertise in direct mail and to building its position as one of the most successful children's publishers in the country. Her team dedicated all of its energy to creating brands that girls loved and parents trusted. Twelve years after Pleasant Company began, when the brand had grown strong enough, it was time to open American Girl Place and bring the company's products and the values they represented together in one location. "This was the last piece of the business plan I had written in the boathouse in Minocqua fourteen years earlier. The last thing on the list," Pleasant recalls.

> "I can remember the opening of American Girl Place like it was yesterday. It was so beautiful. **It was absolutely every single thing I ever dreamed it could be.** And it was so fun to see all that we had done. That wonderful team of smart, committed, hardworking people pulled this together, and **suddenly, the world knew we were there.**"
>
> PLEASANT ROWLAND

The first American Girl Place opened on November 19, 1998. It was located at 111 East Chicago Avenue, in downtown Chicago's North Michigan Avenue shopping district. At last, customers could see and touch Pleasant Company's products in person and speak with staff members face-to-face. The store reflected the past and present of American girlhood, offering a place where girls could share unforgettable experiences with their families and friends and make lasting memories.

As part of the grand opening celebration, Pleasant Company held a benefit for the Chicago Public Library Foundation to support its children's programming. In addition, each of the seventy-eight branches of the Chicago Public Library received a doll and a complete set of hardcover books from The American Girls Collection. Pleasant Company had always placed a high priority on education and literacy, so the Chicago Public Library was a natural choice for a celebration partner. Pleasant said, "Because Pleasant Company's books are the heart of what we do and are found in nearly nine out of ten public libraries throughout the country, it is a meaningful partnership for us."

To celebrate the store's opening, American Girl made a doll T-shirt (left) and a doll-sized Chicago Public Library card (right).

Welcome!

The first American Girl Place was approximately 35,000 square feet spread across three levels. On the main floor, girls could browse the bookstore—filled with the American Girl books they loved—or visit the Photo Studio to have their picture taken for the cover of a personalized souvenir issue of *American Girl* magazine.

American Girl shopping bags quickly became as recognizable as Tiffany & Co. bags—and even more numerous up and down Michigan Avenue.

The photos at left and above show the bookstore designs in progress.

Shoppers found the Photo Studio so much fun at the store that the company made one for Take Your Child to Work Day in 2009. Here, employee Lisa Bunescu's daughter, Bailey, poses with her doll.

The store's upper level celebrated contemporary girls and their interests through product lines such as American Girl Today and Bitty Baby.

The store's lower level celebrated girls of yesterday. It featured The American Girls Collection of historical books, dolls, and accessories, and it was the only place in the country where girls could see the entire collection on display.

A Peek Into the Past

A Peek Into the Past historical exhibits brought each character's world to life with authentically re-created corners of her home, allowing girls to glimpse what life was like during their favorite character's time.

AGC History Wall

Felicity

Period: 1774 - Colonial America (colonial Williamsburg)

Setting: Merriman's parlor

Season: Fall

Time of Day: Daytime

Moment: Felicity sitting at parlor window with her copybook, open to the pages of pictures of Penny (could be sitting on window seat). Her fingers are inky, and she's looking outside at Penny galloping in corral instead of practicing her penmanship. Very dreamy expression. Head tipped to one side. **Mother**, is looking over Felicity's shoulder, dismayed at her lack of progress (holding vase of flowers, candles,or teapot).

Josefina

Period: 1824 - Spanish (Mexican) colonial in Santa Fe, NM

Setting: Montoya's weaving room

Season: Summer

Time of Day: Daytime

Moment: Tia Dolores teaching Josefina to weave. Josefina seated. Tia Dolores standing. Josefina is weaving the blanket that shows the colors and features of the rancho (snow-capped mountains, flying geese, cottonwood trees). Door is open to show courtyard--horno, Mama's flower garden w/hollyhocks, evil Florecita hovering dangerously close to flowers. Big blue sky mandatory.

The art director's notes helped designers imagine each setting.

SAMANTHA

KIRSTEN

MOLLY

ADDY

FELICITY

JOSEFINA

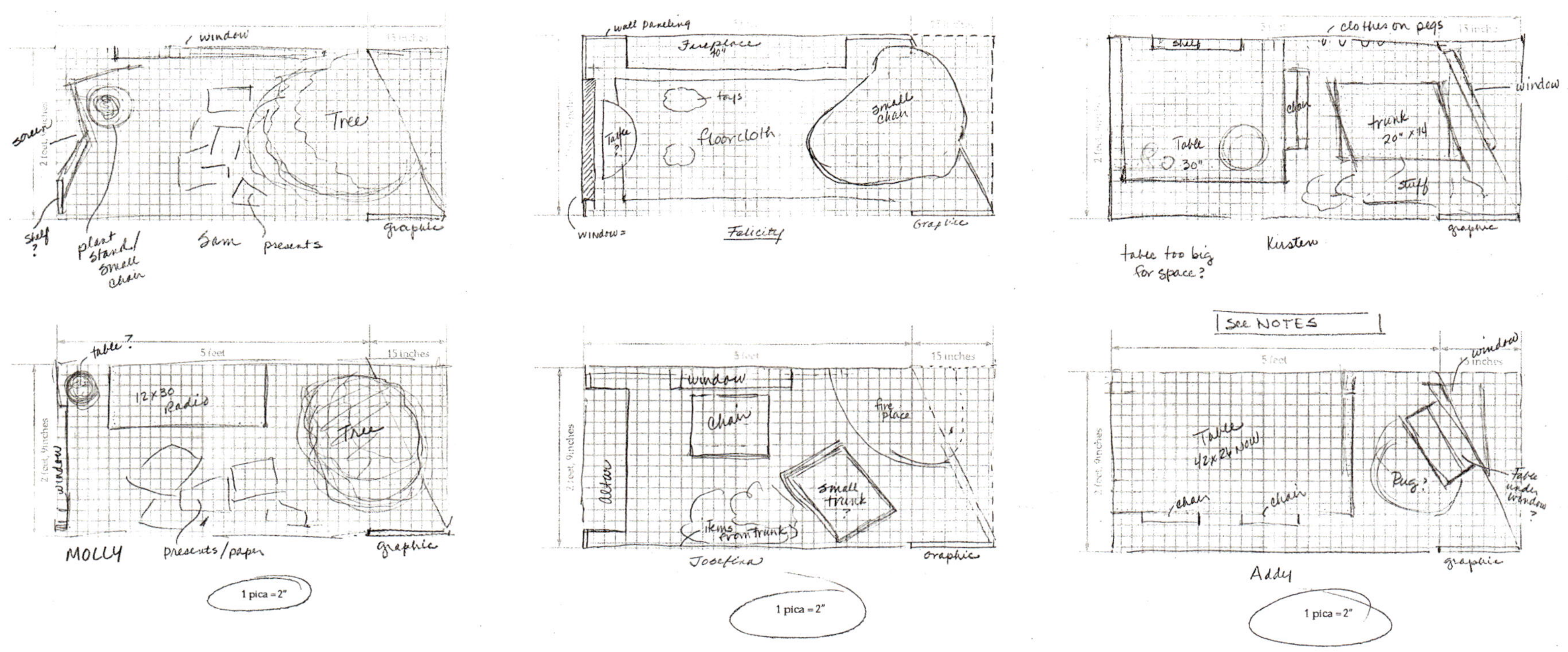

Plans for the first holiday scenes (above).
Felicity, Addy, and Josefina take a peek into the past of Kirsten's, Addy's, and Samantha's holiday scenes (below).

A PEEK INTO THE PAST

Cafe

The original American Girl Cafe offered fancy dining for girls, their mothers, and their dolls, overlooking the historic Water Tower on Michigan Avenue. Guests could enjoy luncheon, tea, or dinner during one of six seatings, each accommodating more than 130 people. Served from an elegant tableside trolley, the delicious girl-sized menu choices included Felicity's tea sandwiches, Josefina's calico corn muffins, and cinnamon buns. Conversation starters, designed to encourage storytelling between generations, were offered at each table. Mothers and daughters answered questions such as, "What did you think was the most fun thing to do when you were ten years old?" or "What would you tell your grown-up self about being a girl right now?"

Birthday parties were held in the Cafe for girls ages eight and up.

These photos show the cafe design in progress. Note the sample of the flowered lampshade, the flat cutout of the chandelier design, the bold striped wallpaper sample, and the polka-dot and striped fabrics used to upholster the dining chairs.

Pleasant's Day to Remember

"I hold dear a memory of a special day almost fifty years ago when my mother took me downtown to hear the Chicago Symphony Orchestra. It was just the two of us—a 'grown-up' experience without my two younger sisters, which, of course, made it particularly meaningful!

First we went for lunch to a restaurant that served delicious, warm cinnamon buns, and then we walked to Orchestra Hall. In my mind's eye, I can still see its pale blue ceiling frosted in gold, gleaming like the instruments of the tuxedoed musicians. I can still remember the music they played that afternoon—especially singing my heart out when the audience was invited to sing along with 'Beautiful Dreamer.'

When the concert was over, we went out into the wintry evening and walked up Michigan Avenue, white-gloved hand in white-gloved hand, squeezing our secret code: three squeezes from Mom meant 'I love you'; four squeezes from me meant 'I love you, too.'"

> "**The inspiration for American Girl Place came from that special day my mother and I had all those years ago.** You'll find it all right here, right down to the cinnamon buns in the cafe and a chance to sing your heart out at *The American Girls Revue.* **When you visit, by all means, don't forget the secret code!**"

PLEASANT ROWLAND

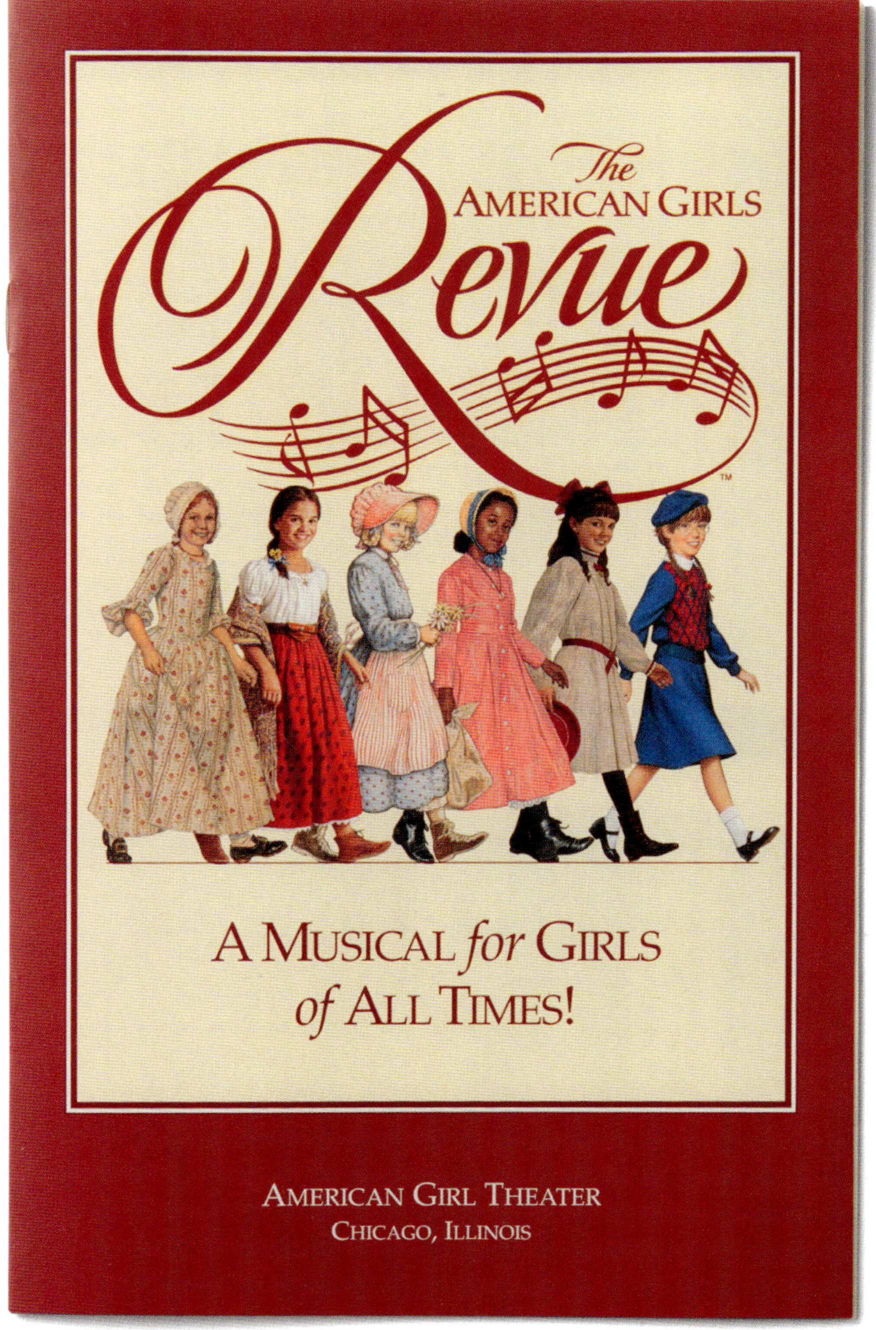

Theater

The voices of girls, past and present, rang strong and true in the intimate 150-seat American Girl Theater. A one-hour original musical for girls, *The American Girls Revue,* written by Broadway playwrights Gretchen Cryer and Nancy Ford, brought the stories of The American Girls Collection to life. The musical was set at a meeting of a modern-day American girls' club. Each club member re-created an episode about her favorite American Girl character, based on the books in the collection. The musical embodied the values and lessons at the heart of The American Girls Collection and helped girls today better understand the lives of American girls throughout history.

Pleasant was very intentional about what the show needed to do: which emotional strings it should pluck, which plotlines to elevate, and which values it had to uphold. She remembers when Gretchen and Nancy presented the show to her, her husband Jerry, and Valerie Tripp for the very first time:

> "They rented a little spinet piano and brought it to my living room. Nancy and Gretchen read the show, and played the music, and sang the songs. **When they had finished, I was in tears at how perfect it was.**"
>
> PLEASANT ROWLAND

Costume Designs

The original renderings and fabric swatches for *The American Girls Revue* show a range of costume interpretations for both the historical and contemporary characters in the production. Adult characters are in the mix, too—you'll find Grandmary, Tía Dolores, Jiggy Nye, and more on these pages.

MOLLY
8-20-1998
BECKY — MOLLY 8-1998
GRANDMARY
8-1998
SAMANTHA
8-1998
PRE-LIM
DESIGN 7-1998
SAMANTHA
scene 5
TIA
MAGDALENA
8-20-1998
ANGELA/
JOSEFINA
8-20-1998
AUNT
CORNELIA
MOTORING
SUIT
8-20-1998
TIA DOLORES
8-1998
ANGELA
JOSEFINA
8-1998
UNCLE
GARD
8-1998

"American Girl Place was the capstone, the cherry on top of it all," Pleasant recalls. With the successful opening complete, she had accomplished all that she had set out to do, and she had seen it all the way through. "It was a beautiful, glorious chapter of my life, but it was closed," she says. Pleasant had decided to usher in a new chapter of American Girl under Mattel, and she accepted a seat on Mattel's Board of Directors to facilitate the transition. In her farewell address, Pleasant included the same words she had shared with her team each holiday season since the company's beginning—words meant to prepare and inspire them for the busy days ahead. "It is a quote from W. B. Yeats, and it crystallizes for me what I dreamed American Girl could be and what I believe it has become."

> "Look up in the sun's eye and give
> What the exultant heart calls good
> That some new day may breed the best
> **Because you gave, not what they would**
> **But the right twigs for an eagle's nest!"**
>
> W. B. YEATS